WORKING WITH
grep, sed, AND awk
Pocket Primer

WORKING WITH
grep, sed, AND awk
Pocket Primer

MERCURY LEARNING AND INFORMATION

Dulles, Virginia
Boston, Massachusetts
New Delhi

Publisher: David Pallai
MERCURY LEARNING AND INFORMATION
22841 Quicksilver Drive
Dulles, VA 20166
info@merclearning.com
www.merclearning.com
1-800-232-0223

O. Campesato. *Working with grep, sed, and awk Pocket Primer.*
ISBN: 978-150152-151-5

The publisher recognizes and respects all marks used by companies, manufacturers, and developers as a means to distinguish their products. All brand names and product names mentioned in this book are trademarks or service marks of their respective companies. Any omission or misuse (of any kind) of service marks or trademarks, etc. is not an attempt to infringe on the property of others.

Library of Congress Control Number: 2023934889
232425321   Printed on acid-free paper in the United States of America.

Our titles are available for adoption, license, or bulk purchase by institutions, corporations, etc. For additional information, please contact the Customer Service Dept. at 800-232-0223 (toll free).

I'd like to dedicate this book to my parents
– may this bring joy and happiness into their lives.

CONTENTS

PREFACE

WHAT IS THE GOAL?

The goal of this book is to introduce readers to three powerful command line utilities that can be combined to create simple yet powerful shell scripts for performing a multitude of tasks. The code samples and scripts use the bash shell, and typically involve small text files, so you can focus on understanding the features of grep, sed, and awk. Aimed at a reader new to working in a bash environment, the book is comprehensive enough to be a good reference and teaches new tricks to those who already have some experience with these command line utilities.

This book takes introductory concepts and demonstrates their use in simple yet powerful shell scripts. Keep in mind that this book does not cover "pure" system administration functionality.

IS THIS BOOK IS FOR ME AND WHAT WILL I LEARN?

This book is intended for general users as well as anyone who wants to perform a variety of tasks from the command line.

You will acquire an understanding of how to use grep, sed, and awk whose functionality is discussed in the first five chapters. Specifically, Chapter 1 introduces the grep command, Chapter 2 introduces the sed command, and Chapters 3 through 5 discuss the awk command. The sixth and final chapter introduces you to regular expressions.

This book saves you the time required to search for relevant code samples, adapting them to your specific needs, which is a potentially time-consuming process.

HOW WERE THE CODE SAMPLES CREATED?

The code samples in this book were created and tested using bash on a MacBook Pro with OS X 10.15.7 (macOS Catalina). Regarding their content: the code samples are derived primarily from scripts prepared by the author, and in some cases, there are code samples that incorporate short sections of code from discussions in online forums. The key point to remember is that the code samples follow the "Four Cs": they must be Clear, Concise, Complete, and Correct to the extent that it is possible to do so, given the size of this book.

WHAT YOU NEED TO KNOW FOR THIS BOOK

You need some familiarity with working from the command line in a Unix-like environment. However, there are subjective prerequisites, such as a desire to learn shell programming, along with the motivation and discipline to read and understand the code samples. In any case, if you're not sure whether or not you can absorb the material in this book, glance through the code samples to get a feel for the level of complexity.

HOW DO I SET UP A COMMAND SHELL?

If you are a Mac user, there are three ways to do so. The first method is to use Finder to navigate to Applications > Utilities and then double click on the Utilities application. Next, if you already have a command shell available, you can launch a new command shell by typing the following command:

```
open /Applications/Utilities/Terminal.app
```

A second method for Mac users is to open a new command shell on a MacBook from a command shell that is already visible simply by clicking command+n in that command shell, and your Mac will launch another command shell.

If you are a PC user, you can install Cygwin (open source *https://cygwin. com/*) that simulates bash commands or use another toolkit such as MKS (a commercial product). Please read the online documentation that describes the download and installation process.

If you use RStudio, you need to launch a command shell inside of RStudio by navigating to Tools > Command Line, and then you can launch bash commands. Note that custom aliases are not automatically set if they are defined in a file other than the main start-up file (such as .bash_login).

WHAT ARE THE "NEXT STEPS" AFTER FINISHING THIS BOOK?

The answer to this question varies widely, mainly because the answer depends heavily on your objectives. The best answer is to try a new tool or technique from the book out on a problem or task you care about, professionally, or personally. Precisely what that might be depends on who you are, as the needs of a data scientist, manager, student, or developer are all different. In addition, keep what you learned in mind as you tackle new data cleaning or manipulation challenges. Sometimes knowing a technique is possible will make finding a solution easier, even if you have to re-read the section to remember exactly how the syntax works.

If you have reached the limits of what you have learned here and want to get further technical depth on these commands, there is a wide variety of literature published and online resources describing the bash `shell`, Unix programming, and the `grep`, `sed`, and `awk` commands.

WORKING WITH GREP

This chapter introduces you to the versatile `grep` command that can process an input text stream to generate a desired output text stream. This command also works well with other Unix commands. This chapter contains many short code samples that illustrate various options of the `grep` command.

The first part of this chapter introduces the `grep` command used in isolation, in conjunction with meta characters (such as `^`, `$`, and so forth), and with code snippets that illustrate how to use some of the options of the `grep` command. Next, you will learn how to match ranges of lines, how to use the back references in `grep`, and how to "escape" meta characters in `grep`.

The second part of this chapter shows you how to use the `grep` command to find empty lines and common lines in datasets, as well as the use of keys to match rows in datasets. Next, you will learn how to use character classes with the `grep` command, as well as the backslash (\) character, and how to specify multiple matching patterns. You will learn how to combine the `grep` command with the `find` command and the `xargs` command, which is useful for matching a pattern in files that reside in different directories. This section contains some examples of common mistakes that people make with the `grep` command.

The third section briefly discusses the `egrep` command and the `fgrep` command, which are related commands that provide additional functionality that is unavailable in the standard `grep` utility. The fourth section contains a use case that illustrates how to use the `grep` command to find matching lines that are then merged to create a new dataset.

What is the grep Command?

The `grep` ("Global Regular Expression Print") command is useful for finding strings in one or more files. Several examples are here:

- `grep abc *sh` displays all the *lines* of `abc` in files with suffix `sh`.
- `grep -i abc *sh` is the same as the preceding query, but case-insensitive.
- `grep -l abc *sh` displays all the *filenames* with suffix `sh` that contain `abc`.
- `grep -n abc *sh` displays all the line numbers of the occurrences of the string `abc` in files with suffix `sh`.

You can perform logical AND and logical OR operations with this syntax:

- `grep abc *sh | grep def` matches lines containing `abc` AND `def`.
- `grep "abc\|def" *sh` matches lines containing `abc` OR `def`.

You can combine switches as well: the following command displays the names of the files that contain the string `abc` (case insensitive):

```
grep -il abc *sh
```

In other words, the preceding command matches filenames that contain `abc`, `Abc`, `ABc`, `ABC`, `abC`, and so forth.

Another (less efficient way) to display the lines containing `abc` (case insensitive) is here:

```
cat file1 |grep -i abc
```

The preceding command involves two processes, whereas the "`grep` using –l switch instead of `cat` to input the files you want" approach involves a single process. The execution time is roughly the same for small text files, but the execution time can become more significant if you are working with multiple large text files.

You can combine the `sort` command, the pipe symbol, and the `grep` command. For example, the following command displays the files with a "`Jan`" date in increasing size:

```
ls -l |grep " Jan " | sort -n
```

A sample output from the preceding command is here:

```
-rw-r--r--  1 oswaldcampesato2  staff      3 Sep 27  2022 abc.txt
-rw-r--r--  1 oswaldcampesato2  staff      6 Sep 21  2022 control1.txt
-rw-r--r--  1 oswaldcampesato2  staff     27 Sep 28  2022 fiblist.txt
```

```
-rw-r--r--  1 oswaldcampesato2  staff     28 Sep 14  2022 dest
-rw-r--r--  1 oswaldcampesato2  staff     36 Sep 14  2022 source
-rw-r--r--  1 oswaldcampesato2  staff    195 Sep 28  2022 Divisors.py
-rw-r--r--  1 oswaldcampesato2  staff    267 Sep 28  2022 Divisors2.py
```

Meta Characters and the grep Command

The fundamental building blocks are the regular expressions that match a single character. Most characters, including all letters and digits, are regular expressions that match themselves. Any meta-character with special meaning may be quoted by preceding it with a backslash.

A regular expression may be followed by one of several repetition operators, as shown here:

"." matches any single character.

"?" indicates that the preceding item is optional and will be matched at most once: Z? matches Z or ZZ.

"*" indicates that the preceding item will be matched zero or more times: Z* matches Z, ZZ, ZZZ, and so forth.

"+" indicates that the preceding item will be matched one or more times: Z+ matches ZZ, ZZZ, and so forth.

"{n}" indicates that the preceding item is matched exactly n times: Z{3} matches ZZZ.

"{n,}" indicates that the preceding item is matched n or more times: Z{3} matches ZZZ, ZZZZ, and so forth.

"{,m}" indicates that the preceding item is matched at most m times: Z{,3} matches Z, ZZ, and ZZZ.

"{n,m}" indicates that the preceding item is matched at least n times, but not more than m times: Z{2,4} matches ZZ, ZZZ, and ZZZZ.

The empty regular expression matches the empty string (i.e., a line in the input stream with no data). Two regular expressions may be joined by the infix operator (|). When used in this manner, the infix operator behaves exactly like a logical "OR" statement, which directs the grep command to return any line that matches either regular expression.

Escaping Meta Characters with the grep Command

Listing 1.1 displays the content of lines.txt that contains lines with words and metacharacters.

LISTING 1.1: lines.txt

```
abcd
ab
abc
cd
defg
.*.
..
```

The following `grep` command lists the lines of length 2 (using the ^ to begin and $ to end, with operators to restrict the length) in `lines.txt`:

```
grep '^..$' lines.txt
```

The following command lists the lines of length two in `lines.txt` that contain two dots (the backslash tells `grep` to interpret the dots as actual dots, not as metacharacters):

```
grep '^\.\.$' lines.txt
```

The result is shown here:

```
..
```

The following command also displays lines of length 2 that begins and ends with a dot. Note that the * matches any text of any length, including no text at all, and is used as a metacharacter because it is not preceded with a backslash:

```
grep '^\.*\.$' lines.txt
```

The following command lists the lines that contain a period, followed by an asterisk, and then another period (the * is now a character that must be matched because it is preceded by a backslash):

```
grep '^\.\*\.$' lines.txt
```

Useful Options for the grep Command

There are many types of pattern matching possibilities with the `grep` command, and this section contains an eclectic mix of such commands that handle common scenarios.

In the following examples, we have four text files (two `.sh` and two `.txt`) and two Word documents in a directory. The string abc is found on one line in `abc1.txt` and three lines in `abc3.sh`. The string ABC is found on two lines in in `ABC2.txt` and four lines in `ABC4.sh`. Notice that abc is not found in ABC files, and ABC is not found in abc files.

```
ls *
ABC.doc    ABC4.sh    abc1.txt    ABC2.txt    abc.doc    abc3.sh
```

The following code snippet searches for occurrences of the string abc in all the files in the current directory that have sh as a suffix:

```
grep abc *sh
abc3.sh:abc at start
abc3.sh:ends with -abc
abc3.sh:the abc is in the middle
```

The "-c" option counts the number of occurrences of a string: even though ABC4.sh has no matches, it still counts them and returns zero:

```
grep -c abc *sh
```

The output of the preceding command is here:

```
ABC4.sh:0
abc3.sh:3
```

The "-e" option lets you match patterns that would otherwise cause syntax problems (the "–" character normally is interpreted as an argument for grep):

```
grep -e "-abc" *sh
abc3.sh:ends with -abc
```

The "-e" option also lets you match multiple patterns:

```
grep -e "-abc" -e "comment" *sh
ABC4.sh:# ABC in a comment
abc3.sh:ends with -abc
```

The "-i" option is to perform a case insensitive match:

```
grep -i abc *sh
ABC4.sh:ABC at start
ABC4.sh:ends with ABC
ABC4.sh:the ABC is in the middle
ABC4.sh:# ABC in a comment
abc3.sh:abc at start
abc3.sh:ends with -abc
abc3.sh:the abc is in the middle
```

The "-v" option "inverts" the matching string, which means that the output consists of the lines that do not contain the specified string (ABC does not match because -i is not used, and ABC4.sh has an entirely empty line):

```
grep -v abc *sh
```

Use the "-iv" options to display the lines that do not contain a specified string using a case insensitive match:

```
grep -iv abc *sh
ABC4.sh:
abc3.sh:this line won't match
```

The "-l" option is to list only the filenames that contain a successful match (note this matches contents of files, not the filenames). The Word document matches because the actual text is still visible to grep, it is just surrounded by proprietary formatting gibberish. You can do similar things with other formats that contain text, such as XML, HTML, CSV, and so forth:

```
grep -l abc *

abc1.txt
abc3.sh
abc.doc
```

The "-l" option is to list only the filenames that contain a successful match:

```
grep -l abc *sh
```

Use the "-il" options to display the filenames that contain a specified string using a case insensitive match:

```
grep -il abc *doc
```

The preceding command is very useful when you want to check for the occurrence of a string in Word documents.

The "-n" option specifies line numbers of any matching file:

```
grep -n abc *sh
abc3.sh:1:abc at start
abc3.sh:2:ends with -abc
abc3.sh:3:the abc is in the middle
```

The "-h" option suppresses the display of the filename for a successful match:

```
grep -h abc *sh
abc at start
ends with -abc
the abc is in the middle
```

For the next series of examples, we will use columns4.txt, as shown in Listing 1.2.

LISTING 1.2: columns4.txt

```
123 ONE TWO
456 three four
ONE TWO THREE FOUR
five 123 six
one two three
four five
```

The "-o" option shows only the matched string (this is how you avoid returning the entire line that matches):

```
grep -o one columns4.txt
```

The "-o" option followed by the "-b" option shows the position of the matched string (returns character position, not line number. The "o" in "one" is the 59th character of the file):

```
grep -o -b one columns4.txt
```

You can specify a recursive search, as shown here (output not shown because it will be different on every client or account. This searches not only every file in directory /etc, but every file in every subdirectory of etc):

```
grep -r abc /etc
```

The preceding commands match lines where the specified string is a substring of a longer string in the file. For instance, the preceding commands will match occurrences of abc as well as abcd, dabc, abcde, and so forth.

```
grep ABC *txt

ABC2.txt:ABC at start or ABC in middle or end in ABC
ABC2.txt:ABCD DABC
```

If you want to exclude everything except for an exact match, you can use the -w option, as shown here:

```
grep -w ABC *txt
ABC2.txt:ABC at start or ABC in middle or end in ABC
```

The --color switch displays the matching string in color:

```
grep --color abc *sh
abc3.sh:abc at start
abc3.sh:ends with -abc
abc3.sh:the abc is in the middle
```

You can use the pair of metacharacters (.*) to find the occurrences of two words that are separated by an arbitrary number of intermediate characters.

The following command finds all lines that contain the strings one and three with any number of intermediate characters:

```
grep "one.*three" columns4.txt
one two three
```

You can "invert" the preceding result by using the -v switch, as shown here:

```
grep -v "one.*three" columns4.txt
```

```
123 ONE TWO
456 three four
ONE TWO THREE FOUR
five 123 six
four five
```

The following command finds all lines that contain the strings one and three with any number of intermediate characters, where the match involves a case-insensitive comparison:

```
grep -i "one.*three" columns4.txt
ONE TWO THREE FOUR
one two three
```

You can "invert" the preceding result by using the -v switch, as shown here:

```
grep -iv "one.*three" columns4.txt
123 ONE TWO
456 three four
five 123 six
four five
```

Sometimes you need to search a file for the presence of either of two strings. For example, the following command finds the files that contain start or end:

```
grep -l 'start\|end' *
ABC2.txt
ABC4.sh
abc3.sh
```

Later in the chapter, you will see how to find files that contain a pair of strings via the grep and xargs commands.

Character Classes and the grep Command

This section contains some simple one-line commands that combine the grep command with character classes.

```
echo "abc" | grep '[:alpha:]'
abc
echo "123" | grep '[:alpha:]'
(returns nothing, no match)
echo "abc123" | grep '[:alpha:]'
abc123
echo "abc" | grep '[:alnum:]'
abc
echo "123" | grep '[:alnum:]'
(returns nothing, no match)
echo "abc123" | grep '[:alnum:]'
abc123
echo "123" | grep '[:alnum:]'
(returns nothing, no match)
echo "abc123" | grep '[:alnum:]'
abc123
```

```
echo "abc" | grep '[0-9]'
(returns nothing, no match)
echo "123" | grep '[0-9]'
123
echo "abc123" | grep '[0-9]'
abc123
echo "abc123" | grep -w '[0-9]'
(returns nothing, no match)
```

Working with the −c Option in grep

Consider a scenario in which a directory (such as a log directory) has files created by an outside program. Your task is to write a shell script that determines which (if any) of the files that contain two occurrences of a string, after which additional processing is performed on the matching files (e.g., use email to send log files containing two or more errors messages to a system administrator for investigation).

One solution involves the −c option for grep, followed by additional invocations of the grep command.

The command snippets in this section assume the following data files whose contents are shown below.

The file hello1.txt contains the following:

```
hello world1
```

The file hello2.txt contains the following:

```
hello world2
hello world2 second time
```

The file hello3.txt contains the following:

```
hello world3
hello world3 two
hello world3 three
```

Now launch the following commands, where warnings and errors are redirected to 2>/dev/null, and therefore you will not see them:

```
grep -c hello hello*txt 2>/dev/null
hello1.txt:1
hello2.txt:2
hello3.txt:3
grep -l hello hello*txt 2>/dev/null
hello1.txt
hello2.txt
hello3.txt
grep -c hello hello*txt 2>/dev/null |grep ":2$"
hello2.txt:2
```

Note how we use the "ends with" $ metacharacter to grab just the files that have exactly two matches. We also use the colon :2$ rather than just 2$ to prevent grabbing files that have 12, 32, or 142 matches (which would end in :12, :32 and :142).

What if we wanted to show "two or more" (as in the "2 or more errors in a log")? In this case, you would use the invert (-v) command to exclude counts of exactly 0 or exactly 1.

```
Grep -c hello hello*txt 2>/dev/null |grep -v ':[0-1]$'
hello2.txt:2
hello3.txt:3
```

In a real world application, you would want to strip off everything after the colon to return only the filenames. There are a many ways to do so, but we will use the cut command, which involves defining : as a delimiter with -d":" and using -f1 to return the first column (i.e., the part before the colon in the return text):

```
grep -c hello hello*txt 2>/dev/null | grep -v ':[0-1]$'| cut
-d":" -f1
hello2.txt
hello3.txt
```

Matching a Range of Lines

The head and tail commands display a range of lines in a text file. Now suppose that you want to search a range of lines for a string. For instance, the following command displays lines 9 through 15 of longfile.txt:

```
cat -n longfile.txt |head -15|tail -9
```

The output is here:

```
 7   and each line
 8   contains
 9   one or
10   more words
11   and if you
12   use the cat
13   command the
14   file contents
15   scroll
```

This command displays the subset of lines 9 through 15 of longfile. txt that contain the string and:

```
cat -n longfile.txt |head -15|tail -9 | grep and
```

The output is here:

```
 7   and each line
11   and if you
13   command the
```

This command includes a whitespace after the word and, thereby excluding the line with the word command:

```
cat -n longfile.txt |head -15|tail -9 | grep "and "
```

The output is here:

```
     7  and each line
    11  and if you
```

Note that the preceding command excludes lines that end in "and" because they do not have the whitespace after "and" at the end of the line. You could remedy this situation with an "OR" operator including both cases:

```
cat -n longfile.txt |head -15|tail -9 | grep " and\|and "
     7  and each line
    11  and if you
    13  command the
```

However, the preceding allows "command" back into the mix. Hence, if you really want to match a specific word, it is best to use the -w tag, which is smart enough to handle the variations:

```
cat -n longfile.txt |head -15|tail -9 | grep -w "and"
     7  and each line
    11  and if you
```

The use of whitespace is safer if you are looking for something at the beginning or end of a line. This is a common approach when reading contents of log files or other structured text where the first word is often important (a tag like ERROR or Warning, a numeric code, or a date). This command displays the lines that start with the word and:

```
cat longfile.txt |head -15|tail -9 | grep "^and "
```

The output is here (without the line number because we are not using cat -n):

```
and each line
and if you
```

Recall that the "use the file name(s) in the command, instead of using cat to display the file first" style is more efficient:

```
head -15 longfile.txt |tail -9 | grep "^and "
and each line
and if you
```

However, the head command does not display the line numbers of a text file, so the "cat first" (cat -n adds line numbers) style was used in the earlier examples when you wanted to see the line numbers, even though this style is less efficient. Hence, add an extra command to a pipe if it adds value, otherwise start with a direct call to the files you want to process with the first command in the pipe (assuming the command syntax is capable of reading in filenames).

Using Backreferences in the grep Command

The `grep` command allows you to reference a set of characters that match a regular expression placed inside a pair of parentheses. For `grep` to parse the parentheses correctly, each has to be preceded with the escape character "\."

For example, `grep 'a\(.\)'` uses the "." meta character to match `ab` or `a3` but not `3a` or `ba`.

The backreference \n, where n is a single digit, matches the substring previously matched by the nth parenthesized sub-expression of the regular expression. For example, `grep '\(a\)\1'` matches `aa` and `grep '\(a\)\2'` matches `aaa`.

When used with alternation, if the group does not participate in the match, then the backreference makes the whole match fail. For example, `grep 'a\(.\)|b\1'` does not match `ba` or `ab` or `bb` (or anything else really).

If you have more than one regular expression inside a pair of parentheses, they are referenced (from left to right) by \1, \2, ..., \9:

```
grep -e '\([a-z]\)\([0-9]\)\1' is the same as this command:
grep -e '\([a-z]\)\([0-9]\)\([a-z]\)'
grep -e '\([a-z]\)\([0-9]\)\2' is the same as this command:
grep -e '\([a-z]\)\([0-9]\)\([0-9]\)'
```

The easiest way to think of it is that the number (for example, \2) is a placeholder or variable that saves you from typing the longer regular expression it references. As regular expressions can become extremely complex, this often helps code clarity.

You can match consecutive digits or characters using the pattern \([0-9]\)\1. For example, the following command is a successful match because the string `1223` contains a pair of consecutive identical digits:

```
echo "1223" | grep  -e '\([0-9]\)\1'
```

Similarly, the following command is a successful match because the string `12223` contains three consecutive occurrences of the digit `2`:

```
echo "12223" | grep  -e '\([0-9]\)\1\1'
```

You can check for the occurrence of two identical digits separated by any character with this expression:

```
echo "12z23" | grep  -e '\([0-9]\).\1'
```

In an analogous manner, you can test for the occurrence of duplicate letters, as shown here:

```
echo "abbc" | grep  -e '\([a-z]\)\1'
```

The following example matches an IP address, and does not use backreferences, just the \d and \. The following are regular expressions to match digits and periods:

```
echo "192.168.125.103" | grep -e '\(\d\d\d\)\.\(\d\d\d\)\.\
    (\d\d\d\)\.\(\d\d\d\)'
```

If you want to allow for fewer than three digits, you can use the expression {1,3}, which matches 1, 2, or 3 digits on the third block. In a situation where any of the four blocks might have fewer than three characters, you must use the following type of syntax in all four blocks:

```
echo "192.168.5.103" | grep -e '\(\d\d\d\)\.\(\d\d\d\)\.\
    (\d\)\{1,3\}\.\(\d\d\d\)'
```

You can perform more complex matches using backreferences. Listing 1.3 displays the content of columns5.txt that contains several lines that are palindromes (the same spelling from left-to-right as right-to-left). Note that the third line is an empty line.

LISTING 1.3: columns5.txt

```
one eno
ONE ENO

ONE TWO OWT ENO
four five
```

The following command finds all lines that are palindromes:

```
grep -w -e '\(.\)\(.\).*\2\1' columns5.txt
```

The output of the preceding command is here:

```
one eno
ONE ENO
ONE TWO OWT ENO
```

The idea is as follows: the first \(.\) matches a set of letters, followed by a second \(.\) that matches a set of letters, followed by any number of intermediate characters. The sequence \2\1 reverses the order of the matching sets of letters specified by the two consecutive occurrences of \(.\).

Finding Empty Lines in Datasets

Recall that the metacharacter ^ refers to the beginning of a line and the metacharacter $ refers to the end of a line. Thus, an empty line consists of the sequence ^$. You can find the single empty in `columns5.txt` with this command:

```
grep -n "^$" columns5.txt
```

The output of the preceding `grep` command is here (use the -n switch to display line numbers, as blank lines will not otherwise show in the output):

```
3:
```

More commonly, the goal is to strip the empty lines from a file. We can do that just by inverting the prior query (and not showing the line numbers)

```
grep -v "^$" columns5.txt

one eno
ONE ENO
ONE TWO OWT ENO
four five
```

As you can see, the preceding output displays four non-empty lines, and as we saw in the previous `grep` command, line #3 is an empty line.

Using Keys to Search Datasets

Data is often organized around unique values (typically numbers) to distinguish otherwise similar things: for example, John Smith the *manager* must not be confused with John Smith the *programmer* in an employee dataset. Hence, each record is assigned a unique number that will be used for all queries related to employees. Moreover, their names are merely data elements of a given record, rather than a means of identifying a record that contains a particular person.

With the preceding points in mind, suppose that you have a text file in which each line contains a single key value. In addition, another text file consists of one or more lines, where each line contains a key value followed by a quantity value.

As an illustration, Listing 1.4 displays the contents of `skuvalues.txt` and Listing 1.5 displays the contents of `skusold.txt`. Note that an SKU is a term often used to refer to an individual product configuration, including its packaging, labeling, and so forth.

LISTING 1.4: skuvalues.txt

```
4520
5530
6550
7200
8000
```

LISTING 1.5: skusold.txt

```
4520 12
4520 15
5530 5
5530 12
6550 0
6550 8
7200 50
7200 10
7200 30
8000 25
8000 45
8000 90
```

The Backslash Character and the grep Command

The \ character has a special interpretation when it is followed by the following characters:

- "\b" = Match the empty string at the edge of a word.

- "\B" = Match the empty string provided it is not at the edge of a word, so:

- '\brat\b' matches the separate word "rat" but not "crate," and

- '\Brat\B' matches "crate" but not "furry rat."

- "\<" = Match the empty string at the beginning of word.

- "\>" = Match the empty string at the end of word.

- "\w" = Match word constituent, it is a synonym for '[_[:alnum:]]'.

- "\W" = Match non-word constituent, it is a synonym for '[^_[:alnum:]]'.

- "\s" = Match whitespace, it is a synonym for '[[:space:]]'.

- "\S" = Match non-whitespace; it is a synonym for '[^[:space:]]'.

Multiple Matches in the grep Command

In an earlier example, you saw how to use the -i option to perform a case insensitive match. However, you can also use the pipe (|) symbol to specify more than one sequence of regular expressions.

For example, the following `grep` expression matches any line that contains one as well as any line that contains ONE TWO:

```
grep "one\|ONE TWO" columns5.txt
```

The output of the preceding `grep` command is here:

```
one eno
ONE TWO OWT ENO
```

Although the preceding `grep` command specifies a pair of character strings, you can specify an arbitrary number of character sequences or regular expressions, as long as you put "\|" between each thing you want to match.

The grep Command and the xargs Command

The `xargs` command is often used in conjunction with the `find` command in bash. For example, you can search for the files under the current directory (including subdirectories) that have the `sh` suffix and then check which one of those files contains the string `abc`, as shown here:

```
find . -print |grep "sh$" | xargs grep -l abc
```

A more useful combination of the `find` and `xargs` command is shown here:

```
find . -mtime -7 -name "*.sh" -print | xargs grep -l abc
```

The preceding command searches for all the files (including subdirectories) with suffix `sh` that have not been modified in at least seven days, and pipes that list to the `xargs` command, which displays the files that contain the string `abc` (case insensitive).

The `find` command supports many options, which can be combined via AND as well as OR to create very complex expressions.

Note that `grep -R hello .` also performs a search for the string `hello` in all files, including subdirectories, and follows the "one process" recommendation. The `find . -print` command searches for all files in all subdirectories, and you can pipe the output to `xargs grep hello` to find the occurrences of the word `hello` in all files (which involves two processes instead of one process).

You can use the output of the preceding code snippet to copy the matching files to another directory, as shown here:

```
cp `find . -print |grep "sh$" | xargs grep -l abc` /tmp
```

Alternatively, you can copy the matching files in the current directory (without matching files in any subdirectories) to another directory with the `grep` command:

```
cp `grep -l abc *sh` /tmp
```

Yet another approach is to use a backtick so that you can obtain additional information:

```
for file in `find . -print`
do
   echo "Processing the file: $file"
   # now do something here
done
```

If you pass too many filenames to the `xargs` command, you will see a "too many files" error message. In this situation, try to insert additional `grep` commands prior to the `xargs` command to reduce the number of files that are piped into the `xargs` command.

If you work with NodeJS, you know that the `node_modules` directory contains a large number of files. In most cases, you probably want to exclude the files in that directory when you are searching for a string, and the `-v` option is ideal for this situation. The following command excludes the files in the `node_modules` directory while searching for the names of the HTML files that contain the string `src` and redirecting the list of file names to the file `src_list.txt` (and also redirecting error messages to `/dev/null`):

```
find . -print |grep -v node |xargs grep -il src >src_list.
   txt 2>/dev/null
```

You can extend the preceding command to search for the HTML files that contain the string `src` and the string `angular` with the following command:

```
find . -print |grep -v node |xargs grep -il src |xargs grep
   -il angular >angular_list.txt 2>/dev/null
```

You can use the following combination of `grep` and `xargs` to find the files that contain both `xml` and `defs`:

```
grep -l xml *svg |xargs grep -l def
```

A variation of the preceding command redirects error messages to `/dev/null`, as shown here:

```
grep -l hello *txt 2>/dev/null | xargs grep -c hello
```

Searching Zip Files for a String

There are at least three ways to search for a string in one or more zip files. As an example, suppose that you want to determine which zip files contain svg documents.

The first way is shown here:

```
for f in `ls *zip`
do
   echo "Searching $f"
   jar tvf $f |grep "svg$"
done
```

When there are many zip files in a directory, the output of the preceding loop can be very verbose, in which case you need to scroll backward and probably copy/paste the names of the files that actually contain svg documents into a separate file. A better solution is to put the preceding loop in a shell and redirect its output. For instance, create the file findsvg.sh whose contents are the preceding loop, and then invoke this command:

```
./findsvg.sh 1>11 2>22
```

Notice that the preceding command redirects error message (2>) to the file 22 and the results of the jar/grep command (1>) to the file 11 (and obviously, you can specify different filenames).

Checking for a Unique Key Value

Sometimes you need to check for the existence of a string (such as a key) in a text file, and then perform additional processing based on its existence. However, do not assume that the existence of a string means that that string only occurs once. As a simple example, suppose the file mykeys.txt has the following content:

```
2000
22000
10000
3000
```

Suppose that you search for the string 2000, which you can do with findkey.sh whose contents are displayed in Listing 1.6.

LISTING 1.6: findkey.sh

```
key="2000"

if [ "`grep $key mykeys.txt`" != "" ]
then
 foundkey=true
else
```

```
   foundkey=false
fi

echo "current key = $key"
echo "found key   = $foundkey"
```

Listing 1.6 contains `if/else` conditional logic to determine whether the file `mykeys.txt` contains the value of `$key` (which is initialized as 2000). Launch the code in Listing 1.6, and you will see the following output:

```
current key = 2000
found key   = true
linecount   = 2
```

While the key value of 2000 does exist in `mykeys.txt`, you can see that it matches *two* lines in `mykeys.txt`. However, if `mykeys.txt` were part of a file with 100,000 (or more) lines, it is not obvious that the value of 2000 matches more than one line. In this dataset, 2000 and 22000 both match, and you can prevent the extra matching line with this code snippet:

```
grep -w $key
```

Thus, in files that have duplicate lines, you can count the number of lines that match the key via the preceding code snippet. Another way to do so involves the use of `wc -l`, which displays the line count.

Redirecting Error Messages

Another scenario involves the use of the `xargs` command with the `grep` command, which can result in "no such ..." error messages:

```
find . -print |xargs grep -il abc
```

Make sure to redirect errors using the following variant:

```
find . -print |xargs grep -il abc 2>/dev/null
```

The egrep Command and fgrep Command

The `egrep` command is extended `grep` that supports added `grep` features like + (1 or more occurrence of previous character), ? (0 or 1 occurrence of previous character) and | (alternate matching). The `egrep` command is almost identical to the `grep -E`, along with some caveats that are described online:

https://www.gnu.org/software/grep/manual/html_node/Basic-vs-Extended.html

One advantage of using the `egrep` command is that it is easier to understand the regular expressions than the corresponding expressions in `grep` (when it is combined with backward references).

The `egrep` ("extended `grep`") command supports extended regular expressions, as well as the pipe (|) to specify multiple words in a search pattern. A match is successful if any of the words in the search pattern appears, so you can think of the search pattern as "any" match. Thus, the pattern 'abc|def' matches lines that contain either `abc` or `def` (or both).

For example, the following code snippet enables you to search for occurrences of the string `abc` as well as occurrences the string `def` in all files with the suffix `sh`:

```
egrep -w 'abc|def' *sh
```

The preceding `egrep` command is an "or" operation: a line matches if it contains either abc *or* def.

You can also use metacharacters in `egrep` expressions. For example, the following code snippet matches lines that start with `abc` or end with four and a whitespace:

```
egrep '^123|four $' columns3.txt
```

A more detailed explanation of `grep`, `egrep`, `fgrep` is online:

https://superuser.com/questions/508881/what-is-the-difference-between-grep-pgrep-egrep-fgrep

Displaying "Pure" Words in a Dataset with egrep

For simplicity, let's work with a text string and that way we can see the intermediate results as we work toward the solution. Let's initialize the variable x as shown here:

```
x="ghi abc Ghi 123 #def5 123z"
```

The first step is to split x into words:

```
echo $x |tr -s ' ' '\n'
```

The output is here:

```
ghi
abc
Ghi
123
#def5
123z
```

The second step is to invoke `egrep` with the regular expression `^[a-zA-Z]+`, which matches any string consisting of one or more uppercase and/or lowercase letters (and nothing else):

```
echo $x |tr -s ' ' '\n' |egrep "^[a-zA-Z]+$"
```

The output is here:

```
ghi
abc
Ghi
```

If you also want to sort the output and print only the unique words, use this command:

```
echo $x |tr -s ' ' '\n' |egrep "^[a-zA-Z]+$" |sort | uniq
```

The output is here:

```
123
123z
Ghi
abc
ghi
```

If you want to extract only the integers in the variable x, use this command:

```
echo $x |tr -s ' ' '\n' |egrep "^[0-9]+$" |sort | uniq
```

The output is here:

```
123
```

If you want to extract alphanumeric words from the variable x, use this command:

```
echo $x |tr -s ' ' '\n' |egrep "^[a-zA-Z0-9]+$" |sort | uniq
```

The output is here:

```
123
123z
Ghi
abc
ghi
```

Note that the ASCII collating sequences places digits before uppercase letters, and the latter are before lowercase letters for the following reason: 0 through 9 are hexadecimal values 0x30 through 0x39, and the uppercase letters in A-Z are hexadecimal 0x41 through 0x5a, and the lowercase letters in a-z are hexadecimal 0x61 through 0x7a.

Now you can replace echo $x with a dataset to retrieve only alphabetic strings from that dataset.

The fgrep Command

The fgrep ("fast grep") is the same as grep -F and although fgrep is deprecated, it is still supported to allow historical applications that rely on them to run unmodified. In addition, some older systems might not support the -F option for the grep command, so they use the fgrep command. If you really want to learn more about the fgrep command, perform an Internet search for tutorials.

Delete Rows with Missing Values

The code sample in this section shows you how to use the awk command to split the comma-separated fields in the rows of a dataset, where fields can contain nested quotes of arbitrary depth.

Listing 1.7 displays some of the rows in titanic.csv and Listing 1.8 displays the content of the file delete-empty-cols-grep.sh that shows you how to create a new dataset that contains only rows that are fully populated with data values.

LISTING 1.7: titanic.csv

```
survived,pclass,sex,age,sibsp,parch,fare,embarked,class,who,
    adult_male,deck,embark_town,alive,alone
0,3,male,22.0,1,0,7.25,S,Third,man,True,,Southampton,no,False
1,1,female,38.0,1,0,71.2833,C,First,woman,False,C,Cherbourg,
    yes,False
1,3,female,26.0,0,0,7.925,S,Third,woman,False,,Southampton,
    yes,True
1,1,female,35.0,1,0,53.1,S,First,woman,False,C,Southampton,
    yes,False
0,3,male,35.0,0,0,8.05,S,Third,man,True,,Southampton,no,True
0,3,male,,0,0,8.4583,Q,Third,man,True,,Queenstown,no,True
// rows omitted for brevity
0,3,male,25.0,0,0,7.05,S,Third,man,True,,Southampton,no,True
0,3,female,39.0,0,5,29.125,Q,Third,woman,False,,Queenstown,
    no,False
0,2,male,27.0,0,0,13.0,S,Second,man,True,,Southampton,no,True
1,1,female,19.0,0,0,30.0,S,First,woman,False,B,Southampton,
    yes,True
0,3,female,,1,2,23.45,S,Third,woman,False,,Southampton,no,False
1,1,male,26.0,0,0,30.0,C,First,man,True,C,Cherbourg,yes,True
0,3,male,32.0,0,0,7.75,Q,Third,man,True,,Queenstown,no,True
```

LISTING 1.8: delete-empty-cols-grep.sh

```
#field5,field4,field3,"field2,foo,bar",field1,field6,
    field7,"fieldZ"
input="titanic.csv"
output="titanic_clean.csv"

row_count1=`wc $input | awk '{print $1}'`
echo "Number of input rows:  $row_count1"

# compare this code with the awk example in chapter 6:
cat $input |grep -v ",," > $output
```

```
row_count2=`wc $output | awk '{print $1}'`
echo "Number of output rows: $row_count2"

echo
echo "=> First five rows in $input:"
cat $input |head -6 |tail -5
echo "-------------------------"
echo

echo "=> First five rows in $output:"
cat $output |head -6 |tail -5
echo ""
```

Listing 1.8 starts by initializing the variables input and output with the values `titanic.csv` and `titanic_clean.csv`, respectively. Next, the variable `row_count1` is initialized with the number of rows from the input file, and then its value is printed.

The next code snippet uses a combination of the `cat` command and the `grep` command to find all rows that do not contain two consecutive commas (which represent missing values) and redirect that list of rows into the output file. In a similar fashion as the variable `row_count1`, the variable `row_count2` is initialized and its value is printed.

The next block of code in Listing 1.8 uses a combination of the `cat`, `head`, and `tail` commands to extract the first six rows of the input file and then the last five rows of the preceding output, which extracts rows 2 through 6 instead of rows 1 through 5.

Similarly, the final block of code in Listing 1.8 uses a combination of the `cat`, `head`, and `tail` commands to extract the first six rows of the output file and then the last five rows of the preceding output, which extracts rows 2 through 6 instead of rows 1 through 5. Now launch the code in Listing 1.8 and you will see the following output:

```
Number of input rows:  892
Number of output rows: 183

=> First five rows in titanic.csv:
0,3,male,22.0,1,0,7.25,S,Third,man,True,,Southampton,no,False
1,1,female,38.0,1,0,71.2833,C,First,woman,False,C,Cherbourg,
    yes,False
1,3,female,26.0,0,0,7.925,S,Third,woman,False,,Southampton,
    yes,True
1,1,female,35.0,1,0,53.1,S,First,woman,False,C,Southampton,
    yes,False
0,3,male,35.0,0,0,8.05,S,Third,man,True,,Southampton,no,True
-------------------------

=> First five rows in titanic_clean.csv:
1,1,female,38.0,1,0,71.2833,C,First,woman,False,C,Cherbourg,
    yes,False
```

```
1,1,female,35.0,1,0,53.1,S,First,woman,False,C,Southampton,
    yes,False
0,1,male,54.0,0,0,51.8625,S,First,man,True,E,Southampton,no,Tr
ue
1,3,female,4.0,1,1,16.7,S,Third,child,False,G,Southampton,
    yes,False
1,1,female,58.0,0,0,26.55,S,First,woman,False,C,Southampton,
    yes,True
```

Later, you will see how to perform the same task using the awk command, and you might be surprised to learn that the solution for this task is actually simpler using the grep command than the awk command.

A Simple Use Case

The code sample in this section shows you how to use the grep command to find specific lines in a dataset and then "merge" pairs of lines to create a new dataset. This is very much like what a "join" command does in a relational database. Listing 1.9 displays the contents of the file test1. csv that contains the initial dataset.

LISTING 1.9: test1.csv

```
F1,F2,F3,M0,M1,M2,M3,M4,M5,M6,M7,M8,M9,M10,M11,M12
1,KLM,,1.4,,0.8,,1.2,,1.1,,,2.2,,,1.4
1,KLMAB,,0.05,,0.04,,0.05,,0.04,,,0.07,,,0.05
1,TP,,7.4,,7.7,,7.6,,7.6,,,8.0,,,7.3
1,XYZ,,4.03,3.96,,3.99,,3.84,4.12,,,,4.04,,
2,KLM,,0.9,0.7,,0.6,,0.8,0.5,,,,0.5,,
2,KLMAB,,0.04,0.04,,0.03,,0.04,0.03,,,,0.03,,
2,EGFR,,99,99,,99,,99,99,,,,99,,
2,TP,,6.6,6.7,,6.9,,6.6,7.1,,,,7.0,,
3,KLM,,0.9,0.1,,0.5,,0.7,,0.7,,,0.9,,
3,KLMAB,,0.04,0.01,,0.02,,0.03,,0.03,,,0.03,,
3,PLT,,224,248,,228,,251,,273,,,206,,
3,XYZ,,4.36,4.28,,4.58,,4.39,,4.85,,,4.47,,
3,RDW,,13.6,13.7,,13.8,,14.1,,14.0,,,13.4,,
3,WBC,,3.9,6.5,,5.0,,4.7,,3.7,,,3.9,,
3,A1C,,5.5,5.6,,5.7,,5.6,,5.5,,,5.3,,
4,KLM,,1.2,,0.6,,0.8,0.7,,,0.9,,,1.0,
4,TP,,7.6,,7.8,,7.6,7.3,,,7.7,,,7.7,
5,KLM,,0.7,,0.8,,1.0,0.8,,0.5,,,1.1,,
5,KLM,,0.03,,0.03,,0.04,0.04,,0.02,,,0.04,,
5,TP,,7.0,,7.4,,7.3,7.6,,7.3,,,7.5,,
5,XYZ,,4.73,,4.48,,4.49,4.40,,,4.59,,,4.63,
```

Listing 1.10 displays the content of the file joinlines.sh that illustrates how to merge the pairs of matching lines in joinlines.csv.

LISTING 1.10: joinlines.sh

```
inputfile="test1.csv"
outputfile="joinedlines.csv"
tmpfile2="tmpfile2"

# patterns to match:
klm1="1,KLM,"
klm5="5,KLM,"
xyz1="1,XYZ,"
xyz5="5,XYZ,"

#output:
#klm1,xyz1
#klm5,xyz5

# step 1: match patterns with CSV file:
klm1line="`grep $klm1 $inputfile`"
klm5line="`grep $klm5 $inputfile`"
xyz1line="`grep $xyz1  $inputfile`"
# $xyz5 matches 2 lines (we want first line):
grep $xyz5 $inputfile > $tmpfile2
xyz5line="`head -1 $tmpfile2`"
echo "klm1line: $klm1line"
echo "klm5line: $klm5line"
echo "xyz1line: $xyz1line"
echo "xyz5line: $xyz5line"

# step 3: create summary file:
echo "$klm1line" | tr -d '\n' >  $outputfile
echo "$xyz1line"                >> $outputfile
echo "$klm5line" | tr -d '\n' >> $outputfile
echo "$xyz5line"                >> $outputfile
echo; echo
```

The output from launching the shell script in Listing 1.10 is here:

```
1,KLM,,1.4,,0.8,,1.2,,1.1,,,2.2,,,1.41,X
YZ,,4.03,3.96,,3.99,,3.84,4.12,,,,4.04,,
5,KLM,,0.7,,0.8,,1.0,0.8,,0.5,,,1.1,,5,K
LM,,0.03,,0.03,,0.04,
0.04,,0.02,,,0.04,,5,XYZ,,4.73,,4.48,,4.49,4.40,,,,4.59,,,,4.
63,
```

As you can see, the task in this section is easily solved via the `grep` command. Note that additional data cleaning is required to handle the empty fields in the output.

This concludes the portion of the chapter devoted to the `grep` command. The next portion discusses the `sed` command, along with various examples that illustrate some of its feature.

Summary

This chapter showed you how to work with the grep utility, which is a very powerful Unix command for searching text fields for strings. You saw various options for the grep command, and examples of how to use those options to find string patterns in text files.

Next, you learned about egrep, which is a variant of the grep command, which can simplify and also expand on the basic functionality of grep, indicating when you might choose one option over another.

Finally, you learned how to use key values in one text file to search for matching lines of text in another file, and perform join-like operations using the grep command.

WORKING WITH SED

This chapter introduces you to the versatile sed command, which can process an input text stream to generate a desired output text stream. This command works well with other Unix commands. This chapter contains many short code samples that illustrate various options of the sed command.

The first section briefly introduces the sed command, which is a command line utility that provides stream-oriented functionality for managing data. This section also shows you some simple patterns for matching strings.

The second section shows you how to substitute string patterns, such as replacing vowels or deleting multiple digits and letters from a string. You will also see how to perform search and replace with sed.

The third section shows you how to replace multiple field delimiters with a single delimiter, along with some useful switches for sed. In addition, you will learn how to print lines, work with character classes, and remove control characters from a text string.

The final section introduces back references in sed, followed by a set of one-line sed commands. This section also shows you how to populate missing values in a dataset and use sed to process a dataset that contains one million rows.

What is the sed Command?

The name sed is an acronym for "stream editor," and the utility derives many of its commands from the ed line-editor (ed was the first Unix text editor). The sed command is a "non-interactive" stream-oriented editor that can be used to automate editing via shell scripts. This ability to modify an entire stream of data (which can be the contents of multiple files, in a manner similar to how grep behaves) as if you were inside an editor. (It is not common in modern programming languages.) This behavior allows some capabilities not easily duplicated elsewhere, while behaving exactly like any other command (grep, cat, ls, find, and so forth) in how it can accept data, output data, and pattern match with regular expressions.

Some of the more common uses for sed include print matching lines, delete matching lines, and find/replace matching strings or regular expressions.

The sed Execution Cycle

Whenever you invoke the sed command, an execution cycle refers to various options that are specified and executed until the end of the file/input is reached. Specifically, an execution cycle performs the following steps:

- Reads an entire line from stdin/file.

- Removes any trailing newline.

- Places the line in its pattern buffer.

- Modifies the pattern buffer according to the supplied commands.

- Prints the pattern buffer to stdout.

Matching String Patterns Using sed

The sed command requires you to specify a string to match the lines in a file. For example, suppose that the file numbers.txt contains the following lines:

```
1
2
123
3
five
4
```

The following sed command prints all the lines that contain the string 3:

```
cat numbers.txt |sed -n "/3/p"
```

Another way to produce the same result is as follows:

```
sed -n "/3/p" numbers.txt
```

In both cases, the output of the preceding commands is as follows:

```
123
3
```

As we saw earlier with other commands, it is always more efficient to just read in the file using the sed command than to pipe it in with a different command. You can "feed" it data from another command if that other command adds value (such as adding line numbers, removing blank lines, or other similar helpful activities).

The −n option suppresses all output, and the p option prints the matching line. If you omit the −n option then every line is printed, and the p option causes the matching line to be printed again. Hence, if you issue the following command,

```
sed "/3/p" numbers.txt
```

the output (the data to the right of the colon) is as follows. Note that the labels to the left of the colon show the source of the data to illustrate the "one row at a time" behavior of sed.

```
Basic stream output :1
Basic stream output :2
Basic stream output :123
Pattern Matched text:123
Basic stream output :3
Pattern Matched text:3
Basic stream output :five
Basic stream output :4
```

It is also possible to match two patterns and print everything between the lines that match:

```
sed -n "/123/,/five/p" numbers.txt
```

The output of the preceding command (all lines between 123 and five, inclusive) is here:

```
123
3
five
```

Substituting String Patterns Using sed

The examples in this section illustrate how to use sed to substitute new text for an existing text pattern.

```
x="abc"
$ echo $x |sed "s/abc/def/"
```

The output of the preceding code snippet is here:

```
def
```

In the prior command, you instructed sed to substitute ("s) the first text pattern (/abc) with the second pattern (/def) and no further instructions (/").

Deleting a text pattern is simply a matter of leaving the second pattern empty:

```
$ echo "abcdefabc" |sed "s/abc//"
```

The result is here:

```
defabc
```

As you see, this only removes the first occurrence of the pattern. You can remove all the occurrences of the pattern by adding the "global" terminal instruction (/g"):

```
$ echo "abcdefabc" |sed "s/abc//g"
```

The result of the preceding command is here:

```
def
```

Note that we are operating directly on the main stream with this command, as we are not using the -n tag. You can also suppress the main stream with -n and print the substitution, achieving the same output if you use the terminal p (print) instruction:

```
$ echo "abcdefabc" |sed -n "s/abc//gp"

def
```

For substitutions, either syntax will do, but that is not always true of other commands.

You can also remove digits instead of letters by using the numeric metacharacters as your regular expression match pattern:

```
$ ls svcc1234.txt |sed "s/[0-9]//g"
ls $ svcc1234.txt |sed -n "s/[0-9]//gp"
```

The result of either of the two preceding commands is here:

```
svcc.txt
```

Recall that the file columns4.txt contains the following text:

```
123 ONE TWO
456 three four
ONE TWO THREE FOUR
five 123 six
one two three
four five
```

The following `sed` command is instructed to identify the rows between 1 and 3, inclusive (`"1,3`), and delete (`d"`) them from the output:

```
$ cat columns4.txt  | sed "1,3d"
```

The output is here:

```
five 123 six
one two three
four five
```

The following `sed` command deletes a range of lines, starting from the line that matches `123` and continuing through the file until reaching the line that matches the string `five` (and also deleting all the intermediate lines). The syntax should be familiar from the earlier matching example:

```
$ sed "/123/,/five/d" columns4.txt
```

The output is here:

```
one two three
four five
```

Replacing Vowels from a String or a File

The following code snippet shows you how simple it is to replace multiple vowels from a string using the `sed` command:

```
$ echo "hello" | sed "s/[aeio]/u/g"
```

The output from the preceding code snippet is here:

```
Hullu
```

Deleting Multiple Digits and Letters from a String

Suppose that we have a variable x that is defined as follows:

```
x="a123zAB 10x b 20 c 300 d 40w00"
```

Recall that an integer consists of one or more digits, so it matches the regular expression `[0-9]+`, which matches one or more digits. However, you need to specify the regular expression `[0-9]*` to remove every number from the variable x:

```
$ echo $x | sed "s/[0-9]//g"
```

The output of the preceding command is here:

```
azAB x b  c  d w
```

The following command removes all lowercase letters from the variable x:

```
$ echo $x | sed "s/[a-z]*//g"
```

The output of the preceding command is here:

```
123AB 10   20   300   4000
```

The following command removes all lowercase and uppercase letters from the variable x:

```
$ echo $x | sed "s/[a-z][A-Z]*//g"
```

The output of the preceding command is here:

```
123 10   20   300   4000
```

Search and Replace with sed

The previous section showed you how to delete a range of rows of a text file based on a start line and end line using either a numeric range or a pair of strings. As deleting is just substituting an empty result for what you match, it should now be clear that a replace activity involves populating that part of the command with something that achieves your desired outcome. This section contains various examples that illustrate how to get the exact substitution you desire.

The following examples illustrate how to convert lowercase abc to uppercase ABC in sed:

```
$ echo "abc" |sed "s/abc/ABC/"
```

The output of the preceding command is here (which only works on one case of abc):

```
ABC
echo "abcdefabc" |sed "s/abc/ABC/g"
```

The output of the preceding command is here (/g" means works on every case of abc):

```
ABCdefABC
```

The following sed expression performs three consecutive substitutions, using -e to string them together. It changes exactly one (the first) a to A, one b to B, one c to C:

```
$ echo "abcde" |sed -e "s/a/A/" -e "s/b/B/" -e "s/c/C/"
```

The output of the preceding command is here:

```
ABCde
```

Obviously, you can use the following sed expression that combines the three substitutions into one substitution:

```
$ echo "abcde" |sed "s/abc/ABC/"
```

Nevertheless, the -e switch is useful when you need to perform more complex substitutions that cannot be combined into a single substitution.

The "/" character is not the only delimiter that sed supports, which is useful when strings contain the "/" character. For example, you can reverse the order of /aa/bb/cc/ with this command:

```
$ echo "/aa/bb/cc" |sed -n "s#/aa/bb/cc#/cc/bb/aa/#p"
```

The output of the preceding sed command is here:

```
/cc/bb/aa/
```

The following examples illustrate how to use the w terminal command instruction to write the sed output to both standard output and also to a named file upper1 if the match succeeds:

```
echo "abcdefabc" |sed "s/abc/ABC/wupper1"
ABCdefabc
```

If you examine the contents of the text file upper1, you will see that it contains the same string ABCdefabc that is displayed on the screen. This two-stream behavior that we noticed earlier with the print ("p") terminal command is unusual, but sometimes useful. It is more common to simply send the standard output to a file using the ">" syntax, as shown below (both syntaxes work for a replace operation), but in that case, nothing is written to the terminal screen. The above syntax allows both at the same time:

```
$ echo "abcdefabc" | sed "s/abc/ABC/" > upper1
$ echo "abcdefabc" | sed -n "s/abc/ABC/p" > upper1
```

Listing 2.1 displays the content of update2.sh that replaces the occurrence of the string hello with the string goodbye in the files with the suffix txt in the current directory.

LISTING 2.1: update2.sh

```
for f in `ls *txt`
do
  newfile="${f}_new"
  cat $f | sed -n "s/hello/goodbye/gp" > $newfile
  mv $newfile $f
done
```

Listing 2.1 contains a for loop that iterates over the list of text files with the txt suffix. For each such file, initialize the variable newfile that is created by appending the string _new to the first file (represented by the variable f). Next, replace the occurrences of "hello" with the string goodbye in each file f, and redirect the output to $newfile. Finally, rename $newfile to $f using the mv command.

If you want to perform the update in matching files in all subdirectories, replace the `for` statement with the following:

```
$ for f in 'find . -print |grep "txt$"'
```

Regular Expressions with sed

Listing 2.2 displays the contents of the CSV file `employees.csv` that will be referenced in various `sed` commands in this section.

LISTING 2.2: employees.csv

```
empid,full_name,start_date,expenses
1000,Jane Jones,12/05/2021,93.55

2000,John Smith,03/08/2020,87.23

3000,Dave Stone,07/15/2022,84.16
```

The following `sed` command displays the lines in `employees.csv` that start with the digit 1:

```
$ sed -n "/^1/p" < employees.csv
1000,Jane Jones,12/05/2021,93.55
```

The following `sed` command displays the lines in `employees.csv` that do not start with the digit 1:

```
$ sed -n "/^[^1]/p" < employees.csv
empid,full_name,start_date,expenses
2000,John Smith,03/08/2020,87.23
3000,Dave Stone,07/15/2022,84.16
```

The following `sed` command displays the number lines in `employees.csv` that do not start with the digit 1:

```
$ sed -n "/^[^1]/p" < employees.csv | wc -l
3
```

However, the preceding `sed` command also includes the header line, which we can remove via the following `sed` command:

```
$ cat employees.csv | sed "1d" | sed -n "/^[^1]/p" |wc -l
2
```

The following `sed` command displays the lines in `employees.csv` that start with a sequence of digits:

```
$ sed -n "/^[0-9].*/p" < employees.csv
1000,Jane Jones,12/05/2021,93.55
2000,John Smith,03/08/2020,87.23
3000,Dave Stone,07/15/2022,84.16
```

The following `sed` command displays the lines in `employees.csv` that start with a sequence of digits followed the letter J:

```
$ sed -n "/^[0-9].*J/p" < employees.csv
1000,Jane Jones,12/05/2021,93.55
2000,John Smith,03/08/2020,87.23
```

The following `sed` command displays the non-empty lines in `employees.csv`:

```
$ sed -n "/./p" < employees.csv
empid,full_name,start_date,expenses
1000,Jane Jones,12/05/2021,93.55
2000,John Smith,03/08/2020,87.23
3000,Dave Stone,07/15/2022,84.16
```

The following `sed` command displays the number of empty lines in `employees.csv`:

```
sed -n "/^$/p" < employees.csv |wc -l
2
```

The following `sed` command displays the number of lines in `employees.csv` that start with either a 1 or a 2:

```
sed -n "/^[1|2]/p" < employees.csv |wc -l
2
```

Datasets with Multiple Delimiters

Listing 2.3 displays the content of the dataset `delimiter1.txt` that contains multiple delimiters "|," ":," and "^." Listing 2.4 displays the content of `delimiter1.sh` that illustrates how to replace the various delimiters in `delimiter1.txt` with a single comma delimiter ",".

LISTING 2.3: delimiter1.txt

```
1000|Jane:Edwards^Sales
2000|Tom:Smith^Development
3000|Dave:Del Ray^Marketing
```

LISTING 2.4: delimiter1.sh

```
inputfile="delimiter1.txt"
cat $inputfile | sed -e 's/:/,/' -e 's/|/,/' -e 's/\^/,/'
```

As you can see, the second line in Listing 2.4 is simple yet very powerful: you can extend the `sed` command with as many delimiters as you require to create a dataset with a single delimiter between values. The output from Listing 2.4 is shown here:

```
1000,Jane,Edwards,Sales
2000,Tom,Smith,Development
3000,Dave,Del Ray,Marketing
```

Do keep in mind that this kind of transformation can be a bit unsafe unless you have checked that your new delimiter is *not* already in use.

For that, a `grep` command is useful (you want the result to be zero):

```
$ grep -c ',' $inputfile
0
```

Useful Switches in sed

The three command line switches `-n`, `-e`, and `-i` are useful when you specify them with the `sed` command. Specify `-n` when you want to suppress the printing of the basic stream output:

```
$ sed -n 's/foo/bar/'
```

Specify `-n` and end with `/p'` when you want to match the result only:

```
$ sed -n 's/foo/bar/p'
```

We briefly touched on using `-e` to do multiple substitutions, but it can also be combined with other commands. This syntax lets us separate the commands in the last example:

```
echo 'myfoo-bar' | sed -n -e 's/foo/bar/' -n -e 's/bar/BAR/p'
```

A more advanced example that hints at the flexibility of `sed` involves the insertion a character after a fixed number of positions. For example, consider the following code snippet:

```
echo "ABCDEFGHIJKLMNOPQRSTUVWXYZ" | sed "s/.\{3\}/&\n/g"
```

The output from the preceding command is here:

```
ABCnDEFnGHInJKLnMNOnPQRnSTUnVWXnYZ
```

While the above example does not seem especially useful, consider a large text stream with no line breaks (everything on one line). You could use something like this to insert newline characters, or something else to break the data into easier-to-process chunks. It is possible to work through exactly what `sed` is doing by looking at each element of the command and comparing to the output, even if you do not know the syntax. (Tip: Sometimes you will encounter very complex instructions for `sed` without any documentation in the code.)

The output is changing after every three characters and we know dot (`.`) matches any single character, so `.{3}` must be telling it to do that (with escape slashes `\` because brackets are a special character for `sed`, and it will not interpret it properly if we just leave it as `.{3}`. The `n` is clear enough in the replacement column, so the `&\` must be somehow telling it to insert a character instead of replacing it. The terminal `g` command means "to repeat." To clarify and confirm those guesses, take what you could infer and perform an Internet search.

Working with Datasets

The `sed` utility is very useful for manipulating the contents of text files. For example, you can print ranges of lines and subsets of lines that match a regular expression. You can also perform search and replace on the lines in a text file. This section contains examples that illustrate how to perform such functionality.

Printing Lines

Listing 2.5 displays the content of `test4.txt` (doubled-spaced lines) that is used for several examples in this section.

LISTING 2.5: test4.txt

```
abc

def

abc

abc
```

The following code snippet prints the first 3 lines in `test4.txt` (we used this syntax before when deleting rows, but it is equally useful for printing):

```
$ cat test4.txt  |sed -n "1,3p"
```

The output of the preceding code snippet is here (the second line is blank):

```
abc

def
```

The following code snippet prints lines 3 through 5 in `test4.txt`:

```
cat test4.txt  |sed -n "3,5p"
```

$ The output of the preceding code snippet is here:

```
def

abc
```

The following code snippet takes advantage of the basic output stream and the second match stream to duplicates every line (including blank lines) in `test4.txt`:

```
$ cat test4.txt  |sed "p"
```

The output of the preceding code snippet is here:

```
abc
abc


def
def


abc
abc


abc
abc
```

The following code snippet prints the first three lines and then capitalizes the string abc, duplicating ABC in the final output because we did not use -n and did end with /p" in the second sed command. Remember that /p" only prints the text that matched the sed command, where the basic output prints the whole file, which is why def does not get duplicated:

```
$ cat test4.txt  |sed -n "1,3p" |sed "s/abc/ABC/p"
ABC
ABC

def
```

Character Classes and sed

You can also use regular expressions with sed. As a reminder, here are the contents of columns4.txt:

```
123 ONE TWO
456 three four
ONE TWO THREE FOUR
five 123 six
one two three
four five
```

As our first example involving sed and character classes, the following code snippet illustrates how to match lines that contain lowercase letters:

```
$ cat columns4.txt | sed -n '/[0-9]/p'
```

The output from the preceding snippet is here:

```
one two three
one two
one two three four
one
one three
one four
```

The following code snippet illustrates how to match lines that contain lowercase letters:

```
$ cat columns4.txt | sed -n '/[a-z]/p'
```

The output from the preceding snippet is here:

```
123 ONE TWO
456 three four
five 123 six
```

The following code snippet illustrates how to match lines that contain the numbers 4, 5, or 6:

```
$ cat columns4.txt | sed -n '/[4-6]/p'
```

The output from the preceding snippet is here:

```
456 three four
```

The following code snippet illustrates how to match lines that start with any two characters followed by one or more E:

```
$ cat columns4.txt | sed -n '/^.\{2\}EE*/p'
```

The output from the preceding snippet is here:

```
ONE TWO THREE FOUR
```

Removing Control Characters

Listing 2.6 displays the content of `controlchars.txt` that contains the ^M control character. The code sample in this section shows you how to remove control characters via the `sed` just like any other character.

LISTING 2.6: controlchars.txt

```
1 carriage return^M
2 carriage return^M
1 tab character^I
```

The following command removes the carriage return and tab characters from the text file `ControlChars.txt`:

```
$ cat controlChars.txt | sed "s/^M//" |sed "s/	//"
```

You cannot see the tab character in the second `sed` command in the preceding code snippet; however, if you redirect the output to the file `nocontrol1.txt`, you can see that there are no embedded control characters in this new file by typing the following command:

```
$ cat -t nocontrol1.txt
```

Counting Words in a Dataset

Listing 2.7 displays the content of `WordCountInFile.sh` that illustrates how to combine various bash commands to count the words (and their occurrences) in a file.

LISTING 2.7: wordcountinfile.sh

```
# The file is fed to the "tr" command, which changes
# uppercase to lowercase
# sed removes commas and periods, then changes whitespace
# to newlines
# uniq needs each word on its own line to count the words
# properly
# Uniq converts data to unique words and the number of times
# they appeared
# The final sort orders the data by the wordcount.

if [ "$1" == "" ]
then
  echo "Please specify an input file"
else
  cat "$1" | xargs -n1 | tr A-Z a-z | \
  sed -e 's/\.//g' -e 's/\,//g' -e 's/ /\ /g' | \
  sort | uniq -c | sort -nr
fi
```

The previous command performs the following operations:

- List each word in each line of the file.

- Shift characters to lowercase.

- Filter out periods and commas.

- Change spaces between words to linefeed.

- Remove duplicates, prefix occurrence count, and sort numerically.

Back References in sed

In the first part of the chapter describing grep, we mentioned back references, and similar functionality is available with the sed command. The main difference is that the back references can also be used in the replacement section of the command.

The following sed command matches the consecutive "a" letters and prints four of them:

```
$ echo "aa" |sed -n "s#\([a-z]\)\1#\1\1\1\1#p"
```

The output of the preceding code snippet is here:

```
aaaa
```

The following `sed` command replaces all duplicate pairs of letters with the letters `aa`:

```
$ echo "aa/bb/cc" |sed -n "s#\(aa\)/\(bb\)/\(cc\)#\1/\1/\1/#p"
```

The output of the previous `sed` command is here (note the trailing "/" character):

```
aa/aa/aa/
```

The following command inserts a comma in a four-digit number:

```
$ echo "1234" |sed -n "s@\([0-9]\)\([0-9]\)\([0-9]\)
    \([0-9]\)@\1,\2\3\4@p"
```

The preceding `sed` command uses the `@` character as a delimiter. The character class `[0-9]` matches one single digit. Since there are four digits in the input string `1234`, the character class `[0-9]` is repeated 4 times, and the value of each digit is stored in `\1`, `\2`, `\3`, and `\4`. The output from the preceding `sed` command is here:

```
1,234
```

A more general `sed` expression that can insert a comma in five-digit numbers is here:

```
$ echo "12345" | sed 's/\([0-9]\{3\}\)$/,\1/g;s/^,//'
```

The output of the preceding command is here:

```
12,345
```

One-Line sed Commands

This section is intended to show more useful problems you can solve with a single line of `sed`, and to expose you to more switches and arguments so you can learn how they can be mixed and matched to solve related tasks.

`sed` supports other options (which are beyond the scope of this book) to perform many other tasks, some of which are sophisticated and correspondingly complex. If you encounter something that none of the examples in this chapter cover, but seems like it is the sort of thing `sed` might do, the odds are decent that it does. An Internet search along the lines of "how do I do <xxx> in sed" will likely either point you in the right direction or at least identify an alternative bash command that will be helpful.

Listing 2.8 displays the content of `data4.txt` that is referenced in some of the `sed` commands in this section. Note that some examples contain options that have not been discussed earlier in this chapter: they are included in case you need the desired functionality (and you can find more details by reading online tutorials).

LISTING 2.8: *data4.txt*

```
hello world4
        hello world5 two
 hello world6 three
                  hello world4  four
line five
line six
line seven
```

Print the first line of `data4.txt` with this command:

```
$ sed q < data4.txt
```

The output is here:

```
hello world3
```

Print the first three lines of `data4.txt` with this command:

```
$ sed 3q < data4.txt
```

The output is here:

```
hello world4
hello world5 two
hello world6 three
```

Print the last line of `data4.txt` with this command:

```
$ sed '$!d' < data4.txt
```

The output is here:

```
line seven
```

You can also use this snippet to print the last line:

```
$ sed -n '$p' < data4.txt
```

Print the last two lines of `data4.txt` with this command:

```
$ sed '$!N;$!D' <data4.txt
```

The output is here:

```
line six
line seven
```

Print the lines of `data4.txt` that do not contain `world` with this command:

```
$ sed '/world/d' < data4.txt
```

The output is here:

Print duplicates of the lines in data4.txt that contain the word world with this command:

```
$ sed '/world/p' < data4.txt
```

The output from the preceding code snippet is here:

```
hello world4
hello world4
    hello world5 two
    hello world5 two
hello world6 three
hello world6 three
        hello world4 four
        hello world4 four
```

Print the fifth line of data4.txt with this command:

```
$ sed -n '5p' < data4.txt
```

The output from the preceding code snippet is here:

```
line five
```

Print the contents of data4.txt and duplicate line five with this command:

```
$ sed '5p' < data4.txt
```

The output from the preceding code snippet is here:

```
hello world4
hello world5 two
hello world6 three
        hello world4 four
line five
line five
line six
line seven
```

Print lines four through six of data4.txt with this command:

```
$ sed -n '4,6p' < data4.txt
```

The output from the preceding code snippet is here:

```
hello world4 four
line five
line six
```

Delete lines four through six of data4.txt with this command:

```
$ sed '4,6d' < data4.txt
```

The output from the preceding code snippet is here:

```
hello world4
hello world5 two
hello world6 three
line seven
```

Delete the section of lines between `world6` and `six` in `data4.txt` with this command:

```
$ sed '/world6/,/six/d' < data4.txt
```

The output from the preceding code snippet is here:

```
hello world4
 hello world5 two
line seven
```

Print the section of lines between `world6` and `six` of `data4.txt` with this command:

```
$ sed -n '/world6/,/six/p' < data4.txt
```

The output from the preceding code snippet is here:

```
hello world6 three
        hello world4 four
line five
line six
```

Print the contents of `data4.txt` *and* duplicate the section of lines between `world6` and `six` with this command:

```
$ sed '/world6/,/six/p' < data4.txt
```

The output from the preceding code snippet is here:

```
hello world4
hello world5 two
hello world6 three
hello world6 three
        hello world4 four
        hello world4 four
line five
line five
line six
line six
line seven
```

Delete the even-numbered lines in `data4.txt` with this command:

```
$ sed 'n;d;' <data4.txt
```

The output from the preceding code snippet is here:

```
    hello world4
 hello world6 three
line five
```

```
line seven
```

Replace letters a through m with a " , " with this command:

```
$ sed "s/[a-m]/,/g" <data4.txt
```

The output from the preceding code snippet is here:

```
    ,,,,o wor,,4
    ,,,,o wor,,5 two
 ,,,,o wor,,6 t,r,,
           ,,,,o wor,,4 ,our
,,n, ,,v,
,,n, s,x
,,n, s,v,n
```

Replace letters a through m with the characters " , @#" with this command:

```
$ sed "s/[a-m]/,@#/g" <data4.txt
```

The output from the preceding code snippet is here:

```
   ,@#,@#,@#,@#o wor,@#,@#4
   ,@#,@#,@#,@#o wor,@#,@#5 two
 ,@#,@#,@#,@#o wor,@#,@#6 t,@#r,@#,@#
           ,@#,@#,@#,@#o wor,@#,@#4 ,@#our
,@#,@#n,@# ,@#,@#v,@#
,@#,@#n,@# s,@#x
,@#,@#n,@# s,@#v,@#n
```

The sed command does not recognize escape sequences such as \t, which means that you must literally insert a tab on your console. In the case of the bash shell, enter the control character ^v and then press the <TAB> key to insert a <TAB> character.

Delete the tab characters in data4.txt with this command:

```
$ sed 's/  //g' <data4.txt
```

The output from the preceding code snippet is here:

```
   hello world4
hello world5 two
 hello world6 three
hello world4 four
line five
line six
line seven
```

Delete the tab characters and blank spaces in data4.txt with this command:

```
$ sed 's/  //g' <data4.txt
```

The output from the preceding code snippet is here:

```
helloworld4
helloworld5two
```

```
helloworld6three
helloworld4four
linefive
linesix
lineseven
```

Replace every line of data4.txt with the word pasta with this command:

```
$ sed 's/.*/\pasta/' < data4.txt
```

The output from the preceding code snippet is here:

```
pasta
pasta
pasta
pasta
pasta
pasta
pasta
```

Insert two blank lines after the third line and one blank line after the fifth line in data4.txt with this command:

```
$ sed '3G;3G;5G' < data4.txt
```

The output from the preceding code snippet is here:

```
hello world4
  hello world5 two
hello world6 three


        hello world4 four
line five

line six
line seven
```

Insert a blank line after every line of data4.txt with this command:

```
$ sed G < data4.txt
```

The output from the preceding code snippet is here:

```
    hello world4

    hello world5 two

 hello world6 three

          hello world4 four

line five

line six

line seven
```

Insert a blank line after every other line of `data4.txt` with this command:

```
$ sed n\;G < data4.txt
```

The output from the preceding code snippet is here:

```
    hello world4
    hello world5 two

 hello world6 three
         hello world4 four

line five
line six

line seven
```

Reverse the lines in `data4.txt` with this command:

```
$ sed '1! G; h;$!d' < data4.txt
```

The output of the preceding `sed` command is here:

```
line seven
line six
line five
         hello world4 four
 hello world6 three
   hello world5 two
   hello world4
```

Populate Missing Values with the sed Command

The example in this section shows you how to update the values in datasets without using Python or Pandas. Although this approach is useful in some cases, Pandas does provide significant functionality that is often simpler than a bash-based counterpart.

Listing 2.9 shows you the content of `missing-titanic-ages.sh` that shows you how to replace missing values in the `titanic.csv` dataset with the string `MISSING` and then count the number of rows whose `age` value is missing.

LISTING 2.9: missing-titanic-ages.sh

```
newfile="titanic-sed.csv"

# this command replaces missing values with MISSING:
$ cat titanic.csv |sed "s/,,/,MISSING,/g" > $newfile

$ cat $newfile | awk -F"," '
BEGIN { count = 0 }
{
    if ($4 ~ /MISSING/) { count += 1 }
}
```

```
END { print "number of missing age values:",count }
'
```

Listing 2.9 initializes the variable `newfile` with the name of the CSV file whose missing values are replaced with the string `MISSING`, and the latter is performed by the subsequent code snippet that starts with the `cat` command.

The next portion of Listing 2.9 is an `awk` script that initializes the variable count with the value 0, and then increments this value whenever a row is encountered with a missing value for the `age` column. Launch the code in Listing 2.9 and you will see the following output:

```
number of missing age values: 177
```

A Dataset with 1,000,000 Rows

The code samples in this section shows you how to use `grep` to perform various comparisons on a dataset that contains 1,000,000 rows.

Numeric Comparisons

Listing 2.10 shows you how to check for a specific number (e.g., 58) and the occurrence of one, two, or three adjacent digits in the first field of each row.

LISTING 2.10: numeric_comparisons.sh

```
filename="1000000_HRA_Records_short.csv"
echo "first loop:"
rownum=0
matches=0

while read line
do
   field1=`echo $line | cut -d"," -f1`
   if [ rownum > 0 ]
   then
     if [ $field1 > 50 ]
     then
        matches=`expr $matches + 1`
     fi
   fi
   rownum=`expr $rownum + 1`
done < $filename
echo "matching records: $matches"

echo "second loop:"
rownum=0
matches=0
while read line
do
   field1=`echo $line | cut -d"," -f1`
   field4=`echo $line | cut -d"," -f4`
```

```
    field5=`echo $line | cut -d"," -f5`

    if [ rownum > 0 ]
    then
      if [ $field1 > 50 -a "$field5" == "Support" ]
      then
        matches=`expr $matches + 1`
      fi
    fi
    rownum=`expr $rownum + 1`
done < $filename
echo "matching records: $matches"
```

Listing 2.10 initializes the variable `newfile` with the name of the CSV file and then initializes some scalar values. Next, a `while` loop processes each row (except for the first row) in the CSV file and initializes the value of the variable `field1` with the contents of the first field of the comma-delimited CSV file. If `field1` is greater than 50, then the variable `matches` is incremented.

The next portion of Listing 2.10 is another `while` loop processes each row (except for the first row) in the CSV file and then extracts the first, fourth, and fifth fields with the following code block:

```
field1=`echo $line | cut -d"," -f1`
field4=`echo $line | cut -d"," -f4`
field5=`echo $line | cut -d"," -f5`
```

Next, a conditional statement checks whether the value of `field1` is greater than 40 and the value of `field5` equals the string `Support`, as shown here:

```
if [ $field1 > 40 -a "$field5" == "Support" ]
```

If the preceding statement is true, the variable `matches` is incremented. The final code snippet in the `while` loop updates the value of the variable `rownum` and then the next row in the CSV file is processed. Launch the code in Listing 2.10 and you will see the following output:

```
first loop:
matching records: 1001
second loop:
matching records: 153
```

Counting Adjacent Digits

Listing 2.11 shows you how to find a specific number (e.g., 58) and the occurrence of one, two, or three adjacent digits in the first field of each row.

LISTING 2.11: adjacent_digits.sh

```
filename="1000000_HRA_Records.csv"
```

```
echo "first:"
grep 58 $filename |wc
echo

echo "second:"
grep "[0-9]" $filename |wc
echo

echo "third:"
grep "[0-9][0-9]" $filename |wc
echo

echo "fourth:"
grep "[0-9][0-9][0-9]" $filename |wc
```

Listing 2.11 initializes the variable `filename` with the name of a CSV file, followed by four code blocks that contain a combination of the `grep` command and the `wc` command.

The first block determines the number of rows that contain the string 58, whereas the second code block determines the number of rows that contain a digit in the CSV file. The third block determines the number of rows that contain two consecutive digits, whereas the fourth code block determines the number of rows that contain three consecutive digit in the CSV file. Launch the code in Listing 2.11 and you will see the following output:

```
first:
  161740   453166 25044202

second:
 1000001 2799978 154857624

third:
 1000001 2799978 154857624

fourth:
 1000000 2799977 154857110
```

Average Support Rate

Listing 2.12 uses the bash commands `echo`, `cut`, and `expr` to calculate the average rate for people who are over 50 and are in the `Support` department.

LISTING 2.12: average_rate.sh

```
filename="1000000_HRA_Records.csv"

rownum=0
matches=0
total=0
num_records=0
min_rate=""
```

```
max_rate=0

while read line
do
  if [ $rownum -gt 0 ]
  then
    field1=`echo $line | cut -d"," -f1`
    field4=`echo $line | cut -d"," -f4`
    field5=`echo $line | cut -d"," -f5`

    if [ $field1 > 40 -a "$field5" == "Support" ]
    then
      total=`expr $total + $field4`
      num_records=`expr $num_records + 1`

      if [ "$min_rate" == "" ]
      then
        min_rate=$field4
      fi

      if [ $min_rate -gt $field4 ]
      then
        min_rate=$field4
      fi
    fi
  fi
  rownum=`expr $rownum + 1`
done < $filename

avg_rate=`expr $total / $num_records`
echo "Number of Records:    $num_records"
echo "Minimum Rate:         $min_rate"
echo "Maximum Rate:         $max_rate"
echo "Sum of All Rates:     $total"
echo "Average Support Rate: $avg_rate"
```

Listing 2.12 initializes the variable `filename` as the name of a CSV file, followed by initializing a set of scalar variables. The main portion of Listing 2.12 consists of a loop that processes each row after the first row in the CSV file, and then extracts the first, fourth, and fifth fields with the following code block:

```
field1=`echo $line | cut -d"," -f1`
field4=`echo $line | cut -d"," -f4`
field5=`echo $line | cut -d"," -f5`
```

Next, a conditional statement checks whether the value of `field1` is greater than 40 and the value of `field5` equals the string `Support`, as shown here:

```
if [ $field1 > 40 -a "$field5" == "Support" ]
```

If the preceding statement is true, the variables `total` and `num_records` are updated accordingly. Another pair of simple `if` statements determines whether the values of the variables `min_rate` and `max_rate` also need to be updated. The final code snippet in the `while` loop updates the value of the variable `rownum`, and then the next row in the CSV file is processed.

The final code block displays the values of the scalar variables that were initialized in the first section of this code sample:

```
avg_rate=`expr $total / $num_records`
echo "Number of Records:    $num_records"
echo "Minimum Rate:         $min_rate"
echo "Maximum Rate:         $max_rate"
echo "Sum of All Rates:     $total"
echo "Average Support Rate: $avg_rate"
```

Launch the code in Listing 2.23 and you will see the following output:

```
Number of Records:    153
Minimum Rate:         107
Maximum Rate:         1489
Sum of All Rates:     118610
Average Support Rate: 775
```

Summary

This chapter started with an introduction to the `sed` command, along with examples of matching string patterns and substituting string patterns. Then you learned how to perform search and replace.

You also learned how to replace multiple delimiters in a dataset with a single delimiter using the `sed` command. Next, you learned about printing lines, removing control characters, and how to work with character classes in `sed`.

In addition, you learned how to use back references in `sed`, followed by a list of useful one-line `sed` commands. Then you learned how to populate missing values in a dataset. Finally, you learned how to work with a dataset that contains one million rows of data.

## CHAPTER 3

WORKING WITH AWK

This chapter introduces you to the `awk` command, which is a highly versatile utility for manipulating data and restructuring datasets. Awk is essentially a programming language in a single command, which accepts standard input, gives standard output, and uses regular expressions and metacharacters in the same way as other Unix commands. This functionality enables you to combine `awk` with other command line tools. You can include commands in `awk` scripts because its versatility can make an `awk` script challenging to understand based on just a quick glance.

The first part of this chapter provides a brief introduction of the `awk` command. You will learn about some built-in variables for `awk` and how to manipulate string variables using `awk`. Note that some of these string-related examples can also be handled using other bash commands.

The second part of this chapter shows you `while` loops and `for` loops in `awk` to manipulate the rows and columns in datasets. Next, you will learn how to use conditional logic in `awk` commands. This section also shows you how to delete lines and merge lines in datasets, and how to print the contents of a file as a single line of text. You will see how to "join" lines and groups of lines in datasets.

The third section contains code samples that illustrate how to use logical operators in `awk`, followed by a code sample that shows you how to check whether a positive integer is a leap year.

The fourth section explains how to specify different types of format for output data, how to work with floating point numbers, truncating and rounding numbers, and numeric functions in `awk`.

The fifth section shows you how to convert strings to lowercase, uppercase, and mixed case. Next, you will see how to count lines that match a character and how to use the `match()` function in `awk`. Finally, you will learn about non-printable characters and hexadecimal numbers in `awk`.

Before you read this chapter, keep in mind that the datasets in this chapter are intentionally very short so that you can focus on learning the rich feature set of the `awk` command. After you have completed this chapter, proceed to the next chapter that contains more `awk`-based code samples.

In case you are wondering, datasets containing 25 terabytes of data have been successfully processed via `awk`. If you work with multi-terabyte datasets, most likely you will process them in a cloud-based environment. Moreover, the `awk` command is very useful for data cleaning tasks involving datasets of almost any size.

The awk Command

The `awk` (Aho, Weinberger, and Kernighan) command has a C-like syntax and you can use this utility to perform very complex operations on numbers and text strings.

As a side comment, there is also the `gawk` command (that is, GNU `awk`), as well as the `nawk` command ("new" `awk`), but neither command is discussed in this book. One advantage of `nawk` is that it allows you to set externally the value of an internal variable.

You can find *The One True Awk*, which is the `awk` written by Aho, Weinberger, and Kernighan, on GitHub:

https://github.com/onetrueawk/awk

Launching awk Commands and File Extensions

The `awk` command allows you to execute `awk`-based scripts in several ways, along with several similar (yet different) ways in which `awk` commands cannot be executed. Many `awk`-based code samples in this book specify an input file, which is described in a later section.

However, there are also `awk` scripts that do not involve an input file, such as an `awk` script that calculates arithmetic sums or geometric sums. Specifically, the following will not work from the command line:

```
awk '{print "hello" }'
```

However, this does work:

```
echo "" | awk '{print "hello" }'
```

You can also invoke an awk script in which the first line is the so-called "shebang" line that also includes the -f option for awk. For example, suppose that the file q1.sh contains this snippet that contains a shebang line and a BEGIN statement:

```
#!/usr/local/bin/awk -f
BEGIN {print "hello"}
```

Then you can launch the preceding awk command after making q1.sh executable with chmod +x q1.sh:

```
./q1.sh
```

Yet another technique involves specifying the -f option from the command line. For example, suppose that the file q2.sh contains this snippet:

```
BEGIN {print "hello"}
```

Then you can launch q2.sh with the following command:

```
awk -f q2.sh
```

As you know, the following technique will also work, which is the technique that is used throughout this book when an input file is not specified:

```
echo "" | awk '{print "hello" }'
```

Another detail to keep in mind is the file extension for shell scripts that contain awk commands. You will often see shell scripts with the extension "sh," and you will also see shell scripts with the extension "awk," which indicates that the shell script contains an awk command. These are conventions that you will often see in code samples that you find during an Internet search.

NOTE *The code samples in this book use the "sh" extension for all executable shell scripts, including those that contain* awk *commands.*

Built-In Variables that Control awk

The awk command provides variables that you can change from their default values to control how awk performs operations. Examples of such variables (and their default values) include:

- FS   (" ")
- RS   ("\n")
- IFS ("\n")
- OFS (" ")
- ORS ("\n")

- NR

- NF

- SUBSEP

- IGNORECASE

The variables FS and RS specify the field separator and record separator, respectively, whereas the variables OFS and ORS specify the output field separator and the output record separator, respectively. If need be, you can change the value of RS, such as text fields whose records span multiple lines.

You can think of the field separators (IFS) as delimiters, whereas the record separators behave in a way similar to how sed treats individual lines. For example, sed can match or delete a range of lines instead of matching or deleting something that matches a regular expression. The default awk record separator is the newline character, so by default, awk and sed have similar ability to manipulate and reference lines in a text file. In addition, NR contains the number of the currently processed record and NF contains the number of fields in the currently processed record.

Other built-in variables include FILENAME (the name of the file that awk is currently reading), FNR (the current record number in the current file), NF (the number of fields in the current input record), and NR (the number of input records awk has processed since the beginning of the program's execution).

Consult the online documentation for additional information regarding these (and other) arguments for the awk command.

How Does the awk Command Work?

The awk command reads the input files one record at a time (by default, one record is one line). If a record matches a pattern (specified by you), then an associated action is performed (otherwise no action is performed). If the search pattern is not given, then awk performs the given actions for each record of the input. The default behavior if no action is given is to print all the records that match the given pattern. Finally, empty braces without any action does nothing; i.e., it will not perform the default printing operation. Note that each statement in actions should be delimited by a semicolon.

Three Important Code Blocks in awk Commands

The structure of an awk command consists of an optional BEGIN block, the main block, and an optional END block. A high-level outline of an awk command looks like this:

```
awk -F"," '
BEGIN { print "BEGIN"; x = 2; y = 5; }
{
    print "MIDDLE","x=",x,"y=",y
    x+=1
    y+=1
}
END { print "END:","x=",x,"y=",y }
' some_input_file.txt
```

Place the preceding code in a file called `template.sh`, and then make this shell script executable by invoking the following command:

```
chmod +x template.sh
```

You also need to replace `some_input_file.txt` with an existing file: let's call this file `one.txt`, which contains just one line of text (the reason will be explained very soon). Now you can launch the shell script `template.sh` from the command line as follows:

```
./template.sh
```

You will see the following output after invoking the preceding command:

```
BEGIN
MIDDLE x= 2 y= 5
END: x= 3 y= 6
```

Here is where it gets interesting: the number of times that the main execution block (i.e., the portion after the BEGIN block and before the END block) is executed equals the number of lines in the text file `one.txt`! Experiment with input files that have a different numbers of lines to convince yourself.

However, the script `template.sh` does not require any input file, so it makes sense to use a different technique that does not require specifying an input file. As you saw, this book uses the "echo" style for `awk`-based scripts that do not require any external input. Feel free to modify those shell scripts if you prefer to use one of the other techniques that are available.

Different Ways to Print Text

The flexibility of the `awk` command allows you to print text in various ways. Listing 3.1 displays the content of `split_awk.sh` that shows you different `awk` commands that generate the same output.

LISTING 3.1: simple_awk.sh
```
echo "1st:"
echo "abc" | awk '{ print "full line:",$0 }'
echo

echo "2nd:"
```

```
echo "abc" | awk '{}'
echo

echo "3nd:"
echo "abc" | awk '{ print }'
echo

echo "4th:"
echo "abc" | awk '{ /abc/ }'
echo

echo "5th:"
echo "abc" | awk '{ if( /abc/ ) {print} }'
echo

echo "6th:"
echo "abc" | awk '{ if($0 ~ /abc/) {print} }'
echo

echo "7th:"
echo "abc" | awk '{ if($1 ~ /abc/) {print} }'
echo

echo "8th:"
echo "abc" | awk '{ if($1 == "abc") {print} }'
echo

echo "9th:"
echo "abc" | awk '{ if($0 == "abc") {print} }'
echo

# error:
#echo "abc" | awk '{ /abc/ {print} }'

echo "10th:"
echo "abc def" | awk '{ if($0 ~ /abc/) {print $2} }'
echo

echo "11th:"
echo "abc def" | awk '{ if($1 ~ /abc/) {print $2} }'
echo
```

Listing 3.1 shows you various awk commands that are similar yet contain important differences. The main details to remember are listed here:

- "==" performs an *exact* match

- "~" performs a *partial* match

- $0 is the entire input line

- $1 is the first field and $2 is the second field (and so on)

Now look at the code in Listing 3.1 again, and you can see why all the awk commands that contain an if keyword will generate an output.

Moreover, the second and fourth `awk` commands do not display any output because they do not contain a print statement. Launch the code in Listing 3.1, and you will see the following output:

```
1st:
full line: abc

2nd:

3nd:
abc

4th:

5th:
abc

6th:
abc

7th:
abc

8th:
abc

8th:
abc

9th:
def

10th:
def
```

Specify the "!" operator to negate the match. For example, none of the following `awk` commands generates any output because the "!" operator negates a match with the string `abc`:

```
$ echo "abc" | awk '{ if($1 != "abc") {print} }'
$ echo "abc" | awk '{ if($1 !~ "abc") {print} }'
$ echo "abc" | awk '{ if($0 !~ "abc") {print} }'
$ echo "abc" | awk '{ if($0 != "abc") {print} }'
```

Working with the -F Switch in awk

This section contains some simple examples involving text strings and the `awk` command (the results are displayed after each code snippet). The `-F` switch sets the field separator to whatever follows it, in this case, a space. Switches will often provide a shortcut to an action that normally needs a command inside a '`BEGIN{}` block):

```
$ x="a b c d e"
$ echo $x |awk -F" "    '{print $1}'
a
```

```
$ echo $x |awk -F" " '{print NF}'
5
$ echo $x |awk -F" " '{print $0}'
a b c d e
$ echo $x |awk -F" " '{print $3, $1}'
c a
$ echo $x |awk -F" " '{NF = 3; print}'
a b c
$ echo $x |awk -F" " '{$3="pasta"; print}'
a b pasta d e
```

Now let's change the FS (record separator) to an empty string to calculate the length of a string, this time using the BEGIN{} code block:

```
$ echo "abcde" | awk 'BEGIN { FS = "" } ; { print NF }'
5
```

The following example illustrates several equivalent ways to specify test.txt as the input file for an awk command:

■ awk < test.txt '{ print $1 }'

■ awk '{ print $1 }' < test.txt

■ awk '{ print $1 }' test.txt

Yet another way is shown here (but as we have discussed earlier, it can be inefficient, so only do it if the cat command adds value in some way):

```
$ cat test.txt | awk '{ print $1 }'
```

Splitting Strings into Characters

The previous section contains several awk commands that you can invoke from the command line. In addition, you can place an awk command in a shell script. Listing 3.2 displays the content of split_chars.sh that splits input strings into a sequence of characters.

LISTING 3.2: split_chars.sh
```
echo abc def ghi | awk '
BEGIN { FS = "" }
{
   for (i = 1; i <= NF; i++)
      print "Field", i, "is", $i
}
'
```

Listing 3.2 contains an echo command that passes a string to the awk command, which in turn specifies an empty string for the field separator FS. Next, the awk command contains a loop that iterates through each input field. Since FS is initialized as "", the number of fields equals the number of characters in the input to the awk command. Launch the code in Listing 3.2, and you will see the following output:

```
Field 1 is a
Field 2 is b
Field 3 is c
Field 4 is
Field 5 is d
Field 6 is e
Field 7 is f
Field 8 is
Field 9 is g
Field 10 is h
Field 11 is i
```

Notice that the following awk command does not split the input strings into a sequence of characters, even though the -FS flag is included:

```
$ echo "abc def" |awk -FS='' '{print}'
abc def
```

In addition, this awk command will not split strings into characters:

```
$ echo "abc def" |awk '{FS=""; print}'
abc def
```

Although we have not discussed conditional logic, it is easy to understand that the content of Listing 3.3 enhances Listing 3.2 by displaying a separating string of dashes and a blank line after each input field.

LISTING 3.3: split_chars2.sh

```
echo abc def ghi | awk '
BEGIN { FS = "" }
{
    for (i = 1; i <= NF; i++) {
      printf("Field %d is %s\n", i, $i)
      if($i == " ")
        print "--------\n"
    }
}
```

Listing 3.3 contains an echo command that passes a string to the awk command, which in turn specifies an empty string for the field separator FS. Next, the awk command contains a loop that iterates through each input field. Since FS is initialized as "", the number of fields equals the number of characters in the input to the awk command.

During each iteration through the loop, the current field position and the value of the field is printed. There is also a conditional statement that printed a sequence of dashes ("-") whenever the current character matches a single white space. Launch the code in Listing 3.3, and you will see the following output:

```
Field 1 is a
Field 1 is a
Field 2 is b
```

```
Field 3 is c
Field 4 is
--------

Field 5 is d
Field 6 is e
Field 7 is f
Field 8 is
--------

Field 9 is g
Field 10 is h
Field 11 is I
```

The PROCINFO Array

The PROCINFO built-in array enables you to check the type of field splitting that is performed on input lines. Listing 3.4 displays the content of procinfo.sh that shows you how to make this determination.

LISTING 3.4: procinfo.sh

```
echo "abc" | awk '
{
  if (PROCINFO["FS"] == "FS")
    print "Regular field splitting"
  else if (PROCINFO["FS"] == "FIELDWIDTHS")
    print "Fixed-width field splitting"
  else if (PROCINFO["FS"] == "FPAT")
    print "Content-based field splitting"
  else
    print "API input parser field splitting"
}
'
```

Listing 3.4 contains a main execution block with conditional logic to check which of the three possible values of PROCINFO["FS"] is in effect.

The value of PROCINFO["FS"] is FS when regular field splitting is being used, whereas the value of PROCINFO["FS"] is FIELDWIDTHS if fixed-width field splitting is being used, or FPAT if content-based field splitting is being used. Launch the code in Listing 3.4, and you will see the following output:

```
Regular field splitting
```

Ignore Case in awk

The command line utilities grep and sed support the "i" option that performs a case insensitive match. The awk utility uses the IGNORECASE option that is specified inside the body of the awk command. Here is an example:

```
$ echo aBC |awk '{ IGNORECASE=1; if($0 ~ /abc/) print $0}'
aBC
```

Although other languages such as Python and Java support the switch i to indicate a case insensitive match, if you specify /i/ in the awk command, no output is displayed:

```
echo aBC |awk '{ if($0 ~ /abc/i) print $0 }'
```

Another option is to use the lowercase() built-in function to perform a case insensitive match, as shown here:

```
$ echo aBC |awk '{if(tolower($0) ~ /abc/) print $0}'
aBC
```

If you want to check whether a string contains all uppercase letters, you can use the following awk command:

```
$ echo ABC |awk '{if($0 ~ toupper($0)) print $0}'
ABC
```

If you want to check whether a string contains all lowercase letters, you can use the following awk command:

```
$ echo abc |awk '{if($0 ~ tolower($0)) print $0}'
abc
```

Another option is to use the lowercase() built-in function to perform a case insensitive match, as shown here:

```
$ echo aBC |awk'{if(tolower($0) ~ /abc/) print $0}'
aBC
```

Working with OFS, ORS, and Linefeed versus "\n"

The awk command provides the built-in variables OFS and ORS to specify the output field separator and output record separator, respectively, whose default values are shown in the following listing. Listing 3.5 displays the content of ofs_ors.sh that shows you how to use these variables.

LISTING 3.5: ofs_ors.sh

```
echo "Default values for OFS and ORS:"
echo "abc def" | awk 'BEGIN { print "OFS = ",OFS,"x",
   " ORS = ", ORS,"x" }'

echo "output string followed by 2 blank lines:"
echo "abc def" | awk 'BEGIN { OFS = "#"; ORS = "\n\n" }
   { print $1, $2 }'
echo

echo "output string followed by Z as line separator:"
echo "abc def" | awk 'BEGIN { OFS = "#"; ORS = "Z" }
   { print $1, $2 }'
echo
```

```
echo "output string followed by Z as line separator:"
echo "abc def" | awk 'BEGIN { OFS = "#"; ORS = "Z" }
   { print $1, $2, "three\nfour" }'
echo
```

Listing 3.5 contains four awk command that set the value of OFS and ORS, which are the output field separators and output records separators, respectively. The first awk command displays their default values, whereas the second awk command sets their values equal to "#" and "\n\n," respectively.

The third and fourth awk commands set their values equal to "#" and "Z," respectively, and then display different output strings. Launch the code and you will see the following output:

```
output string followed by 2 blank lines:
Default values for OFS and ORS:
OFS =    x  ORS =
 x

abc#def


output string followed by Z as line separator:
abc#defZ
output string followed by Z as line separator:
abc#def#three
fourZ
```

Linefeed versus "\n"

The sequence "\n" is treated as two characters when they are embedded in an input string, whereas the print() built-in function of awk will treat "\n" as a linefeed, as shown here:

```
$ awk 'BEGIN { print "one\ntwo\nthree" }'
one
two
three
```

The printf command in conjunction with awk produces the desired result:

```
$ printf "one\ntwo\nthree" | awk '{print}'
one
two
three
```

The printf command treats "\n" as a newline, which is why the following command generates three output lines:

```
$ printf "one\ntwo\nthree"
one
two
three
```

As a result, the earlier `printf` that pipes its output to the `awk` command also displays three output lines. By contrast, compare the preceding output with the output from the following of `awk` command:

```
$ echo "one\ntwo\nthree" | awk '{print}'
one\ntwo\three
```

Moreover, an echo command with a string that contains embedded "\n" sequences that is piped to the `awk` command that specifies `-F"\n"` also does not work:

```
$ echo "one\ntwo\nthree" | awk -F"\n" '{print}'
one\ntwo\nthree

$ echo "one\ntwo\nthree" | awk -F"\\n" '{ print}'
one\ntwo\nthree

$ echo "one\ntwo\nthree" | awk -F"\\\\n" '{ print}'
one\ntwo\nthree
```

Basic awk Examples with Text Files

This section contains a collection of `awk` scripts that will familiarize you with the diverse set of tasks that you can perform via `awk`. Listing 3.6 displays the content of `employees.csv` that will be used in the `awk` code samples in this section.

LISTING 3.6: employees.csv

```
empid,full_name,start_date,expenses
1000,Jane Jones,12/05/2021,93.55

2000,John Smith,03/08/2020,87.23

3000,Dave Stone,07/15/2022,84.16
```

Notice the blank lines in Listing 3.6, which are included because some of the `awk` commands in this section show you how to handle files that contain blank lines.

Display the Contents of a File

There are two simple ways to display the contents of a file using the `awk` command. One way to do so is shown here:

```
$ awk 1 employees.csv
```

Launch the preceding command in a command shell to convince yourself that the output from the preceding command is the content of `employees.csv`. The digit 1 can be replaced by any positive value (including floating point numbers) and the result is the same. If you replace 1 with 0, then nothing is printed. If you replace 1 with a negative number, you will see a list of command line switches for the `awk` command.

Since the default action of `awk` is to print a line, another way to display the contents of the CSV file `employees.csv` is shown here:

```
$ awk '{print}' employees.csv
```

However, the following code snippet is invalid because there is no action specified:

```
$ awk employees.csv
awk: cmd. line:1: employees.csv
awk: cmd. line:1:            ^ syntax error
```

Omit the Header Line of a File

The header line in a text file (if it is present) is the first line, which means that the value of the built-in variable NR equals 1. Therefore, the following example prints the contents of the CSV file `employees.csv` without the header line:

```
$ awk 'NR>1' employees.csv
1000,Jane Jones,12/05/2021,93.55

2000,John Smith,03/08/2020,87.23

3000,Dave Stone,07/15/2022,84.16
```

Display a Range of Lines in a Text File With NR

You have already seen how to display the contents of a text file, and yet another way to do so is by specifying NR, as shown here:

```
$ awk 'NR' employees.csv
```

If you want to skip the first 3 rows and display the remaining rows in a text file, you can use this command:

```
$ awk 'NR > 3' employees.csv
2000,John Smith,03/08/2020,87.23

3000,Dave Stone,07/15/2022,84.16
```

The following `awk` snippet is a slightly longer version of the preceding `awk` command that does the same thing:

```
$ awk 'NR > 3 { print }' employees.csv

awk '/start/,/stop/{if($0 ~ /stop/){print}; if($0 !~ /stop/)
   {printf $0" "}}' file
```

Display a Range of Lines Based on Strings

The preceding section uses the built-in NR variable to display a range of lines, and the following `awk` command specifies text strings as a range of rows to display:

```
$ awk '/two/,/three/ {print}' text_lines.txt
this is line two
this is line one
this is line three
```

Insert Blank Lines

You can print a blank line after each line of a file by changing ORS from the default of one new line to two new lines, as shown here:

```
cat columns.txt | awk 'BEGIN { ORS ="\n\n" } ; { print $0 }'
```

Alternatively, you can include one or more print (or printf) statements in the body of an awk script, depending on the number of blank lines that you want to appear in the output after each input line. In fact, you can use conditional logic to print a different number of blank lines after a given input line.

Remove Blank Lines

The following code snippet prints lines that are not blank:

```
$ awk 'NF' employees.csv
empid,full_name,start_date,expenses
1000,Jane Jones,12/05/2021,93.55
2000,John Smith,03/08/2020,87.23
3000,Dave Stone,07/15/2022,84.16
```

Specifying the Number of Fields

The following code snippet prints the number of fields in each line:

```
awk '{print NF,":",$0}' employees.csv
1 : empid,full_name,start_date,expenses
2 : 1000,Jane Jones,12/05/2021,93.55
0 :
2 : 2000,John Smith,03/08/2020,87.23
0 :
2 : 3000,Dave Stone,07/15/2022,84.16
```

The following code snippet specifies "," as the field delimiter and also prints the number of fields in each line:

```
$ awk -F"," '{print NF,":",$0}' employees.csv
4 : empid,full_name,start_date,expenses
4 : 1000,Jane Jones,12/05/2021,93.55
0 :
4 : 2000,John Smith,03/08/2020,87.23
0 :
4 : 3000,Dave Stone,07/15/2022,84.16
```

The following code snippet prints the rows that contain more than 2 fields:

```
$ awk -F"," '{if(NF > 2) print NF,":",$0}' employees.csv
4 : empid,full_name,start_date,expenses
4 : 1000,Jane Jones,12/05/2021,93.55
4 : 2000,John Smith,03/08/2020,87.23
4 : 3000,Dave Stone,07/15/2022,84.16
```

Here is another way to write the preceding `awk` command that is simpler to read:

```
$ awk -F"," '
{
   if(NF > 2)
     print NF,":",$0
}
' employees.csv
```

The following `awk` command also includes the record number and the fields number using NR and NF, respectively:

```
$ awk -F"," '
{
   if(NF > 2)
     print "Record",NR, "Field Count",NF,":",$0
}
' employees.csv
```

The output from the preceding `awk` command is shown here:

```
Record 1 Field Count 4 : empid,full_name,start_date,expenses
Record 2 Field Count 4 : 1000,Jane Jones,12/05/2021,93.55
Record 4 Field Count 4 : 2000,John Smith,03/08/2020,87.23
Record 6 Field Count 4 : 3000,Dave Stone,07/15/2022,84.16
```

Changing the Field Separator FS

The following code snippet uses the `sed` command to generate a set of rows in which the "," separator has been replaced with a "#" field separator:

```
$ cat employees.csv |sed "s/,/#/g"
empid#full_name#start_date#expenses
1000#Jane Jones#12/05/2021#93.55

2000#John Smith#03/08/2020#87.23

3000#Dave Stone#07/15/2022#84.16
```

The following `awk` command displays a set of rows whose field separator is a "#" symbol instead of a "," symbol:

```
$ awk 'BEGIN { FS=","; OFS="#" } NF { print $1, $3 }'
employees.csv
empid#start_date
1000#12/05/2021
2000#03/08/2020
3000#07/15/2022
```

The preceding `awk` command contains hard-coded fields, whereas Listing 3.7 displays the content of `replace_delimiters.sh` that shows you how to replace the "," delimiter with a "#" for text files that contain an arbitrary number of fields.

LISTING 3.7: replace_delimiters.sh

```
# replace field delimiter "," with "#"
awk -F"," '
{
  for(i=1; i<=NF; i++) {
    printf("%s#",$i)
  }
  print ""
}
' employees.csv
```

Listing 3.7 contains an `awk` command that specifies a comma ",", as a field separator. The main execution block is a loop that iterates through each field in the current input line. During each iteration the current field is printed, along with a "#" character. Launch the code in Listing 3.6, and you will see the following output:

```
empid#full_name#start_date#expenses#
1000#Jane Jones#12/05/2021#93.55#

2000#John Smith#03/08/2020#87.23#

3000#Dave Stone#07/15/2022#84.16#
```

The output from Listing 3.6 contains a trailing "#" character that we can remove as follows:

```
$ ./replace_delimiter.sh   |sed "s/#$//"
empid#full_name#start_date#expenses
1000#Jane Jones#12/05/2021#93.55

2000#John Smith#03/08/2020#87.23

3000#Dave Stone#07/15/2022#84.16
```

Listing 3.8 displays the content of `replace_delimiters2.sh` that shows you how to replace the "," delimiter with a "#" for text files that contain an arbitrary number of fields.

LISTING 3.8: replace_delimiters2.sh

```
# use a "@" as a field delimiter:
awk -F'[:#|^]' '{printf("%s@%s@%s@%s\n",$1,$2,$3,$4)}'
    delimiter1.txt

# use a space as a field delimiter:
#awk -F'[:#|^]' '{print $1, $2, $3, $4}' delimiter1.txt
```

Listing 3.8 contains an `awk` command that specifies the characters ":," "#," "|," and "^" as field delimiters for the input lines. The main execution block is a `print()` statement that prints the fields $1, $2, $3, and $4 with an "@" as a field delimiter. The second `awk` command has been commented out, and the only difference is that a white space is the field delimiter instead of an "@" character. Launch the code in Listing 3.7, and then launch the code in Listing 3.8, and you will see the following output:

```
1000@Jane@Edwards@Sales
2000@Tom@Smith@Development
3000@Dave@Del Ray@Marketing
```

Exclude Fields

The following code snippet excludes the third column:

```
$ awk '{$3=""; print $0}' FILE
```

Print all the other columns, but not the first and the second ones:

```
$ awk '{$1=$2=""; print $0}' FILE
```

The following code snippet prints the even-numbered rows:

```
$ awk -F"," '{if (NR % 2 == 0) print}' employees.csv
1000,Jane Jones,12/05/2021,93.55
2000,John Smith,03/08/2020,87.23
3000,Dave Stone,07/15/2022,84.16
```

The following code snippet prints the even-numbered fields:

```
$ awk -F"," '{print $2,$4}' employees.csv
full_name expenses
Jane Jones 93.55

John Smith 87.23

Dave Stone 84.16
```

The following code snippet prints the even-numbered fields in non-blank rows:

```
$ awk -F"," '{if(NF > 0) print $2,$4}' employees.csv
full_name expenses
Jane Jones 93.55
John Smith 87.23
Dave Stone 84.16
```

The preceding code snippets only print the second and fourth fields, whereas Listing 3.9 displays the content of even_fields.sh, which prints the even-numbered fields for rows that contain any number of fields.

LISTING 3.9: even_fields.sh

```
awk -F"," '
{
   for(i=1; i<=NF; i+=2) {
     printf("%s:",$i)
   }
```

```
    print
}
' employees.csv

#one-line version:
#awk -F"," ' { for(i=1; i<=NF; i+=2) { printf("%s:",$i) }
print } ' employees.csv
```

Listing 3.9 contains an awk command that specifies a comma (","") for the field separator. Next, the awk command contains a loop that iterates through each input field and uses the printf() statement to print the contents of the even-numbered fields. Notice that the bottom line of code specifies the CSV file employees.csv as the input file. Launch the code in Listing 3.9, and you will see the following output:

```
empid:start_date:empid,full_name,start_date,expenses
1000:12/05/2021:1000,Jane Jones,12/05/2021,93.55

2000:03/08/2020:2000,John Smith,03/08/2020,87.23

3000:07/15/2022:3000,Dave Stone,07/15/2022,84.16
```

Listing 3.10 displays the content of even_fields2.sh that prints the even-numbered fields for non-empty rows that contain any number of fields.

LISTING 3.10: even_fields2.sh
```
awk -F"," '
{
   if(NF > 0) {
       for(i=1; i<=NF; i+=2) {
         printf("%s:",$i)
       }
       print
   }
}
' employees.csv
```

Listing 3.10 contains almost the same code as Listing 3.9: the only difference is that Listing 3.10 skips the first row of the input file employees.csv. Launch the code in Listing 3.10, and you will see the following output:

```
empid:start_date:empid,full_name,start_date,expenses
1000:12/05/2021:1000,Jane Jones,12/05/2021,93.55
2000:03/08/2020:2000,John Smith,03/08/2020,87.23
3000:07/15/2022:3000,Dave Stone,07/15/2022,84.16
```

Switch Adjacent Fields

Listing 3.11 displays the content of switch_fields.sh that switches adjacent fields in employees.csv.

LISTING 3.11: switch_fields.sh

```
# switch adjacent fields
awk -F"," '
{
  if(NF > 0) {
      for(i=1; i<=NF; i+=2) {
        printf("%s#%s#",$(i+1),$i)
      }
      print ""
  }
}
' employees.csv
```

Listing 3.11 is similar to Listing 3.10, except that *every* field is printed, along with a "#" as a field delimiter because of the following code snippet:

```
printf("%s#%s#",$(i+1),$i)
```

Launch the code in Listing 3.10, and you will see the following output:

```
full_name#empid#expenses#start_date#
Jane Jones#1000#93.55#12/05/2021#
John Smith#2000#87.23#03/08/2020#
Dave Stone#3000#84.16#07/15/2022#
```

Display Fields in Reverse Order

The following code snippet displays the fields in `employees.csv` in reverse order:

```
$ awk -F"," '{print $4,$3,$2,$1}' employees.csv
expenses start_date full_name empid
93.55  12/05/2021 Jane Jones 1000

87.23 03/08/2020 John Smith 2000

84.16 07/15/2022 Dave Stone 3000
```

The following code snippet displays the fields of the non-empty rows in `employees.csv` in reverse order:

```
$ awk -F"," '{if(NF > 0) print $4,$3,$2,$1}' employees.csv
expenses start_date full_name empid
93.55  12/05/2021 Jane Jones 1000
87.23 03/08/2020 John Smith 2000
84.16 07/15/2022 Dave Stone 3000
```

The preceding examples contain hard-coded field values, whereas Listing 3.12 will work for rows that contain any number of fields.

LISTING 3.12: reverse_fields.sh

```
# print non-empty rows in reverse order
awk -F"," '
{
```

```
   if(NF > 0) {
      for(i=NF; i>=1; i--) {
        printf("%s,",$i)
      }
      print ""
   }
}
' employees.csv
```

Listing 3.12 reverses the order in which the fields of an input line are printed because the `for` loop iterates from `NF` to 1, as shown here:

```
for(i=NF; i>=1; i--) {
   printf("%s,",$i)
}
```

Launch the code in Listing 3.12, and you will see the following output:

```
expenses,start_date,full_name,empid,
93.55,12/05/2021,Jane Jones,1000,
87.23,03/08/2020,John Smith,2000,
84.16,07/15/2022,Dave Stone,3000,
```

Notice that the rows in the preceding output have a trailing "," character, which we can remove by piping the output from Listing 3.12 to the `sed` command, as shown here:

```
$ ./reverse_fields.sh |sed "s/,$//"
expenses,start_date,full_name,empid
93.55,12/05/2021,Jane Jones,1000
87.23,03/08/2020,John Smith,2000
84.16,07/15/2022,Dave Stone,3000
```

Count Non-Empty and Empty Rows

The following code snippet counts the number of non-empty rows in `employees.csv`:

```
$ awk '/./ { count+=1 } END { print "Non-empty rows:",count
}' employees.csv
Non-empty rows: 4
```

The preceding `awk` command uses the metacharacter "." to match a single character, which means that the variable count (whose initial value is 0 by default) is incremented for each line that contains at least one character.

The following `awk` command counts the number of empty lines:

```
$ awk '/^$/ { count+=1 } END { print "Empty rows:",count }'
    employees.csv
Empty rows: 2
```

Detecting Transfer Protocols

Listing 3.13 displays the contents of `protocols.txt`, and Listing 3.14 displays the contents of `awk_protocols.sh`

LISTING 3.13: protocols.txt

```
http
https
ftp
Listing 3.14: awk_protocols.sh
awk '{ if ($1 ~ /http/)     print "HTTP-like protocol"}'
    protocols.txt
awk '{ if ($1 ~ /^http$/)   print "Only HTTP protocol"}'
    protocols.txt
awk '{ if ($1 ~ /http|https|ftp/) print $1}' protocols.txt
```

Listing 3.14 contains three `awk` command, where the first one prints a message if $1 matches the string `http`. The second `awk` command checks if an input line starts with the string `https`, after which another message is displayed. The third `awk` command checks if $1 matches any of the three strings in the pattern `http|https|ftp`, and then prints another string if a match is successful. Note that the text file `protocol.txt` is specified as the input file for each of the three `awk` commands. Launch the code in Listing 3.14, and you will see the following output:

LISTING 3.14: awk_protocols.sh

```
HTTP-like protocol
HTTP-like protocol
Only HTTP protocol
http
https
```

Detecting Number Formats

Listing 3.15 displays the contents of `numbers.txt`, and Listing 3.16 displays the contents of `awk_numbers.sh`.

LISTING 3.15: numbers.txt

```
FA13
1234
192.168.12.40
```

LISTING 3.16: awk_numbers.sh

```
awk '
{
  if($1 ~ /^[0-9]+$/)            { print "Decimal:     ",$1}
  else if ($1 ~ /^[A-F|0-9]+$/) { print "Hexadecimal:",$1}
  else if ($1 ~ /^[0-9]{3}.[0-9]{3}.[0-9]{2}.[0-9]{2}$/) {
    print "IPV4:        ",$1
  }
}
' numbers.txt
```

Listing 3.16 contains an awk command that contains if-else logic to make comparisons of $1 with various patterns. The first pattern is ^[0-9]+$, which matches any line that consists exclusively of decimal digits. If a match occurs, then a message is displayed.

The second code snippet contains the pattern ^[A-F|0-9]+$, which matches any line that consists of any combination of decimal digits and the uppercase letters A through F, inclusive. This pattern matches any hexadecimal number with an arbitrary number of digits.

The third pattern matches an IP address with a format that involves a decimal delimiter that follows three digits, another set of three digits, and then a pair of digits, which is followed by another pair of digits. Note that a matching digit is a hexadecimal digit. Launch the code, and you will see the following output:

```
Hexadecimal: FA13
Decimal:     1234
IPV4:        192.168.12.40
```

Working with Record Lengths

Recall that the file text_lines.txt contains the following data:

```
this is line one
this is line two
this is line one
this is line three
this is line four
```

The following awk command displays the lengths of each line in text_lines.txt:

```
awk '{print length($0), $0}' text_lines.txt
16 this is line one
16 this is line two
16 this is line one
18 this is line three
17 this is line four
```

The following awk command displays all the lines whose length is greater than 20:

```
$ awk 'length($0) > 16' text_lines.txt
this is line three
this is line four
```

The following awk command displays the length of the longest line in text_lines.txt:

```
$ awk '{ if (length($0) > max) max = length($0) }
     END { print max }' text_lines.txt
18
```

The following awk command is a variation of the preceding awk command that includes a comment:

```
$ awk '{ if (x < length($0)) x = length($0) }
     END { print "The longest line length = " x }'
          text_lines.txt
The longest line length = 18
```

The following awk command displays the total file size in the current directory:

```
$ ls -l * | awk '{ x += $5 } END { print "total bytes: " x }'
total bytes: 6572358
```

Aligning Text with the printf() Statement

Since awk is a programming language inside a single command, it also has its own way of producing formatted output via the printf() statement.

Listing 3.17 displays the contents of columns2.txt, and Listing 3.18 displays the content of the shell script AlignColumns1.sh that shows you how to align the columns in a text file.

LISTING 3.17: columns2.txt

```
one two
three four
one two three four
five six
one two three
four five
```

LISTING 3.18: AlignColumns1.sh

```
awk '
{
    # left-align  $1 on a 10-char column
    # right-align $2 on a 10-char column
    # right-align $3 on a 10-char column
    # right-align $4 on a 10-char column
    printf("%-10s*%10s*%10s*%10s*\n", $1, $2, $3, $4)
}
' columns2.txt
```

Listing 3.18 contains a printf() statement that displays the first four fields of each row in the file columns2.txt, where each field is 10 characters wide.

The output from launching the code in Listing 3.18 is here:

```
one        *       two*          *          *
three      *      four*          *          *
one        *       two*    three*      four*
five       *       six*          *          *
one        *       two*    three*          *
four       *      five*          *          *
```

Keep in mind that `printf()` is reasonably powerful and as such has its own syntax, which is beyond the scope of this chapter. A search online can find the manual pages and also discussions of "how to do X with `printf()`."

Working with Loops in awk

The `awk` command supports the following types of loops:

- `for`

- `while`

- `do-while`

The following subsections contain examples of each type of loop in the preceding list.

A for Loop in awk

Listing 3.19 displays the content of `Loop.sh` that illustrates how to print a list of numbers in a loop. Note that "i++" is another way of writing "i=i+1" in `awk` (and most C-derived languages).

LISTING 3.19: Loop.sh

```
echo "" | awk '
BEGIN {}
{
   for(i=0; i<5; i++) {
     printf("%3d", i)
   }
}
END { print "\n" }
'
```

Listing 3.19 contains a `for` loop that prints numbers on the same line via the `printf()` statement. Notice that a new line is printed only in the END block of the code. The output from Listing 3.19 is here:

```
0  1  2  3  4
```

Exponents in a for Loop

Listing 3.20 displays the content of `awk-for-loop.sh` that shows you how to use a `for` loop in `awk`.

LISTING 3.20: awk-for-loop.sh

```
echo "" | awk '
BEGIN {
   for(i=1; i<=10; i++)
```

```
    print "The cube of", i, "is", i*i*i;
} '

# as a single line awk command:
# awk 'BEGIN { for(i=1; i<=10; i++) print "The cube of", i,
# "is", i*i*i;}'
```

Listing 3.20 contains an awk command that starts with a BEGIN block with a loop that iterates through the values between 1 and 10, inclusive. Each iteration prints the value of the loop variable as well as the cube of the loop variable. Launch the code in Listing 3.20, and you will see the following output:

```
The cube of 1 is 1
The cube of 2 is 8
The cube of 3 is 27
The cube of 4 is 64
The cube of 5 is 125
The cube of 6 is 216
The cube of 7 is 343
The cube of 8 is 512
The cube of 9 is 729
The cube of 10 is 1000
```

A for Loop with a break Statement

Listing 3.21 displays the content of awk-loop-break.sh that illustrates how to use a break statement in a for loop in awk.

LISTING 3.21: awk-loop-break.sh

```
echo "" | awk '
{
   for(x=1; x<4; x++) {
      print "x:",x
      if(x == 2) {
         break;
      }
   }
}
'
```

The preceding code block prints output only until the variable x has the value 2, after which the loop exits (because of the break statement inside the conditional logic). The following output is displayed:

```
x:1
x:2
```

Working with while Loops in awk

Listing 3.22 displays the content of awk-while-loop.sh that shows you how to use a while loop in awk.

LISTING 3.22: awk-while-loop.sh

```
echo "" | awk '
BEGIN {
  x=1; max=10
  while(1) {
    print "The cube of",x,"is",x*x*x
      if ( x == max ) break; x++;
  }
}'

# as a single line awk command:
# awk 'BEGIN { for(i=1; i<=10; i++) print "The cube of", i,
# "is", i*i*i;}'
```

Listing 3.22 contains an awk command with a BEGIN block that initializes the variables x and max to 1 and 10, respectively. Next, a while loop prints the value of x and x cubed, and then increments the value of x. When x reaches the value 10, an if statement causes the loop to terminate. Launch the code in Listing 3.22, and you will see the following output:

```
The cube of 1 is 1
The cube of 2 is 8
The cube of 3 is 27
The cube of 4 is 64
The cube of 5 is 125
The cube of 6 is 216
The cube of 7 is 343
The cube of 8 is 512
The cube of 9 is 729
The cube of 10 is 1000
```

A do-while Loop in awk

Listing 3.23 displays the content of awk-dowhile.sh that shows you how to use a do-while loop in awk.

LISTING 3.23: awk-dowhile.sh

```
echo "" | awk '
{
  x = 0

  do {
    print "x:",x
    x = x + 1
  } while(x < 4)
}
'
```

The preceding code block generates the following output:

```
x:0
x:1
x:2
x:3
```

Conditional Logic and Control Statements

Like other programming languages, awk provides support for conditional logic (if/else) and control statements (for/while loops). Listing 3.24 shows you how to use if/else logic.

LISTING 3.24: if-else.sh

```
echo "" | awk '
BEGIN { x = 10 }
{
  if (x % 2 == 0) {
      print "x is even"
  }
  else {
      print "x is odd"
  }
}
'
```

The preceding code block initializes the variable x with the value 10 and prints "x is even" if x is divisible by 2; otherwise, it prints "x is odd."

The break, continue, and next Keywords in awk

The following code snippet illustrates how to use next and continue in a for loop in awk:

```
awk '
{
   /expression1/ { var1 = 5; next }
   /expression2/ { var2 = 7; next }
   /expression3/ { continue }
   // some other code block here
' somefile
```

When the current line matches expression1, then var1 is assigned the value 5 and awk reads the next input line: hence, expression2 and expression3 will not be tested. If expression1 does not match and expression2 *does* match, then var2 is assigned the value 7 and then awk will read the next input line. If only expression3 results in a positive match, then awk skips the remaining block of code and processes the next input line.

Listing 3.25 displays the contents of next_lines.txt, and Listing 3.26 displays the content of next_lines.sh that illustrates the effect of the next keyword in an awk command.

LISTING 3.25: next_lines.txt

```
one two
one two three
one two three four
```

LISTING 3.26: next_lines.sh

```
echo "" | awk '
{
   if($1 ~ /one/) {
     print "Skipping line:", NR
     next
   }

   print "lines containing 'one' are skipped"
}
' next_lines.txt
```

Listing 3.26 contains an `echo` command that passes an empty string to the `awk` command, which in turn contains a conditional statement that checks whether $1 matches the string `one`. If there is a match, then a message is displayed, and the next keyword causes `awk` to process the next input line. Since every line in `next_lines.txt` contains the string `one`, the second print statement will not be executed. Launch the code in Listing 3.26, and you will see the following output:

```
Skipping line: 1
Skipping line: 2
Skipping line: 3
```

Listing 3.27 displays the content of `control_flow1.sh` that illustrates the effect of the `break`, `continue`, and `next` keywords in a loop.

LISTING 3.27: control_flow1.sh

```
echo "" | awk '
{
   printf("all values:        ")
   for(i=0; i<5; i++) {
      printf("%s ",i)
   }
   print ""

   printf("break keyword:     ")
   for(i=0; i<5; i++) {
      printf("%s ",i)
      if(i == 2)
        break
   }
   print ""

   printf("continue keyword: ")
   for(i=0; i<5; i++) {
```

```
        printf("%s ",i)
        if(i == 2)
           continue
     }
     print ""

     printf("next keyword:       ")
     for(i=0; i<5; i++) {
        printf("%s ",i)
        if(i == 2)
           next
     }
     print ""
}
'
```

Listing 3.27 contains a `for` loop that prints numbers on the same line via the `printf()` statement. Notice that a new line is printed only in the END block of the code. The output from Listing 3.27 is here:

```
all values:        0 1 2 3 4
break keyword:     0 1 2
continue keyword: 0 1 2 3 4
next keyword:      0 1 2
```

Listing 3.28 displays the content of `control_flow2.sh` that places the conditional logic before the `printf()` statement in each loop in Listing 3.28.

LISTING 3.28: control_flow2.sh

```
echo "" | awk '
{
     printf("all values:        ")
     for(i=0; i<5; i++) {
        printf("%s ",i)
     }
     print ""

     printf("break keyword:       ")
     for(i=0; i<5; i++) {
        if(i == 2)
           break
        printf("%s ",i)
     }
     print ""

     printf("continue keyword: ")
     for(i=0; i<5; i++) {
        if(i == 2)
           continue
        printf("%s ",i)
     }
     print ""
```

```
        printf("next keyword:      ")
        for(i=0; i<5; i++) {
            if(i == 2)
                next
            printf("%s ",i)
        }
        print ""
    }
    '
```

Listing 3.28 contains a `for` loop that prints numbers on the same line via the `printf()` statement. Notice that a new line is printed only in the END block of the code. The output from Listing 3.28 is here:

```
all values:        0 1 2 3 4
break keyword:     0 1
continue keyword:  0 1 3 4
next keyword:      0 1
```

The exit Keyword

Listing 3.29 displays the content of `exit_keyword.sh` that shows you how to use a `while` loop in `awk`.

LISTING 3.29: exit_keyword.sh

```
echo "" | awk '
{
    for(i=1;i<10;i++) {
        if(i==1)
            exit 2
        elif(i==2)
            exit 4
        elif(i==3)
            exit 8
        print(i)
    }
}
'
```

Listing 3.29 contains a `for` loop that iterates from 1 to 9 inclusive. prints numbers on the same line. Notice that when the loop variable I equals 1, 2, or 4 that an `exit` statement is executed with the values 2, 4, and 8, respectively. By contrast, all the other values of the loop variable i are printed. Now, launch the following command:

```
$ ./exit_keyword.sh; echo "rc=$?"
```

The output from the preceding command is shown here:

```
2
```

Conditionally Displaying Fields

Listing 3.30 displays the content of `conditional_fields1.sh` that shows you how to use a `while` loop in `awk`.

LISTING 3.30: conditional_fields1.sh

```
awk '
{
   for ( j=1; j<=NF; j++ ) {
     if ( j < 3)
       continue
     printf( "%s ", $j )
   }
}
' columns4.txt
```

Listing 3.30 contains an awk command with a for loop that processes every field of every input line. If the value of the loop variable j is less than 3, then the code simply returns to the for statement and processes the next field. If j is not less than 3, then the value of the current field is printed. The file columns4.txt is specified for the input to the awk command. Launch the code in Listing 3.26, and you will see the following output:

```
TWO four THREE FOUR six three
```

Listing 3.31 displays the content of conditional_fields2.sh that shows you how to use a while loop in awk.

LISTING 3.31: conditional_fields2.sh

```
awk '
{
   for ( j=1; j<=NF; j++ ) {
     if ( j < 3)
       continue
     printf( "%s ", $j )

     if ( j == NF) {
       print ""
     }
   }
}
' columns4.txt
```

Listing 3.31 contains an awk command that contains a for loop that processes every field of every input line. If the value of the loop variable j is less than 3, then the code simply returns to the for statement and processes the next field. If j is not less than 3, then the value of the current field is printed. In addition, if the value of j equals the value of NF, then a new line is printed. The file columns4.txt is specified for the input to the awk command. Launch the code in Listing 3.31, and you will see the following output:

```
TWO
four
```

```
THREE FOUR
six
three
Abcd
```

Logical Operators in awk

The logical operators &&, ||, and ! represent AND, OR, and NOT, respectively. These operators are useful for creating compound expressions to select a subset of the rows in a text file that satisfy a set of logical criteria. For example, the following code snippet uses || to exclude rows 2 and 3:

```
$ awk 'NR < 2 || NR > 4' employees.csv
empid,full_name,start_date,expenses

3000,Dave Stone,07/15/2022,84.16
```

The following code snippet uses && to display only rows 2, 3, and 4:

```
$ awk 'NR > 1 && NR < 5' employees.csv
1000,Jane Jones,12/05/2021,93.55

2000,John Smith,03/08/2020,87.23
```

The following code snippet displays all rows except the second row:

```
$ awk 'NR != 1' employees.csv
1000,Jane Jones,12/05/2021,93.55

2000,John Smith,03/08/2020,87.23

3000,Dave Stone,07/15/2022,84.16
```

The following code snippet displays all rows that are not greater than 2 (i.e., the first and second rows):

```
$ awk '!(NR > 2)' employees.csv
empid,full_name,start_date,expenses
1000,Jane Jones,12/05/2021,93.55
```

Logical Operators and Partial Matches

The preceding section showed you how to compose simple expressions using logical operators, and this section contains examples that combine logical operators with partial matches.

For example, the following awk command matches the rows in employees.csv whose name starts with the letter J:

```
$ awk -F"," '{if($2 ~ /J/) print}' employees.csv
1000,Jane Jones,12/05/2021,93.55
2000,John Smith,03/08/2020,87.23
```

The following awk command matches the rows in employees.csv whose name do *not* start with the letter J:

```
$ $ awk -F"," '{if(($2 !~ /J/)&&(NF > 1)) print}' employees.csv
empid,full_name,start_date,expenses
3000,Dave Stone,07/15/2022,84.16
```

The following awk command matches the rows in employees.csv whose name starts with the letter J and ends with the letter h:

```
$ awk -F"," '{if($2 ~ /J/ && ($2 ~ /h/)) print}' employees.csv
2000,John Smith,03/08/2020,87.23
```

The following awk command matches the rows in employees.csv whose name starts with the sequence Jan:

```
$ awk -F"," '{if($2 ~ /Jan/) print}' employees.csv
1000,Jane Jones,12/05/2021,93.55
```

The following awk command matches the rows in employees.csv whose name starts with the letter J *and* whose empid is greater than 1000:

```
$ awk -F"," '{if($2 ~ /J/ && ($1 > 1000)) print}' employees.csv
1000,Jane Jones,12/05/2021,93.55
```

The following awk command matches the rows in employees.csv whose name starts with the letter J *or* whose empid is greater than 1000:

```
$ awk -F"," '{if($2 ~ /J/ || ($1 > 1000)) print}' employees.csv
empid,full_name,start_date,expenses
1000,Jane Jones,12/05/2021,93.55
2000,John Smith,03/08/2020,87.23
3000,Dave Stone,07/15/2022,84.16
```

The following awk command matches the rows in employees.csv whose name starts with the letter J *and* whose empid is greater than 2000 *or* whose empid equals 3000:

```
$
awk -F"," '{if(($2 ~ /J/ && ($1 > 1000))|| ($1 == "3000"))
print}' employees.csv
2000,John Smith,03/08/2020,87.23
3000,Dave Stone,07/15/2022,84.16
```

The && operator has higher precedence than the || operator, which means that the following awk command has the same output as the preceding awk command:

```
$
awk -F"," '{if($2 ~ /J/ && ($1 > 1000)|| ($1 == "3000"))
    print}' employees.csv
2000,John Smith,03/08/2020,87.23
3000,Dave Stone,07/15/2022,84.16
```

However, the following does require the given parentheses if you want to perform the || operation separate from the && operation (and the output is different):

```
$ awk -F"," '{if($2 ~ /J/ && (($1 > 1000)|| ($1 == "3000")))
```

```
       print}' employees.csv
2000,John Smith,03/08/2020,87.23
```

The following `awk` command matches the rows in `employees.csv` whose name starts with either Jane or John:

```
$ awk -F"," '{if($2 ~ /Jane|John/) print}' employees.csv
1000,Jane Jones,12/05/2021,93.55
2000,John Smith,03/08/2020,87.23
```

In addition, you can display blank lines with the following `awk` command:

```
$ awk -F"," '{if(NF == 0) print}' employees.csv
```

Invert the logic in the preceding `awk` command to display the non-blank lines with the following `awk` command:

```
$ awk -F"," '{if(NF != 0) print}' employees.csv
empid,full_name,start_date,expenses
1000,Jane Jones,12/05/2021,93.55
2000,John Smith,03/08/2020,87.23
3000,Dave Stone,07/15/2022,84.16
```

Remove the header line in the preceding output with the following `awk` command:

```
$ awk -F"," '{if((NF != 0) && (NR > 1)) print}' employees.csv
1000,Jane Jones,12/05/2021,93.55
2000,John Smith,03/08/2020,87.23
3000,Dave Stone,07/15/2022,84.16
```

Count the number of non-blank data lines with the following `awk` command:

```
$ awk -F"," '{if((NF != 0) && (NR > 1)) count++} END { print count}' employees.csv
3
```

Checking for Leap Years

A nice example of nested conditional statements involves checking for leap years. Listing 3.32 displays the contents of `dates.txt`, and Listing 3.33 displays the content of `leap_years.sh` that shows you how to determine whether a year is a leap year.

LISTING 3.32: dates.txt

```
02/29/2000
02/29/2002
03/15/1900
12/08/1904
```

LISTING 3.33: leap_year.sh

```
#####################################
# check for leap years
```

```
# given a date mm/dd/yyyy
# if year % 4 == 0:
#   if year % 100 == 0:
#     if year % 400 == 0:
#       print date,"is a leap year"
#     else:
#       print date,"is not a leap year"
# else:
#   print date,"is not a leap year"
#####################################

cat dates.txt | awk -F"/" '
{
  date=$0
  month=substr($0,1,2)
  day=substr($0,4,2)
  year=substr($0,7,4)
  print "month:",month,"day:",day,"year:",year

  if(year % 4 == 0) {
    if(year % 100 == 0) {
      if(year % 400 == 0) {
        print date,"is a leap year A"
      } else {
        print date,"is not a leap year B"
        if((day == 29) && (month == 2)) {
          print date,"is an invalid date ***"
        }
      }
    } else {
      print date,"is not a leap year C"
      if((day == 29) && (month == 2)) {
        print date,"is an invalid date ***"
      }
    }
  } else {
    print date,"is not a leap year D"
    if((day == "29") && (month == "02")) {
      print date,"is an invalid date ***"
    }
  }
  print "-------------\n"
}
'
```

Listing 3.33 contains an initial command block with pseudocode that specifies how to determine whether a positive integer is a leap year. The awk command in Listing 3.33 contains the implementation of the pseudocode, and also specifies the file dates.txt as the input to the awk command.

Notice that there are four print statements that have one of the letters A, B, C, or D in the final portion of the output: these have been included just to show the logical path of execution that leads to the determination of whether a given year is a leap year. Launch the code in Listing 3.33, and you will see the following output:

```
Field 1 is a
month: 02 day: 29 year: 2000
02/29/2000 is a leap year A
------------

month: 02 day: 29 year: 2002
02/29/2002 is not a leap year D
02/29/2002 is an invalid date ***
------------

month: 03 day: 15 year: 1900
03/15/1900 is not a leap year B
------------

month: 12 day: 08 year: 1904
12/08/1904 is not a leap year C
------------
```

Formatting Output

The awk command supports several types of output formats. The following list shows you the different format options that are available and a brief description of their purpose:

- %a, %A: prints a floating point number with C99 hexadecimal floating point format
- %c: prints a number as a character
- %d, %i: prints a decimal integer
- %e, %E: prints a number in scientific (exponential) notation
- %f: prints a number in floating point notation
- %F: similar to $f (POSIX extension)
- %g, %G: prints a number in scientific notation or floating point notation
- %o: prints an unsigned octal integer
- %s: prints a string
- %u: prints an unsigned decimal integer
- %x, %X: prints an unsigned hexadecimal integer

Listing 3.34 displays the content of formats.sh that shows you how an integer is displayed using different formats (many outputs are the same).

LISTING 3.34: formats.sh

```
echo "123" | awk '
{
    print "=> number:",$0
    printf("a: %a\n", $0)
    printf("A: %A\n", $0)
    printf("c: %c\n", $0)
    printf("d: %d\n", $0)
    printf("e: %e\n", $0)
    printf("f: %f\n", $0)
    printf("F: %F\n", $0)
    printf("g: %g\n", $0)
    printf("G: %G\n", $0)
    printf("i: %i\n", $0)
    printf("o: %o\n", $0)
    printf("s: %s\n", $0)
    printf("u: %u\n", $0)
    printf("x: %s\n", $0)
    printf("X: %X\n", $0)
}
'
```

Listing 3.34 contains a set of `printf()` statements that specify different formats for displaying the contents of $0, which in this example is a string. Launch the code in Listing 3.34, and you will see the following output:

```
=> number: 123
a: 0x1.ecp+6
a: 0X1.ECP+6
c: {
d: 123
e: 1.230000e+02
f: 123.000000
F: 123.000000
g: 123
G: 123
i: 123
o: 173
s: 123
u: 123
x: 123
X: 7B
```

Listing 3.35 is similar to Listing 3.34, except that the input $0 is a floating point number instead of a string.

LISTING 3.35: formats2.sh

```
echo "123.45" | awk '
{
    print "=> number:",$0
    printf("a: %a\n", $0)
    printf("c: %c\n", $0)
    printf("d: %d\n", $0)
```

```
    printf("e: %e\n", $0)
    printf("f: %f\n", $0)
    printf("F: %F\n", $0)
    printf("g: %g\n", $0)
    printf("G: %G\n", $0)
    printf("i: %i\n", $0)
    printf("o: %o\n", $0)
    printf("s: %s\n", $0)
    printf("u: %u\n", $0)
    printf("x: %s\n", $0)
    printf("X: %X\n", $0)
}
'
```

Launch the code in Listing 3.35, and you will see the following output:

```
=> number: 123.45
a: 0x1.edccccccccccdp+6
c: {
d: 123
e: 1.234500e+02
f: 123.450000
F: 123.450000
g: 123.45
G: 123.45
i: 123
o: 173
s: 123.45
u: 123
x: 123.45
X: 7B
```

Listing 3.36 displays the content of formats3.sh that shows you how to perform left and right alignment for output strings and numbers.

LISTING 3.36: formats3.sh

```
awk '{ printf("%-10s\n", $1) }' thousands.txt
echo

awk '{ printf("%+10s\n", $1) }' thousands.txt
echo

awk '{ printf("%+10.5s\n", $1) }' thousands.txt
echo

awk '{ printf("%+10.5f\n", $1) }' thousands.txt
echo
```

Listing 3.36 contains four awk commands that print the rows in the text file thousands.txt using different formats. The first awk command specifies a left-justified format whereas the second awk command specifies a right-justified format.

The third `awk` command also specifies a right-justified format, with a decimal position for strings, which does not affect the output. The fourth `awk` command specifies a left-justified format for numbers, so the decimal position appears in the output. Now launch the code, and you will see the following output:

```
10
100
1000
10000
1000000
10000000

        10
       100
      1000
     10000
   1000000
  10000000

        10
       100
      1000
     10000
     10000
     10000

 +10.00000
+100.00000
+1000.00000
+10000.00000
+1000000.00000
+10000000.00000
```

Floating Point Output

Listing 3.37 displays the content of `numeric_strings.txt` that contains floating point numbers.

LISTING 3.37: numeric_strings.txt

```
3.5
3.12
3.123
```

Listing 3.38 displays the content of `numeric_strings1.sh` that illustrates how to add the rows of numbers in Listing 3.37.

LISTING 3.38: numeric_strings.sh

```
#######################################
# the format string specifies:
# %f = format a floating point value
```

```
# 06 = 6 character field padded with leading zeroes
# .1 = 1 digit  after the decimal point
# .2 = 2 digits after the decimal point
# .3 = 3 digits after the decimal point
##########################################

echo "" | awk '
{
   printf("%f :%06.1f\n", $1,$1)
   printf("%f :%06.2f\n", $1,$1)
   printf("%f :%06.3f\n", $1,$1)
   print "----------\n"
}
' numeric_strings.txt
```

Listing 3.38 contains three `printf()` statements that specify slightly different floating point formats for each floating point number in the file `numeric_strings.txt`. Launch the code in Listing 3.38, and you will see the following output:

```
3.500000 :0003.5
3.500000 :003.50
3.500000 :03.500
----------

3.500000 :   3.5
3.500000 :   3.50
3.500000 : 3.500
----------

3.120000 :0003.1
3.120000 :003.12
3.120000 :03.120
----------

3.120000 :   3.1
3.120000 :   3.12
3.120000 : 3.120
----------

3.123000 :0003.1
3.123000 :003.12
3.123000 :03.123
----------

3.123000 :   3.1
3.123000 :   3.12
3.123000 : 3.123
----------
```

Listing 3.39 displays the content of `numeric_strings.txt` that contains floating point numbers.

LISTING 3.39: numeric_strings2.txt

```
8.120
8.1230
8.12340
8.000
8.0000
```

Listing 3.40 displays the content of numeric_strings1.sh that illustrates how to add the rows of numbers in Listing 3.39.

LISTING 3.40: numeric_strings2.sh

```
awk '/^[0-9]+[.][0-9][1-9]*0/' numeric_strings2.txt
```

Listing 3.35 contains an awk command that involves the following regular expression:

1. The left-most character is a digit, followed by

2. One or more digits may appear, followed by

3. A plus sign, followed by

4. A decimal point, followed by

5. A digit in the range [0-9], followed by

6. Zero or more digits, followed by

7. Terminating in the digit 0

Now launch the code in Listing 3.40, and you will see the following output:

```
8.120
8.1230
8.12340
```

Inserting a Thousands Separator

Listing 3.41 displays the content of thousands.txt that contains floating point numbers.

LISTING 3.41: thousands.txt

```
10
100
1000
10000
1000000
10000000
```

Listing 3.42 displays the content of `thousands-separator.sh` that illustrates how to round each number in Listing 3.41.

LISTING 3.42: thousands-separator.sh

```
awk '
{
   len=length($0); result="";
   for (i=0;i<=len;i++) {
      TH=substr($0,len-i+1,1) TH; if (i > 0 && i < len && i
% 3 == 0) { TH = "," TH }
   }
   printf("Initial: %10d formatted: %s\n",$0,TH)
}' thousands.txt
```

Listing 3.42 contains an `awk` command that initializes the variables `len` and `result` with the length of the input string and the "" string, respectively. The next portion is a loop with a loop variable `i` that varies from 0 to the value of `len`, inclusive. During each iteration, the variable `TH` is pre-pended with the character in position `len-i+1` of $0, as shown here:

```
TH=substr($0,len-i+1,1) TH
```

If the loop variable `i` is between 0 and `len` (exclusive) and it is also a multiple of three, then `TH` is pre-pended with a comma (","). Notice that the loop proceeds in a right-to-left fashion while processing the characters in the input string $0, which is the manner in which commas are correctly inserted into a positive integer. The final code snippet prints the contents of the input string $0 and the formatted version of $0 (i.e., as a comma-separated number). Launch the code in Listing 3.42, and you will see the following output:

```
Initial:         10 formatted: 10
Initial:        100 formatted: 100
Initial:       1000 formatted: 1,000
Initial:      10000 formatted: 10,000
Initial:    1000000 formatted: 1,000,000
Initial:   10000000 formatted: 10,000,000
```

Scientific Notation

Listing 3.43 displays the content of `scientific1.sh` that illustrates how to work with scientific notation.

LISTING 3.43: scientific1.sh

```
echo "=> 12.34e-5:"
echo 12.34e-5  | awk '{printf("%.10f\n", $1)}'
echo 12.34e-5  | awk '{printf("%.10f\n", $1*1e4)}'
echo 12.34e-12 | awk '{printf("%.15f\n", $1*1e4)}'
echo
```

```
echo "=> 12.34e-12:"
echo 12.34e-12 | awk -M -v PREC=134 '{printf("%.40g\n", $1)}'
echo

# specify 40 decimal digits:
echo "=> 12.34e-12:"
echo 12.34e-12 | awk -M -v PREC=134 '{printf("%.40f\n", $1)}'
echo

echo "=> 5.0000000000e+02:"
echo "5.0000000000e+02" | awk '{printf("%d\n",$0);}'
echo

echo "=> 1.234567000e+02:"
echo "1.234567000e+02"  | awk '{printf("%0.2f\n",$0);}'
echo

# extract the exponent value (can be done with "cut"):
echo '=> 12.34e-12:'
echo '12.34e-12' |awk -F"e" '{ print "Base: " $1 " exponent: "
$2 }'
echo
```

Listing 3.43 contains 8 awk commands, each of which demonstrates how to format the output of scientific numbers using the floating point format that you have seen in previous code samples in this chapter. Compare each awk command with its corresponding output below. Launch the code in Listing 3.43, and you will see the following output:

```
=> 12.34e-5:
0.0001234000
1.2340000000
0.000000123400000

=> 12.34e-12:
1.234e-11

=> 12.34e-12:
0.0000000000012340000000000000000000000000000

=> 5.0000000000e+02:
500

=> 1.234567000e+02:
123.46

=> 12.34e-12:
Base: 12.34 exponent: -12
```

Listing 3.44 displays the contents of mixed_numbers.txt, and Listing 3.45 displays the content of Listing 3.40 that illustrates how to compare decimal numbers and numbers with scientific notation.

LISTING 3.44: mixed_numbers.txt

```
7E-1
7E-2
7E-3
40
4E1
4000
4E3
40000
4000000
4E6
40000000
4E7
```

LISTING 3.45: scientific2.sh

```
echo "=> Less than 1E-2:"
awk '($1 + 0) < 1E-2' mixed_numbers.txt
echo
echo "=> Greater than 1E3:"
awk '($1 + 0) > 1E3' mixed_numbers.txt
```

Listing 3.45 contains two awk commands: the first command prints the lines in mixed_numbers.txt whose value is less than 1E-2, whereas the second command prints the lines in mixed_numbers.txt whose value is greater than 1E3. Launch the code in Listing 3.45, and you will see the following output:

```
10
=> Less than 1E-2:
7E-3

=> Greater than 1E3:
4000
4E3
40000
4000000
4E6
40000000
4E7
100
1000
10000
1000000
10000000
```

Rounding and Truncating Numbers

Rounding a number involves finding the closest integer value to the given number, whereas truncating a number involves removing the decimal portion (if any) of a given number.

Rounding Numbers

Listing 3.46 displays the content of `rounding_numbers.txt` that contains floating point numbers.

LISTING 3.46: rounding_numbers.txt

```
3.12
3.5
3.9
-4.3
-4.5
-4.9
```

Listing 3.47 displays the content of `rounding_numbers.sh` that illustrates how to round each number in Listing 3.40.

LISTING 3.47: rounding_numbers.sh

```
awk '
{
   print "number:",$0,"rounded:",int($1   + 0.5)
}
' rounding_numbers.txt
```

Listing 3.47 contains an `awk` command that prints the value of an input floating point number and its rounded value, which is calculated by invoking the built-in function `int()` on the value of `$0 + 0.5`. Launch the code in Listing 3.47, and you will see the following output:

```
number:  3.12 rounded:  3
number:  3.5 rounded:  4
number:  3.9 rounded:  4
number:  -4.3 rounded:  -3
number:  -4.5 rounded:  -4
number:  -4.9 rounded:  -4
```

Truncating Numbers

Listing 3.48 displays the content of `truncating_numbers.sh`   that illustrates how to round each number in Listing 3.47.

LISTING 3.48: truncating_numbers.sh

```
awk '
{
   print "number:",$0,"truncated:",int($1)
}
' rounding_numbers.txt
```

Listing 3.48 contains an `awk` command that prints the value of an input floating point number and its rounded value, which is calculated by invoking the built-in function `int()` on the value of $0. Launch the code in Listing 3.48, and you will see the following output:

```
number: 3.12 truncated: 3
number: 3.5 truncated: 3
number: 3.9 truncated: 3
number: -4.3 truncated: -4
number: -4.5 truncated: -4
number: -4.9 truncated: -4
```

Numeric Functions in awk

The int(x) function returns the integer portion of a number. If the number is not already an integer, it falls between two integers. Of the two possible integers, the function will return the one closest to zero. This is different from a rounding function, which chooses the closer integer.

For example, int(3) is 3, int(3.9) is 3, int(-3.9) is -3, and int(-3) is -3 as well. An example of the int(x) function in an awk command is here:

```
awk 'BEGIN {
   print int(3.534);
   print int(4);
   print int(-5.223);
   print int(-5);
} '
```

The output is here:

```
3
4
-5
-5
```

The exp(x) function gives you the exponential of x, or reports an error if x is out of range. The range of values x can have depends on your machine's floating point representation.

```
awk 'BEGIN{
   print exp(123434346);
   print exp(0);
   print exp(-12);
} '
```

The output is here:

```
inf

1

6.14421e-06
```

The log(x) function gives you the natural logarithm of x, if x is positive; otherwise, it reports an error (inf means infinity and nan in output means "not a number").

```
awk 'BEGIN{
  print log(12);
  print log(0);
  print log(1);
  print log(-1);
}'
```

The output is here:

```
2.48491
-inf
0
nan
```

The `sin(x)` function gives you the sine of x, and `cos(x)` gives you the cosine of x, with x in radians:

```
awk 'BEGIN {
   print cos(90);
   print cos(45);
}'
```

The output is here:

```
-0.448074
0.525322
```

The `rand()` function gives you a random number. The values of `rand()` are uniformly-distributed between 0 and 1: the value is never 0 and never 1.

Often, you want random integers instead. Here is a user-defined function you can use to obtain a random nonnegative integer less than n:

```
function randint(n) {
    return int(n * rand())
}
```

The product produces a random real number greater than 0 and less than n. We then make it an integer (using `int`) between 0 and n - 1.

Here is an example where a similar function is used to produce random integers between 1 and n:

```
awk '
# Function to roll a simulated die.
function roll(n) { return 1 + int(rand() * n) }
# Roll 3 six-sided dice and print total number of points.
{
     printf("%d points\n", roll(6)+roll(6)+roll(6))
}'
```

Note that `rand()` starts generating numbers from the same point (or "seed") each time `awk` is invoked. Hence, a program will produce the same results each time it is launched. If you want a program to do different things each time it is used, you must change the seed to a value that will be different in each run.

Use the `srand(x)` function to set the starting point, or seed, for generating random numbers to the value x. Each seed value leads to a particular sequence of "random" numbers. Thus, if you set the seed to the same value a second time, you will get the same sequence of "random" numbers again. If you omit the argument x, as in `srand()`, then the current date and time of day are used for a seed.

This is how to obtain random numbers that are unpredictable. The return value of `srand()` is the previous seed. This makes it easy to keep track of the seeds for use in consistently reproducing sequences of random numbers.

The `time()` function (not in all versions of `awk`) returns the current time in seconds since January 1, 1970. The function `ctime` (not in all versions of `awk`) takes a numeric argument in seconds and returns a string representing the corresponding date, suitable for printing or further processing.

The `sqrt(x)` function gives you the positive square root of x. It reports an error if x is negative. Thus, `sqrt(4)` is 2.

```
awk 'BEGIN{
    print sqrt(16);
    print sqrt(0);
    print sqrt(-12);
}'
The output is here:
4
0
nan
```

Convert Base 10 to Binary

Listing 3.49 displays the contents of `baseten.txt`, and Listing 3.50 displays the content of `decimal2binary.sh` that shows you how to convert decimal numbers to binary values.

LISTING 3.49: baseten.txt

```
10
100
1234
1023
10000
```

LISTING 3.50: decimal2binary.sh

```
awk '
```

```
function dec2bin(dec, bin) {
  while(dec) {
      bin = dec % 2bin
      dec = int(dec/2)
  }
  return(bin)
}
{
   dec = $0
   bin = dec2bin($0)
   printf("Decimal %6d = Binary %12d\n",dec, bin)
}' baseten.txt
```

Listing 3.50 contains an `awk` command that defines the function `dec2bin()` that converts a decimal number to its binary representation. This function contains a `while` loop that computes the modulus of the input parameter `dec` divided by 2. The result is either 0 or 1, which is then pre-pended to the string `bin` (which is initially an empty string). Next, the variable `dec` is divided by 2, and the process repeats until `dec` has the value 0, at which point the `while` loop is complete and the string `bin` is returned.

The next portion of Listing 3.50 initializes the variable `dec` with the value of $0 and invokes the function `dec2bin` with $0. The result is used to initialize the variable `bin`, after which the decimal value and the binary value of $0 are printed. Note that the input field for this `awk` command is the file `baseten.txt` that is shown in Listing 3.50. Launch the code in Listing 3.50, and you will see the following output:

```
Decimal     10 = Binary         1010
Decimal    100 = Binary      1100100
Decimal   1234 = Binary  10011010010
Decimal   1023 = Binary   1111111111
Decimal  10000 = Binary 10011100010000
```

Built-In String Functions in awk

There are several string functions that are available in awk, some of which are listed here:

```
toupper()
tolower()
substr()
split()
sub()
gsub()
getline()
match()
```

The functions `toupper()` and `tolower()` convert strings to uppercase and lowercase, respectively. The `substr()` function allows you to extract a substring of a string. The `split()` function enables you to split a given string into substrings that dynamically populate an array, after which you can select different substrings from that array. Chapter 6 contains an example of using the substring() functions on date fields. The sub() and gsub() functions enable you to perform search-and-replace on strings, which is discussed later in this chapter.

Convert Strings to Lowercase in awk

The following awk command uses the toupper() function to convert all letters in employees.csv to uppercase letters:

```
$ awk '{$0 = tolower($0); print }' < employees.csv
EMPID,FULL_NAME,START_DATE,EXPENSES
1000,JANE JONES,12/05/2021,93.55

2000,JOHN SMITH,03/08/2020,87.23

3000,DAVE STONE,07/15/2022,84.16
```

Convert Strings to Uppercase in awk

The following awk command converts all letters in employees.csv to uppercase letters:

```
$ awk '{$0 = toupper($0); print }' < employees.csv
empid,full_name,start_date,expenses
1000,jane jones,12/05/2021,93.55

2000,john smith,03/08/2020,87.23

3000,dave stone,07/15/2022,84.16
```

Convert Strings to Mixed Case in awk

Suppose that we want to capitalize the first letter of each person's first name. Since the first names in employees.csv is already mixed case, let's convert all letters to lowercase using a combination of the tr command and awk, as shown here:

```
$ cat employees.csv | tr [A-Z] [a-z]
empid,full_name,start_date,expenses
1000,jane jones,12/05/2021,93.55

2000,john smith,03/08/2020,87.23

3000,dave stone,07/15/2022,84.16
```

Now we can convert the first letter of each person's name to uppercase, and then append the remaining portion of each person's name, as shown here:

```
$ cat employees.csv | tr [A-Z] [a-z] | awk
   '{ $2 = toupper(substr($2,1,1)) substr($2,2) } $2 }'
1000,Jane Jones,12/05/2021,93.55
2000,John Smith,03/08/2020,87.23
3000,Dave Stone,07/15/2022,84.16
```

Counting Lines that Match a Character

You can count the number of lines that begin with a given character, such as the following `awk` command that counts the number of lines that start with the digit 1:

```
$ awk '/^1/ { count+=1 } END { print "Rows starting with
1:",count }' employees.csv
Rows starting with 1: 1
```

The following `awk` command counts the number of lines that start with the digit 1 or 2:

```
$ awk '/^[1|2]/ { count+=1 } END { print "Rows starting with
1 or 2:",count }' employees.csv
Rows starting with 1 or 2: 2
```

The following `awk` command counts the number of non-empty lines that do not start with the digit 1:

```
$ awk '/^[^1]/ { count+=1 } END { print "Rows not starting
with 1:",count }' employees.csv
Rows not starting with 1: 3
```

The following `awk` command counts the number of lines that start with one or more digits, followed by a comma, followed by the letter J:

```
$ awk '/^[0-9]+,J/ { count+=1 } END { print "Rows starting
with a J in the second field1:",count }' employees.csv
Rows starting with a J in the second field1: 2
```

Working with the match() Function

The `match()` function enables you to determine the start and end indices in which a string matches a regular expression; if no match occurs, then the values 0 and -1 are returned. Here are examples:

```
$ echo "abcdef" | awk '{ match($1, "bcd"); print RSTART,
RLENGTH}'
2 3
```

```
$ echo "abcdef" | awk '{ match($1, "zbcd"); print RSTART,
RLENGTH}'
0 -1
```

Listing 3.52 displays the contents of the text file `days.txt`, and Listing 3.53 displays the contents of `days.sh`.

LISTING 3.52: days.txt

```
echo
yesterday
today
tomorrow
day
this
```

LISTING 3.53: days.sh

```
awk '{ match($1,"day");printf RSTART "," RLENGTH "\n" }'
    days.txt
```

Listing 3.53 contains an awk command that invokes the built-in match() function to check whether the value of $1 contains the string days. If so, then a printf statement displays the start and end position of the string days in $1 via the built-in variables RSTART and RLENGTH, respectively. Launch the code in Listing 3.53, and you will see the following output:

```
7,3
3,3
0,-1
1,3
0,-1
```

Keep in mind that the first index value is 1 (not 0).

Characters and Hexadecimal Numbers in awk

The awk command works as expected with printable characters and decimal-valued numbers. However, there are some considerations involved when working with non-printable characters and hexadecimal numbers, as discussed in the following subsections.

Non-Printable Characters

Most of the code samples in this book involve printable ASCII characters, which includes uppercase letters, lowercase letters, digits, and punctuation characters. In addition, sometimes you might encounter non-printable characters in a text file, in which case you need special character sequences to match those characters in a regular expression. Specifically, use the following sequences:

- \t for a tab character (ASCII 0x09)

- \r for a carriage return (0x0D)

- \n for a line feed (0x0A)

Hexadecimal Numbers

A hexadecimal number is specified with the prefix \0x or \x, such as \xA for decimal 10 and \xF for decimal 15. Hence, the number 255 is represented as \xFF.

Next, the echo and printf commands handle hexadecimal numbers in a different manner, as shown here:

```
$ awk 'BEGIN {print "\x61"}'
a

$ printf '\x61' | awk '{print}'
a
```

However, the following does not work as desired:

```
$ echo '\x61' | awk '{print}'
\x61
```

A workaround involves using awk with the strtonum() and substr() built-in functions, as shown here:

```
$ printf '%s\n' '\x61' | awk -n '{printf "%c\n",
strtonum("0x" substr($0,3))}'
a
```

The gawk command supports a command line switch for processing hexadecimal numbers, as shown here:

```
$ echo 0x12345678 | gawk --non-decimal-data '{ printf "%s:
%x\n", $1, $1 }'
0x12345678: 12345678
```

The awk command, and the gawk command without the preceding command line switch, return the value 0:

```
$ echo 0x12345678 | awk  '{ printf "%s: %x\n", $1, $1 }'
0x12345678: 0
```

```
$ echo 0x12345678 | gawk '{ printf "%s: %x\n", $1, $1 }'
0x12345678: 0
```

```
$ echo 0x12345678 | gawk '{ printf "%s: %x - %x\n", $1, $1,
    $ strtonum($1) }'
0x12345678: 0 - 12345678
```

Summary

This chapter introduced the awk command, which is essentially an entire programming language that is available as a single Unix command, along with many awk-related features.

Then you learned about while loops and for loops in awk to manipulate the rows and columns in datasets. Next, you saw how to use conditional logic in awk commands. In addition, you learned how to delete lines and merge lines in datasets, and also how to print the contents of a file as a single line of text.

Furthermore, you saw how to use logical operators in awk, as well as a code sample that shows you how to check whether a positive integer is a leap year. Next, you learned how to specify different types of format for output data, how to work with floating point numbers, truncating and rounding numbers, and numeric functions in awk.

In addition, you saw awk-based code samples for converting strings to lowercase, uppercase, and mixed case. Finally, you learned how to work with non-printable characters and hexadecimal numbers in awk.

## CHAPTER 4

WORKING WITH AWK, PART 2

This chapter is the second of three chapters that contains examples of various features of the `awk` command.

The first part of this chapter shows you how to perform operations with arrays, such as initializing them and displaying their contents. You will also learn how to add the numeric values in an array and how to determine the maximum and minimum numeric value in an array. In addition, you will see how to initialize multi-dimensional arrays.

The second section shows you how to perform various tasks with datasets, such as deleting alternate lines, printing a range of strings or dates in a dataset, and joining alternate lines. You will also learn how to work with duplicate rows in a dataset and how to ensure uniformity of data values.

The third section explains how to implement the bubble sort and how to determine whether a pair of strings are anagrams. You will also learn how to sort an array in linear time, which is possible under certain conditions. In addition, you will see how to perform a linear search and a binary search via an iterative algorithm as well as a recursive algorithm.

Working with Arrays in awk

This section contains several subsections that show you how to perform various operations involving arrays, such as initializing, deleting, and iterating through the contents of an array via the `awk` command.

Initializing and Printing the Contents of an Array

Listing 4.1 displays the content of `simple_array1.sh` that shows you how to initialize an array and use a `for` loop to iterate through the values.

LISTING 4.1: simple_array1.sh

```
awk "" | awk '

BEGIN {
  arr[0] = 10; arr[1] = 20; arr[2] = 30;

  printf("Contents of array:\n")
  print("arr[0]:",arr[0])
  print("arr[1]:",arr[1])
  print("arr[2]:",arr[2])
  print("arr[3]:",arr[3])

  printf("Contents of array:\n")
  for (var in arr) {
    printf("%s ", arr[var])
  }
  print ""
}
'
```

Listing 4.1 contains an `awk` command with a `BEGIN` block that starts with the initialization the array `arr` with three numeric values. The next portion of the `BEGIN` block contains a set of `print` statements that prints the value of each element of the array `arr`. In addition, a `for` loop prints the contents of the array `arr` as a single line. Launch the code in Listing 4.1 as follows:

```
awk -f simple_array1.sh
```

The preceding command generates the following output:

```
Contents of array:
arr[0]: 10
arr[1]: 20
arr[2]: 30
arr[3]:
Contents of array:
10 20 30
```

Initializing and Deleting the Contents of an Array

Listing 4.2 displays the content of `delete_array1.sh` that shows you how to initialize an array and use a `for` loop to iterate through the values.

LISTING 4.2: delete_array1.sh

```
echo "" | awk '
    BEGIN {
```

```
    arr[0] = 10; arr[1] = 20; arr= 30;

    # method #1:
    delete arr[0];
    delete arr[1];
    delete arr[2];

    # method #2:
    #for (var in arr) {
    #   delete arr[var]
    #}

    # method #3 using gawk:
    # delete arr

    print "Contents of array:"
    arr[0] = 10; arr[1] = 20; arr= 30;
    for (var in arr) {
      printf("%s ", arr[var])
    }
    print ""
  }
'
```

Listing 4.2 contains an awk command with a BEGIN block that starts with the initialization the array arr with three numeric values. The next portion of the BEGIN block contains a set of delete statements that delete each element of the array arr. In addition, a commented-out for loop shows you a scalable way to delete the elements of the array arr. Launch the code in Listing 4.2 as follows:

```
$ awk -f delete_arr1.sh
```

The preceding command generates the following output:

```
Contents of array:
arr[0]: 10
arr[1]: 20
arr[2]: 30
arr[3]:
Contents of array:
10 20 30
```

Adding an Array of Numbers

Listing 4.3 displays the content of sum_array1.sh that shows you how to initialize an array with numbers and calculate the sum of the numbers in the array.

LISTING 4.3: sum_array1.sh

```
echo "" | awk '
# note that arris not initialized:
BEGIN { arr[0] = 10; arr= 20; arr[3] = 30; }
{
```

```
   sum = 0
   for (idx=0; idx<length(arr); idx++) {
      sum += arr[idx]
   }
}
END { print "Sum of array elements:",sum }
'
```

Listing 4.3 contains an echo command that passes a string to the awk command, which in turn contains a BEGIN block that initializes the array arr with three numeric values. Next, the main execution block initializes the variable sum with the value 0, followed by a loop that iterates through each element of the array arr and adds each value to the variable sum. The final portion of Listing 4.3 contains an END block that prints the value of the variable sum. Launch the code in Listing 4.3, and you will see the following output:

```
Sum of array elements: 60
```

Find the Maximum and Minimum of an Array of Numbers

Listing 4.4 displays the content of max_min_array1.sh that shows you how to initialize an array with numbers and calculate the sum of the numbers in the array.

LISTING 4.4: max_min_array1.sh

```
echo "" | awk '
BEGIN { arr[0] = 10; arr[1] = 20; arr[2] = 30; max=0; min=0}
{
   min = arr[0]
   max = arr[0]
   for (idx=1;idx<length(arr);idx++) {
      if(max < arr[idx]) {
         max = arr[idx]
      }

      if(min > arr[idx]) {
         min = arr[idx]
      }
   }
}
END { print "Max:",max,"min:",min}
'
```

Listing 4.4 contains an echo command that passes a string to the awk command, which in turn contains a BEGIN block that initializes the array arr with three numeric values. This block also initializes the variables max and min with the values 0 and 99999, respectively.

The next portion Listing 4.4 is the main execution block that contains a loop that iterates through the elements of the array arr. During each iteration, the value of max is updated if the current field is larger than the value of max. In addition, the value of min is updated if the current field is smaller than the value of min.

The last portion of Listing 4.4 consists of an END block that prints the values of the variables max and min. Launch the code in Listing 4.4, and you will see the following output:

```
Max: 30 min: 10
```

Concatenating an Array of Strings

Listing 4.5 displays the content of concat_array1.sh that shows you how to initialize an array with strings and concatenate the strings in the array.

LISTING 4.5: concat_array1.sh

```
echo "" | awk '
BEGIN { arr[0] = "abc"; arr[1] = "def"; arr[2] = "ghi"; }
{
  concat = ""
  for (idx=0;idx<length(arr);idx++) {
    concat = concat arr[idx]
  }
}
END { print "Concatenated array elements:",concat}
'
```

Listing 4.5 contains an echo command that passes an empty string to the awk command, which in turn contains a BEGIN block that initializes the array arr with four strings. The next portion Listing 4.5 is the main execution block that initializes the variable concat as an empty string, followed by a loop that iterates through the elements of the array arr. During each iteration, the current array element is appended to the string variable concat.

The last portion of Listing 4.5 consists of an END block that prints the string of concatenated array values. Launch the code in Listing 4.5, and you will see the following output:

```
Concatenated array elements: abcdefghi
```

Generating Arrays from Input Strings

Previous sections showed you how to initialize an array with strings, and the following sections show you how to use the split() function to populate an array with values.

The split() Function with Linefeed Strings

The following awk commands show you how to work with input strings that appear to contain a linefeed character. The first awk command treats "\n" as a sequence of two distinct characters "\" and "\n:"

```
$ echo "AAA\nBBB" | awk -F"\\\\n" '{print $1}'
   AAA\nBBB
```

The following command specifies "-e" for the echo command, which treats the sequence "\n" as a linefeed, after which the awk command treats its input string as two strings on separate input lines:

```
$ echo -e "AAA\nBBB" | awk -F"\\\\n" '{print $1}'
AAA
BBB
```

The preceding technique also works correctly when there are embedded spaces, as shown in these examples:

```
$ echo "AAA \n BBB" | awk '{split($0,a,"\\\\n"); print a[1]}'
AAA

$ echo "AAA \n BBB" | awk '{split($0,a,"\\\\n"); print a[2]}'
  BBB
```

Another approach involves the split() function that splits $0 based on an escaped character sequence, as shown here:

```
$ echo "AAA\nBBB" | awk '{split($0,a,"\\\\n"); print a[1]}'
AAA

$ echo "AAA\nBBB" | awk '{split($0,a,"\\\\n"); print a[2]}'
BBB
```

However, the preceding escaped character sequence does not work when it is specified in the -F switch:

```
$ echo "AAA\nBBB" | awk -F"\\\\n" '{print $1}'
   AAA\nBBB
```

Using the split() Function with the case Statement

Listing 4.6 displays the content of switch1.sh that shows you how to process an array of characters and use the switch statement to determine the value of each character.

LISTING 4.6: switch1.sh

```
echo "" | awk '
BEGIN { split("abcdef",arr, "") }
{
  for (idx=0;idx<4;idx++) {
    ch = arr[idx]
    #print "Processing character:",ch
    switch (ch) {
```

```
        case "a": print "=> found a"; break
        case "b": print "=> found b"; break
        case "c": print "=> found c"; break
        default:  break
    }
  }
}
'
```

Listing 4.6 contains an `echo` command that passes a string to the `awk` command, which in turn contains a `BEGIN` block that invokes the `split()` method on a specified string to populate the array `arr` with each character in the input string.

The next portion Listing 4.6 is the main execution block that contains a loop that iterates through the elements of the array `arr`. During each iteration, the current array element (which is a single character) is processed in a switch statement that prints a message whenever the current character is either a, b, or c. Launch the code in Listing 4.6, and you will see the following output:

```
=> found a
=> found b
=> found c
```

The patsplit() Function

The `split()` function involves a separator, whereas the `patsplit()` function matches a pattern between separators. The following example involves the `split()` function:

```
$ echo 'spicy,food' | awk '{n = split($0,a,/,/);
for(i=1;i<=n;i++) print a[i]}'
spicy
food
```

By comparison, the following `awk` command contains the `patsplit()` function:

```
$ echo 'spicy,food' | awk '{n = patsplit($0,a,/[^,]*/);
for(i=1;i<=n;i++) print a[i]}'
spicy
food
```

Multi-Dimensional Arrays

Listing 4.7 displays the content of `multi_dim_array1.sh` that shows you how to initialize a multi-dimensional array and then display its contents.

LISTING 4.7: multi_dim_array1.sh

```
echo "" | awk '
BEGIN {
  row=1; col=1;
  arr[1,1] = 10; arr[1,2] = 20; arr[1,3] = 30;
```

```
    print "Contents of array:"
    for (var in arr) {
      printf("%s ", arr[var])
    }
    print ""

    arr[2,1] = 10; arr[2,2] = 20; arr[2,3] = 30;
    arr[3,1] = 10; arr[3,2] = 20; arr[3,3] = 30;

    print "Contents of array:"
    for (var in arr) {
      printf("%s ", arr[var])
    }
    print ""
}
'
```

Listing 4.7 contains an awk command that contains a BEGIN block that initializes the variables row and col with the value 1, and then initializes the initial row in the array arr with three integer values. The next portion Listing 4.7 is a for loop that prints the content of the array arr, followed by two code snippets that initialize the second and third rows of the array arr. The last portion of the BEGIN block displays a single line of output that consists of all the elements in the array arr. Launch the code in Listing 4.7 as follows:

```
awk -f multi_dim_array1.sh
```

The preceding command generates the following output:

```
Contents of array:
10 20 30
Contents of array:
10 20 30 10 20 30 10 20 30
```

Listing 4.8 displays the content of multi_dim_array2.sh that shows you how to initialize a multi-dimensional array and then display its contents.

LISTING 4.8: multi_dim_array2.sh

```
BEGIN {
  row=1; col=1; maxrow=4; maxcol=4;

  for(row=1;row<maxrow;row++) {
    for(col=1;col<maxcol;col++) {
        arr[row,col] = row+col
    }
  }

  print "Contents of array:"
  for (var in arr) {
    printf("%s ", arr[var])
  }
  print ""
```

```
    print "Contents of array:"
    for(row=1;row<maxrow;row++) {
        for(col=1;col<maxcol;col++) {
            printf("%d ", arr[row,col])
        }
        print ""
    }
}
```

Listing 4.8 contains an awk command that contains a BEGIN block that initializes the variables row and col with the value 1, and then initializes the variables maxrow and maxcol with the value 4. The next portion of the BEGIN block contains a nested look that initializes each "cell" of the array arr with the sum of the current values of the two loop variables.

The next portion of the BEGIN block contains a loop that invokes the printf() statement to display a one-line string consisting of the values of the elements in the array arr. The final portion of the BEGIN block contains a nested loop that prints the contents of the array arr, where each row of arr is displayed on a separate line. Launch the code in Listing 4.8 as follows:

```
$ awk -f multi_dim_array1.sh
```

The preceding command generates the following output:

```
Contents of array:

3 4 5 4 5 6 2 3 4
Contents of array:
2 3 4
3 4 5
4 5 6
```

Listing 4.9 displays the content of multi_dim_array3.sh that shows you how to initialize a multi-dimensional array and then display its contents.

LISTING 4.9: multi_dim_array3.sh

```
echo "" | awk '
BEGIN {
    row=1; col=1; maxrow=4; maxcol=4;

    for(row=1;row<maxrow;row++) {
        for(col=1;col<maxcol;col++) {
            arr[row,col] = row+col
        }
    }

    print "Contents of array:"
    for (var in arr) {
        printf("%s ", arr[var])
    }
```

```
print ""

print "Contents of array:"
for(row=1;row<maxrow;row++) {
    for(col=1;col<maxcol;col++) {
        printf("%d ",arr[row,col])
    }
    print ""
}

print "Contents of array:"
for(row=1;row<maxrow;row++) {
    for(col=1;col<maxcol;col++) {
        printf("%s ",arr[row,col])
    }
    print ""
}
}
'
```

Listing 4.9 is almost the same as the contents of Listing 4.8. The only difference is another nested loop that displays the contents of the array arr via the printf() statement that specifies each array element as a string. The output is the same as the earlier nested loop that prints the elements of the array arr as integer values. Launch the code in Listing 4.9 as follows:

```
$ awk -f multi_dim_array3.sh
```

The preceding command generates the following output:

```
Contents of array:
3 4 5 4 5 6 2 3 4
Contents of array:
2 3 4
3 4 5
4 5 6
Contents of array:
2 3 4
3 4 5
4 5 6
```

Higher Dimensionality Arrays

Listing 4.10 displays the content of multi_dim_array3.sh that shows you how to initialize a multi-dimensional array and then display its contents.

LISTING 4.10: *higher_dim_array1.sh*

```
echo "" | awk '
    BEGIN {
        row=1; col=1; dep=1;
        maxrow=4; maxcol=4; maxdep=4;
```

```
for(row=1;row<maxrow;row++) {
   for(col=1;col<maxcol;col++) {
      for(dep=1;dep<maxdep;dep++) {
         arr[row,col,dep] = row+col+dep
      }
   }
}

print "Contents of array:"
for (var in arr) {
   printf("%s ", arr[var])
}
print ""

print "Contents of array:"
for(row=1;row<maxrow;row++) {
   for(col=1;col<maxcol;col++) {
      for(dep=1;dep<maxdep;dep++) {
         printf("%d ", arr[row,col,dep])
      }
      print ""
   }
   print "--------"
}
}
'
```

Listing 4.10 is similar to Listing 4.9, except that the nested loops are replaced with triply-nested loops that initialize the contents of the array arr. Launch the code in Listing 4.10 as follows:

```
$ awk -f higher_dim_array1.sh
```

The preceding command generates the following output:

```
Contents of array:
8 5 9 5 6 5 6 7 6 7 3 7 4 5 6 6 7 7 8 4 8 4 5 5 6 6 7
Contents of array:
3 4 5
4 5 6
5 6 7
--------
4 5 6
5 6 7
6 7 8
--------
5 6 7
6 7 8
7 8 9
--------
```

Calculating Invoice Totals (1)

This section contains examples of awk commands that generate reports. Listing 4.11 displays the contents of invoices.txt, and Listing 4.12

displays the content of `invoices_totals.txt` that calculates totals for each customer.

LISTING 4.11: invoices.txt

```
1000,10000,01/02/2022,123.45
1000,10100,04/03/2022,456.78
1000,10200,06/05/2022,999.99
2000,20000,01/02/2022,100.45
2000,20100,02/03/2022,222.78
2000,20200,03/05/2022,333.99
3000,30000,02/02/2022,500.45
3000,30100,05/03/2022,666.78
3000,30200,08/05/2022,777.99
```

LISTING 4.12: invoices_totals.sh

```
# cust_id, purch_id, date, amount
awk -F"," '
{
    # add a customer id:
    #print "customer id:",$1
    cust_ids[$1] = $1;

    # increment invoice:
    #print "invoice:",$4
    cust_invoices[$1] += int($4)
}
END {
    printf("Customer Invoice\n")
    for (i in cust_ids) {
        printf("%5s:    %7.3f\n",cust_ids[i],cust_invoices[i])
    }
}
' invoices.txt
```

Listing 4.12 contains an `awk` command whose main execution block sets the value of the arrays `cust_ids` and `cust_invoices` equal to the values of $1 and $4, respectively. The final portion of Listing 4.12 contains an `END` block that contains a loop that iterates through the elements of the array `cust_ids` to print the value of the array element and the corresponding array element in the array `cust_invoices`. Launch the code in Listing 4.12, and you will see the following output:

```
Customer Invoice
 1000:    1578.000
 2000:    655.000
 3000:    1943.000
```

Calculating Invoice Totals (2)

Listing 4.13 displays the content of `invoice_totals2.sh` that extends the example in the previous section to provide more report-related information.

LISTING 4.13: invoices_totals2.sh

```
# cust_id, purch_id, date, amount
awk -F"," '
{
    # add a customer id:
    cust_ids[$1] = $1;

    # increment invoice:
    cust_invoices[$1] += int($4)

    # current invoice date:
    min_inv_dates[$1] = $3
    max_inv_dates[$1] = $3

    if( min_inv[$1] == "") {
        min_inv[$1] = $4
    }

    if( int($4) < min_inv[$1] ) min_inv[$1] = $4;
    if( int($4) > max_inv[$1] ) max_inv[$1] = $4;
}
END {
    printf("Customer Invoice    Minimum     Maximum
            Min Date    Max Date\n")
    for (i in cust_ids) {
        printf("%5s:    %7.2f %9.2f   %9.2f",cust_ids[i],
               cust_invoices[i],min_inv[i],max_inv[i])
        printf("%15s  %9s\n",min_inv_dates[i],
               max_inv_dates[i])
    }
}
' invoices.txt
```

Listing 4.13 contains the same code as Listing 4.12, along with additional code blocks for keeping track of the minimum and maximum invoice dates in the arrays min_inv_dates and max_inv_dates, respectively. A pair of conditional code snippets keep track of the maximum and minimum invoice quantities. Another pair of conditional statements updates these values accordingly.

The final portion of Listing 4.13 is an END block that iterates through the elements in the cust_ids array and points the corresponding values in the arrays cust_id, cust_invoices, min_inv, max_inv, min_inv_dates, and max_inv_dates. Launch the code in Listing 4.13, and you will see the following output:

```
Customer Invoice    Minimum     Maximum    Min Date     Max Date
  1000:    1578.00    123.45     999.99     06/05/2022   06/05/2022
  2000:     655.00    100.45     333.99     03/05/2022   03/05/2022
  3000:    1943.00    500.45     777.99     08/05/2022   08/05/2022
```

Calculating Invoice Averages

Listing 4.14 displays the content of invoice_averages.sh that calculates the average invoice for each customer.

LISTING 4.14: invoices_averages.sh

```
# cust_id, purch_id, date, amount

awk -F"," '
{
   #print "customer id:",$1
   # add a customer id:
   cust_ids[$1] = $1;

   # increment # of invoices:
   cust_counts[$1]++

   # increment invoice:
   #print "invoice:",$4
   cust_invoices[$1] += int($4)
}
END {
   printf("Customer Invoice   Average\n")
   for (i in cust_ids) {
     printf("%5s:   %7.2f   %7.2f\n",cust_ids[i],
         cust_invoices[i],cust_invoices[i]/cust_counts[i])
   }
}
' invoices.txt
```

Listing 4.14 contains the same code as Listing 4.13, along with a code snippet in the END block that prints the average invoice for each customer. Launch the code in Listing 4.14, and you will see the following output:

```
Customer Invoice    Average
  1000:   1578.00    526.00
  2000:    655.00    218.33
  3000:   1943.00    647.67
```

Counting Fields in Text Files

This section contains examples of awk commands that count and compare the number of fields of the rows in text files. Listing 4.15 displays the content of variable_fields.txt that is used in the awk commands.

LISTING 4.15: variable_lines.txt

```
this is a line
second line is here
new york manhattan
san francisco downtown
deep dish chicago pizza
short line
```

Displaying the Number of Fields in Text Files

Listing 4.16 displays the content of `field_counts1.sh` that illustrates how to print the number of fields in a line and then the line itself.

LISTING 4.16: field_counts1.sh

```
# print number of fields
awk '
{
   print "NF:",NF,$0
}
' variable_lines.txt

#one-line version:
#awk ' { print "NF:",NF,$0} }' variable_lines.txt
```

Listing 4.16 contains an `awk` command that prints the number of fields in each row, along with the contents of each row. Launch the code in Listing 4.16, and you will see the following output:

```
NF: 4 this is a line
NF: 4 second line is here
NF: 3 new york manhattan
NF: 3 san francisco downtown
NF: 4 deep dish chicago pizza
NF: 2 short line
```

Listing 4.17 displays the content of `field_counts2.sh` that illustrates how to print the number of fields in a line and then the line itself.

LISTING 4.17: field_counts2.sh

```
awk '
BEGIN { arr= ""; first_count = 0 }
{
   arr[NR] = $0

   if( NR == 1 ) {
     first_count = NF
     print "=> Length of first line:",NF
   }

   if(NF == first_count) {
     print "Line",NR,"matches field count",first_count
   } else if (NF > first_count) {
     print "Line",NR,"is longer than",first_count,":",NF
   } else {
     print "Line",NR,"is shorter than",first_count,":",NF
   }
}
END {
  print "=> Initial array:"
  for (i=1; i<=NR; i++) {
    print "Row",i,arr[i]
```

```
    }

    print "=> Sorted array:"
    row_count = asorti(arr, sorted)
    for (i=1; i<=row_count; i++) {
        print sorted[i] ":" arr[sorted[i]]
    }
}
' variable_lines.txt
```

Listing 4.17 contains the code in Listing 4.16, along with additional code blocks that update the array variable arr with each input line, followed by a code snippet that keeps track of the number of fields in the first input line, followed by a conditional code block that checks the number of fields in each subsequent input line. The conditional code block also displays an appropriate message when the number of fields in each input line is the same as the first input line, as well as input lines that have more fields and input lines that have fewer fields than the first input line.

The last portion of Listing 4.17 is an END block that contains two loops: the first loop printed all the input lines, and the second loop prints the input lines in sorted order. Launch the code in Listing 4.17, and you will see the following output:

```
=> Length of first line: 4
Line 1 matches field count 4
Line 2 matches field count 4
Line 3 is shorter than 4 : 3
Line 4 is shorter than 4 : 3
Line 5 matches field count 4
Line 6 is shorter than 4 : 2
=> Initial array:
Row 1 this is a line
Row 2 second line is here
Row 3 new york manhattan
Row 4 san francisco downtown
Row 5 deep dish chicago pizza
Row 6 short line
=> Sorted array:
1:this is a line
2:second line is here
3:new york manhattan
4:san francisco downtown
5:deep dish chicago pizza
6:short line
```

Deleting Alternate Lines in Datasets

Listing 4.18 displays the contents of linepairs.csv, and Listing 4.19 displays the content of deletelines.sh that illustrates how to print alternating lines from the dataset linepairs.csv that have exactly two columns.

LISTING 4.18: linepairs.csv

```
a,b,c,d
e,f,g,h
1,2,3,4
5,6,7,8
```

LISTING 4.19: deletelines.sh

```
inputfile="linepairs.csv"
outputfile="linepairsdeleted.csv"
awk ' NR%2 {printf "%s", $0; print ""; next}' < $inputfile
> $outputfile
```

Listing 4.19 specifies NR%2 to determine whether the current record number NR is divisible by 2, in which case it prints the current line and then specifies next to skip the next line in the dataset. The output is redirected to the specified output file, the contents of which are here:

```
a,b,c,d
1,2,3,4
```

Print a Range of Strings in Datasets

Listing 4.20 displays the contents of report.txt, and Listing 4.21 displays the content of line_range.sh that prints a range of lines from a CSV file.

LISTING 4.20: report.txt

```
This is a sample report.
Some relevant details were presented yesterday.
Several people likes to work from home.
However, some people prefer the office.
In addition, parking is easier now.
The WFM topic has different appeal.
```

LISTING 4.21: line_range.sh

```
awk '
   /Some/,/However/ { print }
' report.txt

echo "--------------------------"
echo ""

awk '
{
   if(NR > 1 && NR < 3) { print }
}
' report.txt
```

Listing 4.21 contains an awk command whose execution block specifies the pattern /Some/,/However/ that acts as a start-end pair of strings: awk will print the contents of the row that starts with the token Some and ends with the token `However`, as well as all the rows (if any) between this pair of rows.

The next portion of Listing 4.21 displays a string consisting of "-," followed by another `awk` command that prints the value of $2 for text lines that contain exactly two fields. Note that both `awk` commands process the text file `report.txt`. Launch the code in Listing 4.21, and you will see the following output:

```
Some relevant details were presented yesterday.
Several people like to work from home.
However, some people prefer the office.
-------------------------

Some relevant details were presented yesterday.
```

Keep in mind that the first row containing `Some` is the first row that is printed, and the first row that contains `However` is the last row that is printed. Just to be clear, the following text block shows the matching rows in bold:

```
This is a sample report.
Some relevant details were presented yesterday.
Several people likes to work from home.
However, some people prefer the office.
In addition, parking is easier now.
```

The following rows (shown in bold) match the pattern `/Some/,/However/`:

```
Some sample report.
Some relevant details were presented yesterday.
Several people likes to work from home.
However, some people prefer the office.
In addition, parking is easier now.
```

The following rows (shown in bold) also match the pattern `/Some/,/However/`:

```
Some sample report.
Some relevant details were presented yesterday.
Several people like to work from home.
However, some people prefer the office.
However, this does not match the pattern.
In addition, parking is easier now.
```

The following rows (shown in bold) also match the pattern `/Some/,/However/`:

```
Some relevant details were presented yesterday.
However, some people prefer the office.
In addition, parking is easier now.
```

Print a Range of Dates in Datasets

Listing 4.22 displays the contents of `dates2.txt`, and Listing 4.23 displays the contents of `dates3.txt`.

LISTING 4.22: dates2.txt

```
01/31/1000
02/29/1200
07/15/1800
03/21/1900
12/08/1904
02/29/2000
03/31/2024
```

LISTING 4.23: dates3.txt

```
01:31:1000
02:29:1200
07:15:1800
03:21:1900
12:08:1904
02:29:2000
03:31:2024
```

Listing 4.25 displays the content of date_range.sh that prints a range of lines from two text files.

LISTING 4.25: date_range.sh

```
echo "Date range from dates2.txt:"
awk '
   /02\/29\/1200/,/02\/29\/2000/ { print }
' dates2.txt

# this will not work:
#awk '
#BEGIN { start_date = "/02\/29\/1200"
#        end_date   = "/02\/29\/2000"
#}
#{
#   /start_date/,/end_date/ { print }
#' dates2.txt

echo
echo "Date range from dates3.txt:"
awk '
   /02:29:1200/,/02:29:2000/ { print }
' dates3.txt
```

Listing 4.25 contains an awk command whose execution block specifies two date ranges in the pattern /02\/29\/1200/,/02\/29\/2000/ that act as a start-end pair of dates: awk will print the contents of the row that matches the pattern /02\/29\/1200/ up to the line of text that matches the pattern /02\/29\/2000/, as well as all the rows (if any) between this pair of rows). Note that this awk command process the text file dates2. txt.

The next portion of Listing 4.25 contains a commented-out code block that is self-explanatory. The final portion of Listing 4.25 is similar to the first awk command: the difference is that the dates in the former use the "/" delimiter, whereas the dates in the latter use a ":" delimiter. Note that this awk command processes the text file dates2.txt. Launch the code in Listing 4.25, and you will see the following output:

```
Date range from dates2.txt:
02/29/1200
07/15/1800
03/21/1900
12/08/1904
02/29/2000

Date range from dates3.txt:
02:29:1200
07:15:1800
03:21:1900
12:08:1904
02:29:2000
```

A slightly more common task involves merging consecutive lines, which is the topic of the next section.

Merging Lines in Datasets

Listing 4.26 displays the contents of columns.txt, and Listing 4.27 displays the content of ColumnCount1.sh that illustrates how to print the lines from the text file columns.txt that have exactly two columns.

LISTING 4.26: columns.txt

```
one two three
one two
one two three four
one
one three
one four
```

LISTING 4.27: ColumnCount1.sh

```
awk '
{
   if( NF == 2 ) { print $0 }
}
' columns.txt
```

Listing 4.27 is straightforward: if the current record contains an even number of fields, then the current line is printed (i.e., odd-numbered rows are skipped). The output from launching the code in Listing 4.27 is here:

```
one two
one three
one four
```

If you want to display the lines that do *not* contain 2 columns, use the following code snippet:

```
if( NF != 2 ) { print $0 }
```

Printing File Contents as a Single Line

The contents of test4.txt are here (note the blank lines):

```
abc

def

abc

abc
```

The following code snippet illustrates how to print the contents of test4.txt as a single line:

```
$ awk '{printf("%s", $0)}' test4.txt
```

The output of the preceding code snippet is here. See if you can tell what is happening before reading the explanation in the next paragraph:

```
abcdefabcabc
```

Explanation: %s here is the record separator syntax for printf() with an ending quotation mark after it, which means the record separator is the empty field "". Our default record separator for awk is /n (newline), what the printf is doing is stripping out all the new lines. The blank rows will vanish entirely, as all they have is the new line, so the result is that any actual text will be merged together with nothing between them. Had we added a space between the %s and the ending quotation mark, there would be a space between each character block, plus an extra space for each new line.

Notice how the following comment helps the comprehension of the code snippet:

```
# Merging all text into a single line by removing the new lines
$ awk '{printf("%s", $0)}' test4.txt
```

Joining Groups of Lines in a Text File

Listing 4.28 displays the contents of digits.txt, and Listing 4.29 displays the content of digits.sh that "joins" three consecutive lines of text in the file digits.txt.

LISTING 4.28: digits.txt

```
1
2
3
4
5
6
7
8
9
```

LISTING 4.29: digits.sh

```
awk -F" " '{
  printf("%d",$0)
  if(NR % 3 == 0) { printf("\n") }
}' digits.txt
```

Listing 4.29 prints three consecutive lines of text on the same line, after which a linefeed is printed. This has the effect of "joining" every three consecutive lines of text. The output from launching digits.sh is here:

```
123
456
789
```

Joining Alternate Lines in a Text File

Listing 4.30 displays the contents of columns2.txt, and Listing 4.31 displays the content of JoinLines1.sh that "joins" two consecutive lines of text in the file columns2.txt.

LISTING 4.30: columns2.txt

```
one two
three four
one two three four
five six
one two three
four five
```

LISTING 4.31: JoinLines1.sh

```
awk '
{
   printf("%s",$0)
   if( $1 !~ /one/) { print " " }
}
' columns2.txt
```

The output from launching Listing 4.11 is here:

```
one two three four
one two three four five six
one two three four five
```

Notice that the code in Listing 4.31 depends on the presence of the string "one" as the first field in alternating lines of text – we are merging based on matching a simple pattern, instead of tying it to record combinations.

To merge each pair of lines instead of merging based on matching a pattern, use the modified code in Listing 4.32.

LISTING 4.32: JoinLines2.sh

```
awk '
BEGIN { count = 0 }
{
    printf("%s",$0)
    if( ++count % 2 == 0) { print " " }
} columns2.txt
```

Yet another way to "join" consecutive lines is shown in Listing 4.33, where the input file and output file refer to files that you can populate with data. This is another example of an awk command that might be a puzzle if encountered in a program without a comment. It is doing exactly the same thing as Listing 4.32, but its purpose is less obvious because of the more compact syntax.

LISTING 4.33: JoinLines2.sh

```
inputfile="linepairs.csv"
outputfile="linepairsjoined.csv"
$ awk ' NR%2 {printf "%s,", $0; next;}1' < $inputfile > $outputfile
```

Reversing the Lines in a File

Listing 4.34 displays the contents of clients.csv, and Listing 4.35 displays the content of reverse_file.sh that shows you how to reverse the contents of a text file.

LISTING 4.34: clients.csv

```
clientid,fname,lname,start_date,expenses
1000,Jane,Jones,12/05/2021,93.55
1100,John,Jones,12/05/2021,93.55
2000,John,Smith,03/08/2020,87.23
2100,Jane,Smith,03/08/2020,87.23
3000,Dave,Stone,07/15/2022,84.16
3100,Dave,Smith,07/15/2022,84.16
```

LISTING 4.35: reverse_file.sh

```
awk '{ arr[idx++] = $0 }
END {
  for (j=idx-1; j>=0;) {
    print arr[j--]
```

```
    }
  }
' clients.csv
```

The output from launching Listing 4.35 is here:

```
3100,Dave,Smith,07/15/2022,84.16
3000,Dave,Stone,07/15/2022,84.16
2100,Jane,Smith,03/08/2020,87.23
2000,John,Smith,03/08/2020,87.23
1100,John,Jones,12/05/2021,93.55
1000,Jane,Jones,12/05/2021,93.55
clientid,fname,lname,start_date,expenses
```

If you want to omit the header line from the output, then use Listing 4.36.

LISTING 4.36: reverse_file2.sh

```
awk '{
  if(NR > 1)
    arr[idx++] = $0
}
END {
  for (j=idx-1; j>=0;) {
    print arr[j--]
  }
}
' clients.csv
```

The output from launching Listing 4.36 is here:

```
3100,Dave,Smith,07/15/2022,84.16
3000,Dave,Stone,07/15/2022,84.16
2100,Jane,Smith,03/08/2020,87.23
2000,John,Smith,03/08/2020,87.23
1100,John,Jones,12/05/2021,93.55
1000,Jane,Jones,12/05/2021,93.55
```

Working with Duplicate Lines in a File

There are several operations that you can perform regarding duplicate lines in a text file: you can display duplicate rows and also remove duplicate rows, both of which are discussed in the following subsections.

Display Duplicate Rows

The preceding example shows you how to find the unique rows, and the code sample in Listing 4.37 in this section shows you how to find the duplicate rows.

LISTING 4.37: find-duplicates.sh

```
filename1="duplicates.csv"
sorted="sorted.csv"
```

```
unique="unique.csv"
multiple="multiple.csv"

# sorted rows:
cat $filename1 | sort > $sorted

# unique rows:
cat $sorted | uniq > $unique

# duplicates rows:
diff -u $sorted $unique |sed -e '1,3d' -e 's/^
    //' -e 's/-//' > $multiple
```

Listing 4.37 starts by initializing several scalar variables as filenames that will contain CSV-based data. The remaining portion of Listing 4.37 consists of two statements with the `cat` command and another statement with the `diff` command that populate the following three CSV files with data:

```
sorted.csv
unique.csv
multiple.csv
```

The first `cat` command pipes the contents of `duplicates.csv` to the sort command that in turn populates the CSV file `sorted.csv`, which contains the sorted set of rows from `duplicates.csv`. In addition, the duplicate rows (if any) in `sorted.csv` will appear as consecutive rows in `sorted.csv`.

The second `cat` command pipes the contents of `sorted.csv` to the `uniq` command that in turn populates `unique.csv` with the unique rows from `sorted.csv` so that the rows in the file `unique.csv` are unique.

Finally, the `diff` command highlights the differences in the contents of `sorted.csv` and `unique.csv`. The output of the `diff` command is input for the `sed` command, which deletes the first three lines, removes leading white spaces, and also removes any hyphen ("-") characters. In addition, the output of the `diff` command is redirected to the `sed` command that does three things:

- Remove the first three text lines

- Remove an initial space character

- Remove an initial "-" character

After the `sed` command has completed, the output is redirected to the file `$multiple` that contains the duplicate rows. Launch the code in Listing 4.37, and then inspect the contents of `multiple.csv` that are shown here:

```
Female,16,150,0
```

```
Female,16,150,0
Female,17,170,0
Female,17,170,0
Male,15,180,0
Male,15,180,0
Male,19,160,0
Male,19,160,0
Male,19,190,0
Male,19,190,0
```

Remove Duplicate Rows

Data deduplication refers to the task of removing row-level duplicate data values. Listing 4.38 displays the contents of duplicates.csv, and Listing 4.39 displays the content of duplicates.sh that removes the duplicate rows and creates the CSV file no_duplicates.csv that contains unique rows.

LISTING 4.38: duplicates.csv

```
Male,19,190,0
Male,19,190,0
Male,15,180,0
Male,15,180,0
Female,16,150,0
Female,16,150,0
Female,17,170,0
Female,17,170,0
Male,19,160,0
Male,19,160,0
```

LISTING 4.39: remove-duplicates.sh

```
filename1="duplicates.csv"
filename2="no_duplicates.csv"

cat $filename1 | sort |uniq > $filename2
```

Listing 4.39 is straightforward: after initializing the variables filename1 and filename2 with the names of the input and output files, respectively, the only remaining code snippet contains the Unix pipe ("|") with a sequence of commands.

The left-most command displays the contents of the input file, which is redirected to the sort command that sorts the input rows. The result of the sort command is redirected to the uniq command, which removes duplicates rows, and this result set is redirected to the file specified in the variable filename2.

Keep in mind that the sort followed by uniq command is required: this is how the uniq command can remove adjacent duplicate rows. Launch the code in Listing 4.39, and you will see the output that is displayed in Listing 4.40.

LISTING 4.40: no_duplicates.csv

```
Male,19,190,0
Female,16,150,0
Female,17,170,0
Male,15,180,0
Male,19,160,0
Male,19,190,0
Male,19,190,0
```

Uniformity of Data Values

An example of uniformity of data involves verifying that the data in a given feature contains the same units measure. For example, the following set of values have numeric values that are in a narrow range, but the units of measure are incorrect:

```
50mph
50kph
100mph
20kph
```

Listing 4.41 displays the content of same_units.sh that illustrates how to ensure that items in a set of strings have the same unit of measure.

LISTING 4.41: same_units.sh

```
strings="120kph 100mph 50kph"
new_unit="fps"

for x in `echo $strings`
do
  number=`echo $x | tr -d [a-z][A-Z]`
  unit=`echo $x | tr -d [0-9][0-9]`
  echo "initial: $x"
  new_num="${number}${new_unit}"
  echo "new_num: $new_num"
  echo
done
```

Listing 4.41 starts by initializing the variables strings and new_unit, followed by a for loop that iterates through each string in the strings variable. During each iteration, the variables number and unit are initialized with the characters and digits, respectively, in the current string represented by the loop variable x.

Next, the variable new_num is initialized as the concatenation of the contents of number and new_unit. Launch the code in Listing 4.41, and you will see the following output:

```
initial: 120kph
new_num: 120fps
```

```
initial: 100mph
new_num: 100fps

initial: 50kph
new_num: 50fps
```

Count Duplicate Fields in a File

Listing 4.42 displays the content of `duplicate_fields.sh` that shows you how to count duplicate fields in a text file.

LISTING 4.42: duplicate_fields.sh

```
awk -F",", " '
{
    #clientid,fname,lname,start_date,expenses
    if( NR > 1 ) {
      client_dups[$1]++;
      fname_dups[$2]++;
      lname_dups[$3]++;
      date_dups[$4]++;
      expense_dups[$5]++;
    }
}
END {
for(client_id in client_dups)
    print "client id:",client_id
print "-----------\n"

for(fname in fname_dups)
    print "fname:",fname,"count: "fname_dups[fname]
print "-----------\n"

for(lname in lname_dups)
    print "lname:",lname,"count: "lname_dups[lname]
print "-----------\n"

for(date in date_dups)
    print "date:",date,"count: "date_dups[date]
print "-----------\n"

}
' clients.csv
```

The output from launching Listing 4.42 is here:

```
client id : 1000
client id : 1100
client id : 2000
client id: 2100
client id : 3000
client id : 3100


fname: Dave count: 2
```

```
fname: John count: 2
fname: Jane count: 2


lname: Stone count: 1
lname: Smith count: 3
lname: Jones count: 2


date: 12/05/2021 count: 2
date: 03/08/2020 count: 2
date: 07/15/2022 count: 2
```

Calculating Invoice Totals

Listing 4.43 displays the contents of `line_items.csv`, and Listing 4.44 displays the content of `line_items.sh` that calculates the amount due for a purchase order.

LISTING 4.43: line_items.csv

```
item,unit_price,quantity
toothpaste,2.50,5
towels,5.95,2
soap,3.95,6
plates,1.75,8
microwave,60.00,1
chairs,20.00,4
```

LISTING 4.44: line_items.sh

```
awk -F"," '
BEGIN { total = 0 }
{
   #item,unit_price,quantity
   if(NR > 1) {
      print "Line item:",$0
      item_price = $2 * $3
      print "Item cost:",item_price
      total += item_price
   }
}
END {
print "Amount due:",total
}
' line_items.csv
```

Listing 4.44 contains an `awk` command that specifies a common "," as the field separator, followed by a `BEGIN` block that initializes the variables `total` and `col` with the value 0. The `BEGIN` block also contains conditional logic that processes every line *after* the header line. Inside the conditional block, the `item_price` is initialized as the product of $2 and $3, then its value is printed, and then the variable total is incremented with the value of `item_price`.

The final portion of Listing 4.44 contains an END block that prints the value of total. Launch the code in Listing 4.44, and you will see the following output:

```
Line item: toothpaste,2.50,5
Item cost: 12.5
Line item: towels,5.95,2
Item cost: 11.9
Line item: soap,3.95,6
Item cost: 23.7
Line item: plates,1.75,8
Item cost: 14
Line item: microwave,60.00,1
Item cost: 60
Line item: chairs,20.00,4
Item cost: 80
Amount due: 202.1
```

Printing Lines Using Conditional Logic

Listing 4.45 displays the content of products.txt that contains three columns of information.

LISTING 4.45: products.txt

```
MobilePhone 400    new
Tablet       300    new
Tablet       300    used
MobilePhone 200    used
MobilePhone 100    used
```

The following code snippet prints the lines of text in products.txt whose second column is greater than 300:

```
$ awk '$2 > 300' products.txt
```

The output of the preceding code snippet is here:

```
MobilePhone 400    new
```

The following code snippet prints the lines of text in products.txt whose product is "new:"

```
$ awk '($3 == "new")' products.txt
```

The output of the preceding code snippet is here:

```
MobilePhone 400    new
Tablet       300    new
```

The following code snippet prints the first and third columns of the lines of text in products.txt whose cost equals 300:

```
$ awk ' $2 == 300 { print $1, $3 }' products.txt
```

The output of the preceding code snippet is here:

```
Tablet new
Tablet used
```

The following code snippet prints the first and third columns of the lines of text in `products.txt` that start with the string `Tablet`:

```
$ awk '/^Tablet/ { print $1, $3 }' products.txt
```

The output of the preceding code snippet is here:

```
Tablet new
Tablet used
```

Listing 4.46 displays the content of the file `line-numbers.sh` in which the line number precedes the contents of each line of a text file.

LISTING 4.46: line-numbers.sh

```
awk '
{
   print NR, $0
}
' < columns.txt

# the one-line version:
# awk ' { print NR, $0 } ' < columns.txt
```

Listing 4.46 contains an `awk` command that prints each line of text from the text file `columns.txt`, preceded by the row number of each line of text. Launch the code in Listing 4.46, and you will see the following output:

```
1 one two three
2 one two
3 one two three four
4 one
5 one three
6 one four
```

Listing 4.47 displays the content of the file `field-counts.sh` in which each output line is preceded by the number of fields in that output line.

LISTING 4.47: field-counts.sh

```
awk '
{
   print NF, $0
}
' < columns.txt

# the one-line version:
# awk ' { print NF, $0 } ' < columns.txt
```

Listing 4.47 contains an `awk` command that prints each line of text from the text file `columns.txt`, preceded by the row number of each line of text. Launch the code in Listing 4.47, and you will see the following output:

```
3 one two three
2 one two
4 one two three four
1 one
2 one three
2 one four
```

Listing 4.48 displays the content of the file `character-counts.sh` in which each output line is preceded by the number of characters in that output line.

LISTING 4.48: character-counts.sh

```
awk '
{
    print NF, length($0), $0
}
' < columns.txt

# the one-line version:
# awk ' { print NF, length($0), $0 } ' < columns.txt
```

Listing 4.48 contains an `awk` command that prints each line of text from the text file `columns.txt`, preceded by the number of characters in each line of text. Launch the code in Listing 4.48, and you will see the following output:

```
3 13 one two three
2 7 one two
4 18 one two three four
1 3 one
2 9 one three
2 8 one four
```

Listing 4.49 displays the content of the file `short-rows.sh` in which rows are printed if they do not have a sufficient number of fields, which in this example is 3.

LISTING 4.49: short-rows.sh

```
awk '
BEGIN {
    field_count = 3;
    print "Minimum number of fields:",field_count
}
{
    if( NF < field_count ) {
```

```
        print NF, $0
    }
}
' < columns.txt
```

Listing 4.49 contains an `awk` command that contains a `BEGIN` block that initializes the variables `field_count` with the value 3, followed by a simple print statement. The main execution block contains a conditional statement that prints the number of fields and the contents of a text line, for each line in the text file `columns.txt` that contains fewer than `field_count` columns. Launch the code in Listing 4.49, and you will see the following output:

```
Minimum number of fields: 3
2 one two
1 one
2 one three
2 one four
```

Duplicate and Unique Rows in Text Files

Listing 4.50 displays the contents of the text file `text_lines.txt`.

LISTING 4.50: text_lines.txt

```
this is line one
this is line two
this is line one
this is line three
this is line four
```

The next code snippet is an `awk` command that displays duplicate lines in the text file `text_lines.txt`:

```
$ awk 'arr1[$0]++' text_lines.txt
this is line one
```

The preceding code snippet refers to a dynamically created array called `arr1` that is initially empty. During each "pass" through `text_lines.txt`, the value of `arr1[$0]` is incremented only when there is another matching line in the file. Hence, `arr1[$0]` contains a non-empty value, which can only occur if a duplicate row is detected.

The next code snippet is an `awk` command that displays unique lines in `text_lines.txt`:

```
$ awk '!arr1[$0]++' text_lines.txt
this is line one
this is line two
this is line three
this is line four
```

The next code snippet is an `awk` command that counts the number of unique lines in the text file text_lines.txt:

```
$ awk '!arr1[$0]++' text_lines.txt |wc -l
4
```

Listing 4.51 displays the contents of the text file `datapoints.txt`.

LISTING 4.51: datapoints.txt

```
item1,4,6
item2,5,5
item3,4,6
item4,7,9
item5,8,8
```

Listing 4.52 displays the content of `duplicate-fields.sh` that shows you how to print the rows in which the second and third fields are the same.

LISTING 4.52: duplicate-fields.sh

```
awk -F ',' '
{
   if($2 == $3) {
      print "Duplicate fields in row",NR,":",$1,$2,$3
   }
}' datapoints.txt
```

Listing 4.52 contains an `awk` statement that specifies a common "," as a field separator, followed by the main execution block that prints the values of $1, $2, and $3 for any row in the text file `datapoint.txt` in which the second and third field values are equal. Launch the code in Listing 4.52, and you will see the following output:

```
Duplicate fields in row 2 : item2 5 5
Duplicate fields in row 5 : item5 8 8
```

Splitting Filenames with awk

Listing 4.53 displays the contents of `splitFilename2.sh` that illustrates how to split a filename containing the "." character to increment the numeric value of one of the components of the filename. Note that this code only works for a filename with exactly the expected syntax. It is possible to write more complex code to count the number of segments, or alternately to just say "change the field right before the .zip," which would only require the filename had a format matching the final two sections (`<anystructure>.number.zip`).

LISTING 4.53: SplitFilename2.sh

```
echo "05.20.144q.az.1.zip" | awk -F"." '
{
  f5=$5 + 1
  printf("%s.%s.%s.%s.%s.%s",$1,$2,$3,$4,f5,$6)
}'
```

The output from Listing 4.48 is here:

```
05.20.144q.az.2.zip
```

One-Line awk Commands

The code snippets in this section reference the text file `short1.txt`, which you can populate with any data of your choice.

The following code snippet prints each line preceded by the number of fields in each line:

```
$ awk '{print NF ":" $0}' short1.txt
```

Print the right-most field in each line:

```
$ awk '{print $NF}' short1.txt
```

Print the lines that contain more than 2 fields:

```
$ awk '{if(NF > 2) print }' short1.txt
```

Print the value of the right-most field if the current line contains more than 2 fields:

```
$ awk '{if(NF > 2) print $NF }' short1.txt
```

Remove leading and trailing whitespaces:

```
$ echo " a b c " | awk '{gsub(/^[ \t]+|[ \t]+$/,"");print}'
```

Print the first and third fields in reverse order for the lines that contain at least 3 fields:

```
$ awk '{if(NF > 2) print $3, $1}' short1.txt
```

Print the lines that contain the string one:

```
$ awk '{if(/one/) print }' *txt
```

As you can see from the preceding code snippets, it is easy to extract information or subsets of rows and columns from text files using simple conditional logic and built-in variables in the `awk` command.

Useful Short awk Scripts

This section contains a set of short `awk` -based scripts for performing various operations. Some of these scripts can also be used in other shell scripts to perform more complex operations. Listing 4.54 displays the content of the file data.txt that is used in various code samples in this section.

LISTING 4.54: data.txt

```
this is line one that contains more than 40 characters
this is line two
this is line three that also contains more than 40
characters
four

this is line six and the preceding line is empty

line eight and the preceding line is also empty
```

The following code snippet prints every line that is longer than 40 characters:

```
awk 'length($0) > 40' data.txt
```

Now print the length of the longest line in data.txt:

```
awk '{ if (x < length()) x = length() }
END { print "maximum line length is " x }' < data.txt
```

The input is processed by the expand utility to change tabs into spaces, so the widths compared are actually the right-margin columns.

Print every line that has at least one field:

```
$ awk 'NF > 0' data.txt
```

The output from the preceding code snippet shows you how to create a file whose contents do not include blank lines.

Print seven random numbers from 0 to 100, inclusive:

```
$ awk 'BEGIN { for (i = 1; i <= 7; i++)
              print int(101 * rand()) }'
```

Count the lines in a file:

```
$ awk 'END { print NR }' < data.txt
```

Print the even-numbered lines in the data file:

```
$ awk 'NR % 2 == 0' data.txt
```

If you use the expression 'NR % 2 == 1' in the previous code snippet, the program would print the odd-numbered lines.

Insert a duplicate of every line in a text file:

```
$ awk '{print $0, '\n', $0}' < data.txt
```

Insert a duplicate of every line in a text file and also remove blank lines:

```
$ awk '{print $0, "\n", $0}' < data.txt | awk 'NF > 0'
```

Insert a blank line after every line in a text file:

```
$ awk '{print $0, "\n"}' < data.txt
```

Printing the Words in a Text String in awk

Listing 4.55 displays the content of `Fields2.sh` that illustrates how to print the words in a text string using the `awk` command.

LISTING 4.55: Fields2.sh

```
echo "a b c d e"| awk '
{
  for(i=1; i<=NF; i++) {
     print "Field ",i,":",$i
  }
}
'
```

The output from Listing 4.55 is here:

```
Field  1 : a
Field  2 : b
Field  3 : c
Field  4 : d
Field  5 : e
```

Count Occurrences of a String in Specific Rows

Listing 4.56 and Listing 4.57 display the contents `data1.csv` and `data2.csv`, respectively, and Listing 4.58 displays the content of `checkrows.sh` that illustrates how to count the number of occurrences of the string `past` in column 3 in rows 2, 5, and 7.

LISTING 4.56: data1.csv

```
in,the,past,or,the,present
for,the,past,or,the,present
in,the,past,or,the,present
for,the,paste,or,the,future
in,the,past,or,the,present
completely,unrelated,line1
in,the,past,or,the,present
completely,unrelated,line2
```

LISTING 4.57: data2.csv

```
in,the,past,or,the,present
completely,unrelated,line1
```

```
for,the,past,or,the,present
completely,unrelated,line2
for,the,paste,or,the,future
in,the,past,or,the,present
in,the,past,or,the,present
completely,unrelated,line3
```

LISTING 4.58: checkrows.sh

```
files="`ls data*.csv| tr '\n' ' '`"
echo "List of files: $files"

awk -F"," '
( FNR==2 || FNR==5 || FNR==7 ) {
    if ( $3 ~ "past" ) { count++ }
}
END {
    printf "past: matched %d times (INEXACT) ", count
    printf "in field 3 in lines 2/5/7\n"
}' data*.csv
```

Listing 4.58 looks for occurrences in the string past in columns 2, 5, and 7 because of the following code snippet:

```
( FNR==2 || FNR==5 || FNR==7 ) {
    if ( $3 ~ "past" ) { count++ }
}
```

If a match occurs, then the value of count is incremented. The END block reports the number of times that the string past was found in columns 2, 5, and 7. Note that strings such as paste and pasted will match the string past. The output from Listing 4.58 is here:

```
List of files: data1.csv data2.csv
past: matched 5 times (INEXACT) in field 3 in lines 2/5/7
```

The shell script checkrows2.sh replaces the term $3 ~ "past" with $3 == "past" in checkrows.sh to check for exact matches, which produces the following output:

```
List of files: data1.csv data2.csv
past: matched 4 times (EXACT) in field 3 in lines 2/5/7
```

Well-Known Sorting Algorithms

Sorting algorithms have a best case, average case, and worst case in terms of performance. Interestingly, sometimes an efficient algorithm (such as quick sort) can perform the worst when a given array is already sorted.

The following subsections contain code samples for the following well-known sort algorithms:

▪ bubble sort

- selection sort

- insertion sort

- Merge sort

- Quick sort

- BucketSort

- Shell Sort

- Shell Sort

- Heap Sort

- BucketSort

- InplaceSort

- CountingSort

- RadixSort

If you want to explore sorting algorithms in more depth, perform an Internet search for additional sorting algorithms.

The Bubble Sort

A *bubble sort* involves a nested loop whereby each element of an array is compared with the elements to the right of the given element. If an array element is less than the current element, the values are interchanged ("swapped"), which means that the contents of the array will eventually be sorted from smallest to largest value. Here is an example:

```
arr1 = np.array([40, 10, 30, 20]);
Item = 40;
Step 1: 40 > 10 so switch these elements:
arr1 = np.array([10, 40, 30, 20]);
Item = 40;
Step 2: 40 > 30 so switch these elements:
arr1 = np.array([10, 30, 40, 20]);
Item = 40;
Step 3: 40 > 20 so switch these elements:
arr1 = np.array([10, 30, 20, 40]);
```

As you can see, the smallest element is in the left-most position of the array arr1. Now repeat this process by comparing the second position (which is index 1) with the right-side elements.

```
arr1 = np.array([10, 30, 20, 40]);
Item = 30;
Step 4: 30 > 20 so switch these elements:
arr1 = np.array([10, 20, 30, 40]);
```

```
Item = 30;
Step 4: 30 < 40 so do nothing
```

As you can see, the smallest elements two elements occupy the first two positions in the array `arr1`. Now repeat this process by comparing the third position (which is index 2) with the right-side elements.

```
arr1 = np.array([10, 20, 30, 40]);
Item = 30;
Step 4: 30 < 40 so do nothing
```

The array `arr1` is now sorted in increasing order (in a left-to-right fashion). If you want to reverse the order so that the array is sorted in decreasing order (in a left-to-right fashion), simply replace the ">" operator with the "<" operator in the preceding steps.

Listing 4.59 displays the content of `bubble_sort1.sh` that shows you how to sort an array of numbers using the bubble sort.

LISTING 4.59: bubble_sort1.sh

```
echo "" | awk '
BEGIN {
    arr[0] = 30; arr[1] = 10; arr[2] = 200; arr[3] = -13;
    printf("Array:    ")
    for (i=0;i<length(arr);i++) {
      printf("%d ",arr[i])
    }
    print ""
}
{
  for (i=0;i<length(arr)-1;i++) {
     for (j=i+1;j<length(arr);j++) {
       if(arr[i] > arr[j]) {
           tmp = arr[i]
           arr[i] = arr[j]
           arr[j] = tmp
       }
     }
  }
}
END {
    printf("Sorted: ")
    for (i=0;i<length(arr);i++) {
      printf("%d ",arr[i])
    }
    print ""
}
'
```

You can manually perform the code execution in Listing 4.59 to convince yourself that the code is correct (hint: it is the same sequence of steps that you saw earlier in this section). Launch the code in Listing 4.59, and you will see the following output:

```
Array:   30 10 200 -13
Sorted: -13 10 30 200
```

Find Anagrams in a List of Words

Recall that the variable word1 is an anagram of word2 if word2 is a permutation of word1. Listing 4.60 displays the content of the anagrams2. sh that illustrates how to check if two words are anagrams of each other.

LISTING 4.60: anagrams2.sh

```
echo "" | awk '
function sort_word(str1) {
    split(str1,chars,"")

    word = ""
    for (idx in chars) {
        word = word chars[idx]
    }
    return word
}
function is_anagram(str1, str2) {
  sorted1 = sort_word(str1)
  sorted2 = sort_word(str2)
  return (sorted1 == sorted2)
}
BEGIN {
    PROCINFO["sorted_in"]="@val_str_asc"
    words[1] = "abc";  words[2] = "evil"
    words[3] = "Z";    words[4] = "cab"
    words[5] = "live"; words[6] = "xyz"
    words[7] = "zyx";  words[8] = "bac"
}
{
  for(i=1; i<length(words)-1; i++) {
    for(j=i+1; j<length(words); j++) {
      result = is_anagram(words[i], words[j])
      if(result == 1) {
        printf("%10s and %10s => anagrams\n",
               words[i],words[j])
      } else {
        printf("%10s and %10s => not anagrams\n",
               words[i],words[j])
      }
    }
  }
}
'
```

Listing 4.60 defines the function is_anagram() that takes parameters str1 and str2 whose sorted values are used to initialize the variables sorted1 and sorted2, respectively. The function returns the result of comparing sorted1 with sorted2: if they are equal, then str1 is a palindrome.

The next portion of Listing 4.60 initializes the variable words as a list of strings, followed by a nested loop. The outer loop uses the variable i to range from 0 to len(words)-1, and the inner loop uses the variable j to range from i+1 to len(words). The inner loop initializes the variable result with the value returned by the function is_anagram() that is invoked with the strings words[i] and words[j]. The two words are palindromes if the value of the variable result is True. Launch the code in Listing 4.60, and you will see the following output:

```
abc and     evil => not anagrams
abc and        Z => not anagrams
abc and      cab => anagrams
abc and     live => not anagrams
abc and      xyz => not anagrams
abc and      zyx => not anagrams
evil and       Z => not anagrams
evil and     cab => not anagrams
evil and     live => anagrams
evil and      xyz => not anagrams
evil and      zyx => not anagrams
   Z and     cab => not anagrams
   Z and     live => not anagrams
   Z and      xyz => not anagrams
   Z and      zyx => not anagrams
 cab and     live => not anagrams
 cab and      xyz => not anagrams
 cab and      zyx => not anagrams
live and      xyz => not anagrams
live and      zyx => not anagrams
 xyz and      zyx => anagrams
```

Sort an Array in O(n) Complexity

Listing 4.61 displays the content of simple_sort.sh that shows you how to sort an array of numbers using the bubble sort.

LISTING 4.61: simple_sort.sh

```
echo "" | awk ' BEGIN {
    arr1[1] = 0; arr1[2] = 1; arr1[3] = 2;
    arr1[4] = 2; arr1[5] = 1; arr1[6] = 0;
    arr1[7] = 0; arr1[8] = 1; arr1[9] = 2;
}
{
   printf("Initial: ")
   for(i=1; i<=length(arr1); i++)
     printf("%s ",arr1[i])
   print ""
```

```
    for(i=1; i<=length(arr1); i++) {
      if(arr1[i] == 0)
        zeroes += 1
    }

    third = int(length(arr1)/3)
    for(i=1; i<=third; i++) {
        arr1[i]         = 0
        arr1[third+i]   = 1
        arr1[2*third+i] = 2
    }

    printf("Sorted:   ")
    for(i=1; i<=length(arr1); i++) {
        printf("%s ",arr1[i])
    }
    print ""
}
'
```

Listing 4.61 initializes `arr1` with a list of multiple occurrences the values 0, 1, and 2, and then displays the contents of `arr1`. The second loop counts the number of occurrences the value 0 in the variable `arr1`. The third loop uses a "thirds" technique to assign the values 0, 1, and 2 to contiguous locations: all the 0 values appear first, followed by all the 1 values, and then all the 2 values. The key word in this task is "`equal`," which is shown in bold at the top of this section. Launch the code in Listing 4.61, and you will see the following output:

```
Initial: 0 1 2 2 1 0 0 1 2
Sorted:  0 0 0 1 1 1 2 2 2
```

Find the Median of an Array of Numbers

Instead of using a bubble sort, you can use the built-in `sort()` function in awk to sort numbers or strings. Listing 4.62 displays the content of `median1.sh` that shows you how to find the median of an array of numbers using the built-in `sort()` function.

LISTING 4.62: median1.sh

```
echo "" | awk ' BEGIN {
  arr1[1] = 400
  arr1[2] = 5
  arr1[3] = 1
  arr1[4] = 123
  arr1[5] = 500
  arr1[6] = -55

  print "=> Initial array:"
  for(i=1;i<=length(arr1);i++) print i,":",arr1[i]
}
END {
```

```
    row_count = asort(arr1,arr2)

    print "=> Sorted array:"
    for(i=1;i<=length(arr2);i++) print i,":",arr2[i]

    if (row_count % 2 != 0) {
        middle = int(row_count/2 + 0.5)
        median = arr2[middle]
    } else {
        median = (arr2[row_count/2]+arr2[row_count/2+1])/2
    }
    print "=> Median value:",median
}
'
```

Listing 4.62 starts with an awk command that contains a BEGIN statement that initializes arr1 with multiple integer values and then displays its contents. The next portion of Listing 4.62 invokes the built-in sort() function to popular the array arr2 with the sorted contents of array arr1.

The final portion of Listing 4.67 contains a BEGIN statement that displays the contents of arr2, followed by conditional logic to determine the median. Recall that the median of an array with an odd number of values is the middle value of the array, whereas the median of an array with an even number of values is the average of the two "middle values" of the array. The final code snippet in the END statement displays the median value in the array arr1. Launch the code in Listing 4.62, and you will see the following output:

```
=> Initial array:
1 : 400
2 : 5
3 : 1
4 : 123
5 : 500
6 : -55
=> Sorted array:
1 : -55
2 : 1
3 : 5
4 : 123
5 : 400
6 : 500
=> Median value: 64
```

Linear Search

Listing 4.63 displays the content of linear_search.sh that shows you how to sort an array of numbers using the bubble sort.

LISTING 4.63: linear_search.sh

```
echo "" | awk ' BEGIN {
  item = 123
  arr1[1] = 1
  arr1[2] = 3
  arr1[3] = 5
  arr1[4] = 123
  arr1[5] = 400
}
{

  found = -1
  for(i=1; i<=length(arr1); i++) {
    if (item == arr1[i]) {
      found = i
      break
    }
  }

  if (found >= 0) {
    print "found",item,"in position",found
  } else {
    print item,"not found"
  }
}
'
```

Listing 4.63 starts with the variable found that is initialized with the value -1, followed by the search item 123, and also the array arr1 that contains an array of numbers. Next, a loop that iterates through the elements of the array arr1 of integers, comparing each element with the value of item. If a match occurs, the variable found is set equal to the value of the loop variable i, followed by an early exit.

The last portion of Listing 4.63 checks the value of the variable found: if it is non-negative, then the search item was found (otherwise, it is not in the array). Launch the code in Listing 4.1, and you will see the following output:

```
found 123 in position 3

Keep in mind the following point: although the array arr1
contains a sorted list of numbers, the code works correctly
for an unordered list as well. Launch the code in Listing
4.63, and you will see the following output:
found 123 in position 4
```

Binary Search (Iterative)

A *binary search* requires a sorted array and can be implemented via an iterative algorithm as well as a recursive solution. This type of search involves comparing the middle element of an array of sorted elements with a search element. If they are equal, then the item has been found; if the middle element is smaller than the search element, then the previous step is repeated with the right half of the array. If the middle element is larger than the search element, then the previous step is repeated with the left half of the array. Eventually, the element will be found (if it appears in the array) or the repeated splitting of the array terminates when the subarray has a single element (i.e., no further splitting can be performed).

Binary Search Walkthrough

Let's perform a walkthrough of a binary search that searches for an item in a sorted array of integers.

Example #1: Let `item = 25` and `arr1 = [10,20,25,40,100]`, so the midpoint of the array is 3. Since `arr1[3] == item`, the algorithm terminates successfully.

Example #2: Let `item = 25` and `arr1 = [1,5,10, 15, 20, 25, 40]`, which means that the midpoint is 4.
First iteration: Since `arr1[4]` < item, we search the array `[20,25,40]`.
Second iteration: The midpoint is 1, and the corresponding value is 25.
Third iteration: 25 and the array is the single element `[25]`, which matches the item.

Example #3: `item = 25` and `arr1 = [10, 20, 25, 40, 100,150,400]`, so the midpoint is 4.
First iteration: Since `arr1[4]` > 25, we search the array `[10,20,25]`.
Second iteration: The midpoint is 1, and the corresponding value is 20.
Third iteration: 25 and the array is the single element `[25]`, which matches the item.

Example #4: `item = 25` and `arr1 = [1,5,10, 15, 20, 30, 40]`, so the midpoint is 4.
First iteration: Since `arr1[4]` < 25, we search the array `[20,30,40]`.
Second iteration: The midpoint is 1, and the corresponding value is 30.
Third iteration: 25 and the array is the single element `[20]`, so there is no match.

As mentioned in the first paragraph of this section, a binary search can be implemented with an interactive solution, which is the topic of the next section.

Code for a Binary Search (Iterative)

Listing 4.64 displays the content of the `binary_search1.sh` that illustrates how to perform a binary search with an array of numbers.

LISTING 4.64: binary_search1.sh

```
echo "" | awk ' BEGIN {
```

```
        arr1[1] = 1
        arr1[2] = 3
        arr1[3] = 5
        arr1[4] = 123
        arr1[5] = 400
        found = -1
        item = 123
        left = 0
        right = length(arr1)-1

        printf("array: ")
        for(k=1; k<=length(arr1); k++) {
           printf("%d ",arr1[k])
        }
        print ""
}
{
        while(left <= right) {
          mid = int(left + (right-left)/2)

          if(arr1[mid] == item) {
             found = mid
             break
          } else if (arr1[mid] < item) {
             left = mid+1
          } else {
             right = mid-1
          }
        }

        if( found >= 0) {
          print "found",item,"in position",found
        } else {
          print item,"not found"
        }
}
'
```

Listing 4.64 initializes an array of numbers and some scalar variables to keep track of the left and right index positions of the subarray that we will search each time that we split the array. The next portion of Listing 4.64 contains conditional logic that implements the sequence of steps that you saw in the examples in the previous section. Launch the code in Listing 4.64, and you will see the following output:

```
array: [   1   3   5 123 400]
found 123 in position 3
```

Binary Search (Recursive)

Listing 4.65 displays the content of the `binary_search_recursive.py` that illustrates how to perform a binary search recursively with an array of numbers.

LISTING 4.65: binary_search_recursive.py

```
echo "" | awk '
function binary_search(data, item, left, right) {
  if(left > right) {
    return "Not Found"
  } else {
    # incorrect (can result in overflow):
    # mid = (left + right) / 2
    mid = int(left + (right-left)/2)

    if(item == data[mid]) {
      return "Found"
    } else if (item < data[mid]) {
      # recursively search the left half
      return binary_search(data, item, left, mid-1)
    } else {
      # recursively search the right half
      return binary_search(data, item, mid+1, right)
    }
  }
}
BEGIN {
   arr1[1] = 1
   arr1[2] = 3
   arr1[3] = 5
   arr1[4] = 123
   arr1[5] = 400

   items[1] = -100
   items[2] = 123
   items[3] = 200
   items[4] = 400

   found = -1
   item = 123
   left = 0
   right = length(arr1)-1

   printf("array: ")
   for(k=1; k<=length(arr1); k++) {
      printf("%d ",arr1[k])
   }
   print ""
}
{
   for(i=1; i<=length(items); i++) {
     item  = items[i]
     left  = 0
     right = length(arr1)-1
     result = binary_search(arr1, item, left, right)
     print "item",item, result
   }
}
'
```

Listing 4.65 starts with the function `binary_search()` with parameters `data`, `item`, `left`, and `right` that contain the current array, the search item, the left index of `data`, and the right index of `data`, respectively. If the left index `left` is greater than the right index `right` then the search item does not exist in the original array.

However, if the left index `left` is *less than* the right index `right`, then the code assigns the middle index of `data` to the variable `mid`. Next, the code performs the following three-part conditional test:

* If `item == data[mid]`, then the search item has been found in the array.

* If `item < data[mid]`, then the function `binary_search()` is invoked with the left half of the `data` array.

* If `item > data[mid]`, then the function `binary_search()` is invoked with the right half of the `data` array.

The next portion of Listing 4.65 initializes the sorted array `arr1` with numbers and initializes the array `items` with a list of search items, and also initializes some scalar variables to keep track of the left and right index positions of the subarray that we will search each time that we split the array.

The final portion of Listing 4.65 consists of a loop that iterates through each element of the `items` array and invokes the function `binary_search()` to determine whether the current item is in the sorted array. Launch the code in Listing 4.65, and you will see the following output:

```
array:  [  1   3   5 123 400]
item:   -100  found:  False
item:    123  found:  True
item:    200  found:  False
item:    400  found:  True
```

Summary

The first part of this chapter showed you how to perform operations with arrays, such as initializing them and displaying their contents. Then you saw how to add the numeric values in an array, and how to determine the maximum and minimum numeric values in an array. In addition, you saw how to initialize multi-dimensional arrays.

Next, you learned how to perform various tasks with datasets, such as deleting alternate lines, printing a range of strings or dates in a dataset, and joining alternate lines. In addition, you learned how to work with duplicate rows in a dataset and how to ensure uniformity of data values.

Furthermore, you saw how to implement the bubble sort and how to determine whether a pair of strings are anagrams. In addition, you learned how to sort an array in linear time, which is possible under certain conditions. After that, you saw how to perform a linear search and a binary search via an iterative algorithm as well as a recursive algorithm.

## CHAPTER 5

WORKING WITH AWK, PART 3

This chapter is the third of three chapters that contain examples of various features of the `awk` command.

The first part of this chapter starts with bit operations in `awk`, such as calculating the AND, OR, and XOR of a pair of positive integers. This section also contains code samples to perform various string-related tasks, such as reversing a string, checking for balanced parentheses, and column alignment.

The second part of this chapter shows you how to delete rows with missing values, how to process multiple files, and perform date conversion. You will also learn how to work with a dataset that contains one million records and how to count adjacent digits in such a dataset.

The third portion of this chapter discusses recursion, along with code samples for calculating values of arithmetic series, geometric series, factorial values, and Fibonacci numbers. In addition, you will see how to use Euclid's algorithm to find the greatest common divisor of two positive integers, which can also be used to find the least common multiple of two positive integers.

Bit Operations in awk

This section contains awk statements that perform bit operations on numbers, some of which are listed below, along with the associated `awk` function in parentheses:

- AND (and)

- OR (or)

- XOR (xor)

- NOT (compl)

- Left shift (lshift)

- Right shift (rshift)

Logical AND

Listing 5.1 displays the content of bitwise_and.sh that shows you how to calculate the logical AND of two positive integers.

LISTING 5.1: bitwise_and.sh

```
awk 'BEGIN {
   num1 = 24
   num2 = 10
   printf "(%d AND %d) = %d\n", num1, num2, and(num1, num2)
}'
```

Listing 5.1 contains an awk command with a BEGIN block that initializes the variables num1 and num2 with the values 24 and 10, respectively. The next code snippet is a printf() statement that displays the values of num1, num2, and the logical AND value of num1 and num2. Launch the code in Listing 5.1, and you will see the following output:

```
(24 AND 10) = 8
```

Logical OR

Listing 5.2 displays the content of bitwise_and.sh that shows you how to calculate the logical OR of two positive integers.

LISTING 5.2: bitwise_or.sh

```
awk 'BEGIN {
   num1 = 24
   num2 = 10
   printf "(%d OR %d) = %d\n", num1, num2, or(num1, num2)
}'
```

Listing 5.2 contains an awk command with a BEGIN block that initializes the variables num1 and num2 with the values 24 and 10, respectively. The next code snippet is a printf() statement that displays the values of num1, num2, and the logical R value of num1 and num2. Launch the code in Listing 5.2, and you will see the following output:

```
(24 OR 10) = 26
```

Logical XOR

Listing 5.3 displays the content of bitwise_xor.sh that shows you how to calculate the logical XOR of two positive integers.

LISTING 5.3: bitwise_xor.sh

```
awk 'BEGIN {
    num1 = 24
    num2 = 10
    printf "(%d AND %d) = %d\n", num1, num2, xor(num1, num2)
}'
```

Listing 5.3 contains an `awk` command with a BEGIN block that initializes the variables `num1` and `num2` with the values 24 and 10, respectively. The next code snippet is a `printf()` statement that displays the values of `num1`, `num2`, and the logical XOR value of `num1` and `num2`. Launch the code in Listing 5.3, and you will see the following output:

```
(24 XOR 10) = 18
```

Logical NOT

Listing 5.4 displays the content of `bitwise_not.sh` that shows you how to calculate the logical NOT of two positive integers.

LISTING 5.4: bitwise_comp.sh

```
awk 'BEGIN {
    num1 = 24
    num2 = 10
    printf("COMPLEMENT(%d) = %d\n", num1, compl(num1))
}'
```

Listing 5.4 contains an `awk` command with a BEGIN block that initializes the variables `num1` and `num2` with the values 24 and 10, respectively. The next code snippet is a `printf()` statement that displays the values of `num1`, `num2`, and the logical NOT value of `num1` and `num2`. Launch the code in Listing 5.4, and you will see the following output:

```
COMPLEMENT(24) = 9007199254740967
```

Logical Left Shift

Listing 5.5 displays the content of bitwise_lfshift.sh that shows you how to calculate the logical left shift of a positive integer.

LISTING 5.5: bitwise_lshift.sh

```
awk 'BEGIN {
    num1 = 24
    printf("left shift %d = %d\n", num1, lshift(num1))
}'
```

Listing 5.5 contains an `awk` command with a BEGIN block that initializes the variable `num1` with the values 24. The next code snippet is a `printf()` statement that displays the values of `num1`, `num2`, and the logical left shift value of `num1`. Launch the code in Listing 5.5, and you will see the following output:

```
lshift(24) by 1 = 48
```

Logical Right Shift

Listing 5.6 displays the content of `bitwise_rshift.sh` that shows you how to calculate the logical right shift of a positive integer.

LISTING 5.6: bitwise_rshift.sh

```
awk 'BEGIN {
   num1 = 24
   printf("right shift %d = %d\n", num1, rshift(num1))
}'
```

Listing 5.6 contains an `awk` command with a BEGIN block that initializes the variable `num1` with the value 24. The next code snippet is a `printf()` statement that displays the values of `num1`, `num2`, and the logical right shift value of `num1`. Launch the code in Listing 5.6, and you will see the following output:

```
rshift(24) by 1 = 12
```

Reverse a String

Listing 5.7 displays the content of `reverse1.sh` that shows you how to sort an array of numbers.

LISTING 5.7: reverse1.sh

```
echo "" | awk '
BEGIN {
   str1 = "abcdef"; rev = "";
   print "String:   ", str1
}
{
   for(i=length(str1); i>=1; i--) {
     rev = rev substr(str1,i,1)
   }
}
END { print "Reversed:", rev}
'
```

Listing 5.7 contains an `echo` command that passes an empty string to the `awk` command, which in turn contains a BEGIN block that initializes the variable `str1` and the variable `rev`, and then prints the value of `str1`.

The next portion of Listing 5.7 is the main execution block that contains a loop that processes the contents of the variable `str1` in a right-to-left fashion. During each iteration, the variable `rev` (which is initially an empty string) is updated by appending the current right-most character in str1 to the variable rev. Launch the code in Listing 5.55, and you will see the following output:

```
String:   abcdef
Reversed: fedcba
```

Find Palindromes

Listing 5.8 displays the content of palindrome1.sh that shows you how to determine whether a string is a palindrome.

LISTING 5.8: palindrome1.sh

```
echo "" | awk '
BEGIN {
   str1 = "abcdef"; rev = "";
   print "String: ", str1
}
{
   for(i=length(str1); i>=1; i--) {
     rev = rev substr(str1,i,1)
   }
}
END {
   if (rev == str1) {
     print "Palindrome: TRUE"
   } else {
     print "Palindrome: FALSE"
   }
}
'
```

Listing 5.8 contains the same initialization code as Listing 5.7, along with a new conditional code block in an END block that compares the string str1 with the string rev. If the strings are equal, then str1 is a palindrome, otherwise it is not a palindrome. In both cases, an appropriate message is displayed. Launch the code in Listing 5.8, and you will see the following output:

```
String:   abcdef
Palindrome: FALSE
```

Check for Unique Characters

Listing 5.9 displays the content of unique_chars.sh that shows you how to determine whether a string contains unique characters.

LISTING 5.9: unique_chars.sh

```
#128 characters for ASCII and 256 characters for extended
ASCII
```

```
echo "" | gawk '
function unique_chars(str1) {
  char_set[0] = 0
  for(j=1; j<128; j++) {
    char_set[j] = 0
  }

  str1 = tolower(str1)

  for(i=1; i<length(str1); i++) {
    char = substr(str1,i,1)
    ord_char = ord[char]
    val = ordz - ord_char
    #print i,":",i,"val:",val,"char:",char

    if (char_set[val] == 1) {
      # found duplicate character
      return 0
    } else {
      char_set[val] = 1
    }
  }
  return 1
}
BEGIN {
  for(num=1;num<128;num++) {
    ord[sprintf("%c",num)] = num
  }
  ordz = ord["z"]
}
{
  arr1[1] = "first str1ing"
  arr1[2] = "second str1ing"
  arr1[3] = "friendly world"
  arr1[4] = "abcdefghijklmo"

  for(k=1; k<=length(arr1); k++) {
    str1 = arr1[k]
    unique = unique_chars(str1)

    if(unique == 0) {
      print "duplicate characters =>",str1
    } else {
      print "unique characters =>   ",str1
    }
  }
}
'
```

Listing 5.9 contains an `echo` command that passes an empty string to an `awk` command, which in turn defines the function `unique_characters()` that determines whether its input parameter contains unique characters.

Specifically, the function `unique_characters()` converts its parameter `str` to lowercase letters and then initializes the 1x128 integer array `char_set` whose values are all 0. The next portion of this function iterates through the characters of the string `str` and initializes the integer variable `val` with the offset position of each character from the character `z`.

If this position in `char_set` equals 1, then a duplicate character has been found; otherwise, this position is initialized with the value 1. Note that the value `False` is returned if the string `str` contains duplicate letters, whereas the value `True` is returned if the string `str` contains unique characters. Launch the code in Listing 5.9, and you will see the following output:

```
duplicate characters => first str1ing
duplicate characters => second str1ing
duplicate characters => friendly world
unique characters =>    abcdefghijklmo
```

Check for Balanced Parentheses

Listing 5.10 displays the content of `balanced_parens.sh` that shows you how to determine whether a string contains balanced parentheses.

LISTING 5.10: balanced_parens.sh

```
echo "" | awk '
function check_balanced(text) {
  counter = 0
  text_len = length(text)

  for(i=1; i<=text_len; i++) {
    ch = substr(text,i,1)
    if (ch == "(") {
      counter += 1
    } else {
      if (ch == ")") {
        counter -= 1
      }
    }

    if (counter < 0)
      break
  }

  return counter
}
{
  exprs= "()()()"
  exprs= "(()()())"
  exprs[3] = "()("
  exprs[4] = "(())"
  exprs[5] = "()()("

  for(idx=1; idx<=length(exprs); idx++) {
    str1 = exprs[idx]
```

```
        counter = check_balanced(str1)

        if (counter == 0) {
          print "balanced string:   ",str1
        } else {
          print "unbalanced string:",str1
        }
    }
}'
```

Listing 5.10 starts with the iterative function check_balanced() that uses conditional logic to check the contents of the current character in the input string. The code increments the variable counter if the current character is a left parenthesis "(" and decrements the variable counter if the current character is a right parenthesis ")." The final code snippet in this function returns the value of the variable counter. The only way for an expression to consist of a balanced set of parentheses is for counter to equal 0 when the loop has finished execution.

The second part of Listing 5.10 contains the main execution block that initializes the array exprs with variable strings consisting of a combination of left and right parentheses, followed by a loop that invokes the function check_balanced() with each element of the array exprs. Conditional logic displays a message indicating whether each string is a palindrome. Launch the code in Listing 5.10, and you will see the following output:

```
balanced string:    () () ()
balanced string:    (() () ())
unbalanced string: () (
balanced string:    (())
unbalanced string: () () (
```

Printing a String in a Fixed Number of Columns

Listing 5.11 displays the content of FixedFieldCount1.sh that illustrates how to print the words in a text string using the awk command.

LISTING 5.11: FixedFieldCount1.sh

```
echo "aa bb cc dd ee ff gg hh"| awk '
BEGIN { colCount = 3 }
{

  for(i=1; i<=NF; i++) {
      printf("%s ", $i)
      if(i % colCount == 0) {
          print " "
      }
  }
}
'
```

Listing 5.11 invokes the `echo` command to redirect a string to an `awk` command that initializes the variable `colCount` to 3, followed by the main execution block that contains an array that prints every input field. Note that a new line is printed after three consecutive elements have been printed. Launch the code in Listing 5.11, and you will see the following output:

```
aa bb cc
dd ee ff
gg hh
```

Printing a Dataset in a Fixed Number of Columns

Listing 5.12 displays the content of `VariableColumns.txt` with lines of text that contain a different number of columns.

LISTING 5.12: VariableColumns.txt

```
this is line one
this is line number one
this is the third and final line
```

Listing 5.13 displays the content of `Fields3.sh` that illustrates how to print the words in a text string using the `awk` command.

LISTING 5.13: Fields3.sh

```
awk '{printf("%s ", $0)}' | awk '
BEGIN { columnCount = 3 }
{
  for(i=1; i<=NF; i++) {
    printf("%s ", $i)
    if( i % columnCount == 0 )
      print " "
  }
}
' VariableColumns.txt
```

Listing 5.13 starts with an `awk` command that displays the content of the text file `VariableColumns.txt` as a *single output line* because the `printf` statement omits the "\n" character. If you want to print the exact contents of the text file `VariableColumns.txt`, replace the `printf` statement of the first awk command with following statement:

```
printf("%s\n", $0)
```

Launch the code in Listing 5.13, and you will see the following output:

```
this is line
one this is
line number one
this is the
```

```
third and final
line
```

Aligning Columns in Datasets

If you have read the preceding two examples, the code sample in this section is easy to understand: you will see how to realign columns of data that are correct in terms of their content, but have been placed in different rows (and therefore are misaligned). Listing 5.14 displays the content of mixed-data.csv with misaligned data values. In addition, the first line and final line in Listing 5.14 are empty lines, which will be removed by the shell script in this section.

LISTING 5.14: mixed-data.csv

```
Sara, Jones, 1000, CA, Sally, Smith, 2000, IL,
Dave, Jones, 3000, FL, John, Jones,
4000, CA,
Dave, Jones, 5000, NY, Mike,
Jones, 6000, NY, Tony, Jones, 7000, WA
```

Listing 5.15 displays the content of mixed-data.sh that illustrates how to realign the dataset in Listing 5.14.

LISTING 5.15: mixed-data.sh

```
#------------------------------------------
# 1) remove blank lines
# 2) remove line feeds
# 3) print a LF after every fourth field
# 4) remove trailing ',' from each row
#------------------------------------------

inputfile="mixed-data.csv"

grep -v "^$" $inputfile |awk -F"," '{printf("%s",$0)}' | awk '
BEGIN { columnCount = 4 }
{
   for(i=1; i<=NF; i++) {
     printf("%s ", $i)
     if( I % columnCount  == 0) { print""" }
   }
' > temp-columns

# 4) remove trailing'''' from output:
cat temp-columns | sed''s/, $/'' | sed''s/ $/'' > $outputfile
```

Listing 5.15 starts with a grep command that removes blank lines, followed by an awk command that prints the rows of the dataset as a single line of text. The second awk command initializes the columnCount variable with the value 4 in the BEGIN block, followed by a loop that iterates through the input fields.

After four fields are printed on the same output line, a linefeed is printed, which has the effect of creating an output dataset consisting of rows consisting of four fields. The output from Listing 5.15 is here:

```
Sara, Jones, 1000, CA
Sally, Smith, 2000, IL
Dave, Jones, 3000, FL
John, Jones, 4000, CA
Dave, Jones, 5000, NY
Mike, Jones, 6000, NY
Tony, Jones, 7000, WA
```

Aligning Columns and Multiple Rows in Datasets

The preceding section showed you how to "join" consecutive rows from an input file to create a new output file. Listing 5.16 displays the content of mixed-data2.csv that contains an initial blank row and a final blank row, followed by Listing 5.17 that displays the contents of aligned-data2.csv with the correctly formatted dataset.

LISTING 5.16: mixed-data2.csv

```
Sara, Jones, 1000, CA,
Sally, Smith, 2000, IL,
Dave, Jones, 3000, FL,
John, Jones, 4000, CA,
Dave, Jones, 5000, NY,
Mike, Jones, 6000, NY,
Tony, Jones, 7000, WA
```

LISTING 5.17: aligned-data2.csv

```
Sara, Jones, 1000, CA, Sally, Smith, 2000, IL
Dave, Jones, 3000, FL, John, Jones, 4000, CA
Dave, Jones, 5000, NY, Mike, Jones, 6000, NY
Tony, Jones, 7000, WA
```

Listing 5.18 displays the content of mixed-data2.sh that illustrates how to realign the dataset in Listing 5.16.

LISTING 5.18: mixed-data2.sh

```
#-------------------------------------------
# 1) remove blank lines
# 2) remove line feeds
# 3) print a LF after every 8 fields
# 4) remove trailing'''' from each row
#-------------------------------------------
inputfile""mixed-data2.cs""
outputfile""aligned-data2.cs""

echo""=> Contents of input file""
```

```
cat $inputfile

grep -v""""^""" $inputfile |awk -""""""''{printf""""%"",$0)'' | awk''
BEGIN { columnCount = 4; rowCount = 2; currRow = 0 }
{
   for(i=1; i<=NF; i++) {
     printf""""%s"", $i)
     if( i % columnCount == 0) { ++currRow }
     if( currRow > 0 && currRow % rowCount == 0)
        { currRow = 0; print"""" }
   }
'' > temp-columns

# 4) remove trailing'''' from output:
cat temp-columns | sed''s/, $/'' | sed''s/ $/'' > $outputfile

echo""""=> Contents of output file""
cat $outputfile
echo
```

Listing 5.18 is similar to Listing 5.15. The program prints a linefeed character after a pair of "normal" records have been processed, which is implemented via the code that is shown in bold in Listing 5.18. Launch the code in Listing 5.18, and you will see the following output:

```
=> Contents of input file:

Sara, Jones, 1000, CA,
Sally, Smith, 2000, IL,
Dave, Jones, 3000, FL,
John, Jones, 4000, CA,
Dave, Jones, 5000, NY,
Mike, Jones, 6000, NY,
Tony, Jones, 7000, WA

=> Contents of output file:
Sara, Jones, 1000, CA, Sally, Smith, 2000, IL
Dave, Jones, 3000, FL, John, Jones, 4000, CA
Dave, Jones, 5000, NY, Mike, Jones, 6000, NY
Tony, Jones, 7000, WA
```

Now you can generalize Listing 5.18 very easily by changing the initial value of the rowCount variable to any other positive integer, and the code will work correctly without any further modification. For example, if you initialize rowCount to the value 5, then every row in the new dataset (with the possible exception of the final output row) will contain 5 "normal" data records.

Displaying a Subset of Columns in a Text File

Listing 5.19 displays the contents of the text file products.txt, whose rows contain the same number of columns.

LISTING 5.19: products.txt

```
MobilePhone 400   new
Tablet        300   new
Tablet        300   used
MobilePhone 200   used
MobilePhone 100   used
```

Listing 5.20 displays the content of RemoveColumn.sh that shows the contents of products.txt without the first column from the text file.

LISTING 5.20: RemoveColumn.sh

```
awk '{ for (i=2; i<=NF; i++) printf "%s ", $i; printf "\n";
       }' products.txt
```

The loop ranges from 2 and NF inclusive, which excludes the first input field. In addition, printf explicitly adds new lines after a row of data fields has been printed. The output of the awk command in Listing 5.20 is here:

```
400 new
300 new
300 used
200 used
100 used
```

Listing 5.21 displays the content of RemoveColumns.sh that contains an awk statement that prints all but the third column of a text file, followed by an awk statement that prints all but the third and seventh columns of a text file.

LISTING 5.21: RemoveColumns.sh

```
filename="aligned-data2.csv"
echo "=> contents of $filename:"
cat $filename
echo ""

# print all but the third column:
echo "Skipping field 3:"
awk '
{
  for (i=1; i<=NF; i++) {
     if( i != 3 ) {
        printf("%s ", $i)
     }
  }
  print ""
}' $filename
echo ""

# print all but the third and seventh columns:
echo "Skipping field 3 and field 7:"
```

```
awk '
{
  for (i=1; i<=NF; i++) {
    if( (i != 3 ) && ( i != 7 ) ) {
      printf("%s ", $i)
    }
  }
  print ""
}' $filename
```

Listing 5.21 is an enhancement of the Listing 5.20, and it starts by initializing the variable `filename` with the name of a CSV file. Next, the loop in the first `awk` statement prints each column of each row in the CSV file unless it is the third column. The loop in the second `awk` statement prints each column of each row in the CSV file unless it is the third column or the seventh column. Launch the code in Listing 5.21, and you will see the following output:

```
=> contents of aligned-data2.csv:
Sara, Jones, 1000, CA, Sally, Smith, 2000, IL
Dave, Jones, 3000, FL, John, Jones, 4000, CA
Dave, Jones, 5000, NY, Mike, Jones, 6000, NY
Tony, Jones, 7000, WA

Skipping field 3:
Sara, Jones, CA, Sally, Smith, 2000, IL
Dave, Jones, FL, John, Jones, 4000, CA
Dave, Jones, NY, Mike, Jones, 6000, NY
Tony, Jones, WA

Skipping field 3 and field 7:
Sara, Jones, CA, Sally, Smith, IL
Dave, Jones, FL, John, Jones, CA
Dave, Jones, NY, Mike, Jones, NY
Tony, Jones, WA
```

Subsets of Columns Aligned Rows in Datasets

The code sample in this section illustrates how to extract a subset of the existing columns and a subset of the rows. Listing 5.22 displays the content of `sub-rows-cols.txt` of the desired dataset that contains two columns from every even row of the file `aligned-data.txt`.

LISTING 5.22: sub-rows-cols.txt

```
Sara, 1000
Dave, 3000
Dave, 5000
Tony, 7000
```

Listing 5.23 displays the content of `sub-rows-cols.sh` that illustrates how to generate the dataset in Listing 5.22. Most of the code is the same as Listing 5.21, with the new code shown in bold.

LISTING 5.23: sub-rows-cols.sh

```
#-----------------------------------------
# 1) remove blank lines
# 2) remove line feeds
# 3) print a LF after every fourth field
# 4) remove trailing ',' from each row
#-----------------------------------------

inputfile="mixed-data.csv"
outputfile="sub-rows-cols.csv"

echo "=> Contents of input file:"
cat $inputfile

grep -v "^$" $inputfile |awk -F"," '{printf("%s",$0)}' | awk '
BEGIN { columnCount = 4 }
{
   for(i=1; i<=NF; i++) {
     printf("%s ", $i)
     if( i % columnCount  == 0) { print "" }
   }
}' > temp-columns

# 4) remove trailing ',' from output:
cat temp-columns | sed 's/, $//' | sed 's/$//' > temp-columns2

cat temp-columns2 | awk '
BEGIN { rowCount = 2; currRow = 0 }
{
   if(currRow % rowCount == 0) { print $1, $3 }
   ++currRow
}' > temp-columns3

cat temp-columns3 | sed 's/,$//' | sed 's/ $//' > $outputfile

echo "=> Contents of output file:"
cat $outputfile
```

Listing 5.23 contains a new block of code that redirects the output of Step #4 to a temporary file `temp-columns2` whose contents are processed by another awk command in the last section of Listing 5.23. Notice that that awk command contains a BEGIN block that initializes the variables rowCount and currRow with the values 2 and 0, respectively.

The main block prints columns 1 and 3 of the current line if the current row number is even, and then the value of currRow is then incremented. The output of this awk command is redirected to yet another temporary file that is the input to the final code snippet, which uses the cat command and two occurrences of the sed command to remove a trailing ",", and a trailing space, as shown here:

```
cat temp-columns3 | sed 's/,$//' | sed 's/ $//' > $outputfile
```

Launch the code in Listing 5.23, and you will see the following output:

```
=> Contents of input file:

Sara, Jones, 1000, CA,
Sally, Smith, 2000, IL,
Dave, Jones, 3000, FL,
John, Jones, 4000, CA,
Dave, Jones, 5000, NY,
Mike, Jones, 6000, NY,
Tony, Jones, 7000, WA

=> Contents of output file:
Sara, 1000
Dave, 3000
Dave, 5000
Tony, 7000
```

There are other ways to perform the functionality in Listing 5.22; the main purpose is to show you different techniques for combining various bash commands.

Longest/Shortest Words in Datasets

Listing 5.24 displays the contents of `report.txt`, and Listing 5.25 displays the content of `longest_word.sh` that illustrates how to count the frequency of words in a file.

LISTING 5.24: longest_word.sh

```
This is a sample report.
Some relevant details were presented yesterday.
Several people likes to work from home.
However, some people prefer the office.
In addition, parking is easier now.
The WFM topic has different appeal.
```

LISTING 5.25: longest_word.sh

```
awk '
{
   longest=0
   shortest=""

   for(i=1; i<=NF; i++) {
     if(length($i) > longest) longest = length($i)
     if(shortest == "") shortest = length($i)
     if(length($i) < shortest) shortest = length($i)
   }
   print "Sentence: ",$0
   print "Longest:  ",longest,"Shortest: ",shortest,"\n"
}
' report.txt
```

Listing 5.25 starts by initializing the variables `longest` and `shortest` with the values 0 and "", respectively. The next portion of code contains a loop that iterates through the fields of each sentence. A conditional code block updates the values of longest and shortest whenever the current field is longer than or shorter than, respectively, the current values of `longest` and `shortest`. The output from Listing 5.25 is here:

```
Sentence:   This is a sample report.
Longest:    7 Shortest:  1

Sentence:   Some relevant details were presented yesterday.
Longest:    10 Shortest:  4

Sentence:   Several people likes to work from home.
Longest:    7 Shortest:  2

Sentence:   However, some people prefer the office.
Longest:    8 Shortest:  3

Sentence:   In addition, parking is easier now.
Longest:    9 Shortest:  2

Sentence:   The WFM topic has different appeal.
Longest:    9 Shortest:  3
```

Counting Word Frequency in Datasets

Listing 5.26 displays the content of `WordCounts1.sh` that illustrates how to count the frequency of words in a file.

LISTING 5.26: WordCounts1.sh

```
awk '
# Print list of word frequencies
{
    for (i = 1; i <= NF; i++)
        freq[$i]++
}
END {
    for (word in freq)
        printf "%s\t%d\n", word, freq[word]
}
' columns2.txt
```

Listing 5.26 contains a block of code that processes the lines in `columns2.txt`. Each time that a word (of a line) is encountered, the code increments the number of occurrences of that word in the hash table `freq`. The END block contains a loop that displays the number of occurrences of each word in `columns2.txt`. The output from Listing 5.26 is here:

```
two         3
one         3
```

```
three       3
six         1
four        3
five        2
```

Listing 5.27 displays the contents of `columns4.txt`, and Listing 5.28 displays the content of `WordCounts2.sh` that performs a case insensitive word count.

LISTING 5.27: columns4.txt

```
123 ONE TWO
456 three four
ONE TWO THREE FOUR
five 123 six
one two three
four five
```

LISTING 5.28: WordCounts2.sh

```
awk '
{
    # convert everything to lower case
    $0 = tolower($0)

    # remove punctuation
    #gsub(/[^[:alnum:]_[:blank:]]/, "", $0)

    for(i=1; i<=NF; i++) {
        freq[$i]++
    }
}
END {
    for(word in freq) {
        printf "%s\t%d\n", word, freq[word]
    }
}
' columns4.txt
```

Listing 5.28 includes the following code snippet that converts the text in each input line to lowercase letters:

```
$0 = tolower($0)
```

The output from launching Listing 5.28 with `columns4.txt` is here:

```
456         1
two         3
one         3
three       3
six         1
123         2
four        3
five        2
```

Displaying Only "Pure" Words in a Dataset

For simplicity, let's work with a text string and that way we can see the intermediate results as we work toward the solution. This example will be familiar from prior chapters, but now we see how awk does it.

Listing 5.29 displays the content of onlywords.sh that contains three awk commands for displaying the words, integers, and alphanumeric strings in a text string.

LISTING 5.29: onlywords.sh

```
x="ghi abc Ghi 123 #def5 123z"

echo "Only words:"
echo $x |tr -s ' ' '\n' | awk -F" " '
{
   if($0 ~ /^[a-zA-Z]+$/) { print $0 }
}
' | sort | uniq
echo

echo "Only integers:"
echo $x |tr -s ' ' '\n' | awk -F" " '
{
   if($0 ~ /^[0-9]+$/) { print $0 }
}
' | sort | uniq
echo

echo "Only alphanumeric words:"
echo $x |tr -s ' ' '\n' | awk -F" " '
{
   if($0 ~ /^[0-9a-zA-Z]+$/) { print $0 }
}
' | sort | uniq
echo
```

Listing 5.29 starts by initializing the variable x as a space separated set of tokens:

```
x="ghi abc Ghi 123 #def5 123z"
```

The next step is to split x into words:

```
echo $x |tr -s ' ' '\n'
```

The output from the preceding code snippet is shown here:

```
ghi
abc
Ghi
123
#def5
123z
```

The third step is to invoke `awk` and check for words that match the regular expression `^[a-zA-Z]+`, which matches any string consisting of one or more uppercase and lowercase letters (and nothing else):

```
if($0 ~ /^[a-zA-Z]+$/) { print $0 }
```

The output from the preceding code snippet is here:

```
ghi
abc
Ghi
```

Finally, if you also want to sort the output and print only the unique words, redirect the output from the `awk` command to the `sort` command and the `uniq` command.

The second `awk` command uses the regular expression `^[0-9]+` to check for integers and the third `awk` command uses the regular expression `^[0-9a-zA-Z]+` to check for alphanumeric words. The output from launching Listing 5.29 is here:

```
Only words:
Ghi
abc
ghi

Only integers:
123

Only alphanumeric words:
123
123z
Ghi
abc
ghi
```

You can replace the variable x with a dataset to retrieve only alphabetic strings from that dataset.

Delete Rows with Missing Values

The code sample in this section shows you how to use the `awk` command to split the comma-separated fields in the rows of a dataset, where fields can contain nested quotes of arbitrary depth.

Listing 5.30 displays a subset of the rows in `titanic.csv`, and Listing 5.31 displays the content of the file `delete-empty-cols-awk.sh` that shows you how to create a new dataset whose rows are fully populated with data values.

LISTING 5.30: titanic.csv

```
survived,pclass,sex,age,sibsp,parch,fare,embarked,class,who,
    adult_male,deck,embark_town,alive,alone
0,3,male,22.0,1,0,7.25,S,Third,man,True,,Southampton,no,
    False
1,1,female,38.0,1,0,71.2833,C,First,woman,False,C,
    Cherbourg,yes,False
1,3,female,26.0,0,0,7.925,S,Third,woman,False,,Southampton,
    yes,True
1,1,female,35.0,1,0,53.1,S,First,woman,False,C,Southampton,
    yes,False
0,3,male,35.0,0,0,8.05,S,Third,man,True,,Southampton,no,True
0,3,male,,0,0,8.4583,Q,Third,man,True,,Queenstown,no,True
// rows omitted for brevity
0,3,male,25.0,0,0,7.05,S,Third,man,True,,Southampton,no,True
0,3,female,39.0,0,5,29.125,Q,Third,woman,False,,Queenstown,
    no,False
0,2,male,27.0,0,0,13.0,S,Second,man,True,,Southampton,no,
    True
1,1,female,19.0,0,0,30.0,S,First,woman,False,B,Southampton,
    yes,True
0,3,female,,1,2,23.45,S,Third,woman,False,,Southampton,no,
    False
1,1,male,26.0,0,0,30.0,C,First,man,True,C,Cherbourg,yes,True
0,3,male,32.0,0,0,7.75,Q,Third,man,True,,Queenstown,no,True
```

LISTING 5.31: delete-empty-cols-awk.sh

```
input="titanic.csv"
output="titanic_clean.csv"

row_count1='wc $input | awk '{print $1}''
echo "Number of input rows:  $row_count1"

# compare the awk code with the grep example in chapter 5:
awk -F"," '
{
  if ($0 !~ /,,/) { print $0 }
}' < $input > $output

row_count2=`wc $output | awk '{print $1}'`
echo "Number of output rows: $row_count2"

echo
echo "=> First five rows in $input:"
cat $input |head -6 |tail -5
echo "-------------------------"
echo

echo "=> First five rows in $output:"
cat $output |head -6 |tail -5
echo ""
```

Listing 5.31 starts by initializing the variables input and output with the values `titanic.csv` and `titanic_clean.csv`, respectively. The next code snippet is an `awk` command that extracts the rows from the CSV file that do not contain two consecutive commas (which indicate a missing field value) and redirects those rows to the output file.

The next code snippet initializes the variable `row_count2` with the rows 2 through 6 of the input file and displays their contents, followed by a code snippet that performs the same operation using the input file. Launch the code in Listing 5.31, and you will see the following output:

```
Number of input rows:  892
Number of output rows: 183

=> First five rows in titanic.csv:
0,3,male,22.0,1,0,7.25,S,Third,man,True,,Southampton,no,
   False
1,1,female,38.0,1,0,71.2833,C,First,woman,False,C,
   Cherbourg,yes,False
1,3,female,26.0,0,0,7.925,S,Third,woman,False,,Southampton,
   yes,True
1,1,female,35.0,1,0,53.1,S,First,woman,False,C,Southampton,
   yes,False
0,3,male,35.0,0,0,8.05,S,Third,man,True,,Southampton,no,True
------------------------

=> First five rows in titanic_clean.csv:
1,1,female,38.0,1,0,71.2833,C,First,woman,False,C,
   Cherbourg,yes,False
1,1,female,35.0,1,0,53.1,S,First,woman,False,C,Southampton,
   yes,False
0,1,male,54.0,0,0,51.8625,S,First,man,True,E,Southampton,
   no,True
1,3,female,4.0,1,1,16.7,S,Third,child,False,G,Southampton,
   yes,False
1,1,female,58.0,0,0,26.55,S,First,woman,False,C,
   Southampton,yes,True
```

As a quick refresher, the file `delete-empty-cols-grep.sh` contains the following code snippet that skip any records that contain two consecutive commas, which indicate a missing value for a feature:

```
$ cat $input |grep -v ",," > $output
```

Although the `awk` command is more powerful than `grep`, you can sometimes perform the same task with less (and more intuitive) code using the `grep` command. Hence, it is worthwhile for you to gain proficiency in `grep`, `sed`, and `awk` so that you can create shell scripts that are clear and concise, and can also be enhanced (or debugged) with less effort.

Moreover, you can take advantage of the power of in `grep`, `sed`, and `awk` to perform pre-processing on datasets before you perform data cleaning tasks using utilities such as Pandas.

Working with Multiline Records in awk

Listing 5.32 displays the contents of employees.txt, and Listing 5.33 displays the content of employees.sh that illustrates how to concatenate text lines in a file.

LISTING 5.32: employees.txt

```
Name:  Jane Edwards
EmpId: 12345
Address: 123 Main Street Chicago Illinois

Name:  John Smith
EmpId: 23456
Address: 432 Lombard Avenue SF California
```

LISTING 5.33: employees.sh

```
inputfile="employees.txt"
outputfile="employees2.txt"

echo "=> Input file:"
cat $inputfile

awk '
{
  if($0 ~ /^Name:/) {
    x = substr($0,8) ","
    next
  }

  if( $0 ~ /^Empid:/) {
   #skip the Empid data row
   #x = x substr($0,7) ","
    next
  }

  if($0 ~ /^Address:/) {
    x = x substr($0,9)
    print x
  }
}
' < $inputfile > $outputfile

echo "=> Output file:"
cat $outputfile
```

The output from launching the code in Listing 5.33 is here:

```
=> Input file:
Name:  Jane Edwards
EmpId: 12345
Address: 123 Main Street Chicago Illinois

Name:  John Smith
```

```
EmpId: 23456
Address: 432 Lombard Avenue SF California

=> Output file:
Jane Edwards, 123 Main Street Chicago Illinois
John Smith, 432 Lombard Avenue SF California
```

Now that you have seen `awk` code snippets and shell scripts containing the `awk` command that illustrate various types of tasks that you can perform on files and datasets, you are ready for some use cases. The next section (which is the first use case) shows you how to replace multiple field delimiters with a single delimiter, and the second use case shows you how to manipulate date strings.

CSV Files with Multirow Records

This section contains a CSV file with multirow records such that each field is on a separate line (e.g., `survived:0`) instead of comma-separated field values for each record.

The solution is surprisingly simple when we use `awk`: set RS equal to the string pattern that separates records. In our case, we need to set RS equal to \n\n, after which $0 will contain the contents of each multiline record. In addition, specify FS='\n' so that get each line is treated as a field (i.e., $1, $2, and so forth).

Listing 5.34 displays the contents of the CSV file `multi_line_rows.csv`, and Listing 5.35 display the contents of `multi_line_rows.sh`.

LISTING 5.34: multi_line_rows.csv

```
survived:0
pclass:3
sex:male
age:22.0

survived:1
pclass:1
sex:female
age:38.0

survived:0
pclass:3
sex:male
age:35.0

survived:1
pclass:3
sex:female
age:27.0
```

LISTING 5.35: multi_line_rows.sh

```
filename="multi_line_rows.csv"

cat $filename | awk '
BEGIN { RS="\n\n"; FS="\n" }
{
   # name/value pairs have this format:
   # survived:0 pclass:3 sex:male age:22.0
   split($1,arr,":"); printf("%s,",arr[2]);
   split($2,arr,":"); printf("%s,",arr[2]);
   split($3,arr,":"); printf("%s,",arr[2]);
   split($4,arr,":"); printf("%s\n",arr[2]);
}'
```

The main idea in Listing 5.35 is shown in bold, which specifies the value of RS (record separator) as two consecutive linefeed characters and then specifies FS (field separator) as a linefeed character. The main block of code splits the fields $1, $2, $3, and $4 based on a colon (":") separator, and then prints the second field, which is the actual data value.

Note that arr[1] contains the *name* of the fields, such as survived, pclass, sex, or age, whereas arrcontains the *value* of the fields. Launch the code in Listing 5.35, and you will see the following output:

```
0,3,male,22.0
1,1,female,38.0
0,3,male,35.0
1,3,female,27.0
```

There is one more detail: Listing 5.35 does *not* display the header line with the names of the fields. Listing 5.36 shows you how to modify Listing 5.34 to generate the header line.

LISTING 5.36: multi_line_rows2.sh

```
filename="multi_line_rows.csv"

cat $filename | awk '
BEGIN { RS="\n\n"; FS="\n"; count=0 }
{
   if(count == 0) {
     count += 1
     split($1,arr,":"); header = arr[1]
     split($2,arr,":"); header = header "," arr[1]
     split($3,arr,":"); header = header "," arr[1]
     split($4,arr,":"); header = header "," arr[1]
     print header
   }

   # name/value pairs have this format:
   # survived:0 pclass:3 sex:male age:22.0
   split($1,arr,":"); printf("%s,",arr[2]);
   split($2,arr,":"); printf("%s,",arr[2]);
```

```
    split($3,arr,":"); printf("%s,",arr[2]);
    split($4,arr,":"); printf("%s\n",arr[2]);
}'
```

Listing 5.36 initializes the variable count with the value 0, followed by a conditional block of code that constructs the contents of the variable header (which will contain the names of the fields) by sequentially concatenating the field names. The contents of header are printed, and since the value of count has been incremented, this block of code is executed only once, which prevents the header line from being repeatedly displayed. Launch the code in Listing 5.36, and you will see the following output:

```
survived,pclass,sex,age
0,3,male,22.0
1,1,female,38.0
0,3,male,35.0
1,3,female,27.0
```

Other variations of the preceding code are also possible, such as changing the display order of the fields. Listing 5.37 displays the fields in reverse order: age, sex, pclass, and survived.

LISTING 5.37: multi_line_rows3.sh

```
filename="multi_line_rows.csv"

cat $filename | awk '
BEGIN { RS="\n\n"; FS="\n"; count=0 }
{
    # fields displayed in reverse order:
    if(count == 0) {
      count += 1
      split($4,arr,":"); header = arr[1]
      split($3,arr,":"); header = header "," arr[1]
      split($2,arr,":"); header = header "," arr[1]
      split($1,arr,":"); header = header "," arr[1]
      print header
    }

    # name/value pairs have this format:
    # survived:0 pclass:3 sex:male age:22.0
    split($1,arr,":"); survived = arr[2];
    split($2,arr,":"); pclass = arr[2];
    split($3,arr,":"); sex = arr[2];
    split($4,arr,":"); age = arr[2];

    # fields displayed in reverse order:
    printf("%s,%s,%s,%s\n",age, sex, pclass, survived)
}'
```

Listing 5.37 contains a conditional block of code that constructs the contents of the variable header by sequentially concatenating the field names *in reverse order*. The contents of header are printed, and since the value of count has been incremented, this block of code is executed only once, which prevents the header line from being repeatedly displayed.

The second block of code constructs an output string by initializing the variables survived, pclass, sex, and age, and then printing them *in reverse order*. Launch the code in Listing 5.37, and you will see the following output:

```
age,sex,pclass,survived
22.0,male,3,0
38.0,female,1,1
35.0,male,3,0
27.0,female,3,1
```

Processing Multiple Files with awk

Listing 5.38, Listing 5.39, and Listing 5.40 display the contents of the text files file1.txt, file2.txt, and file3.txt, respectively.

LISTING 5.38: file1.txt

```
deep dish potato garlic pizza file1 line1
deep dish potato garlic pizza file1 line2
deep dish potato garlic pizza file1 line3
```

LISTING 5.39: file2.txt

```
deep pepperoni pizza file2 line1
deep pepperoni pizza file2 line2
deep pepperoni pizza file2 line3
deep pepperoni pizza file2 line4
deep pepperoni pizza file2 line5
```

LISTING 5.40: file3.txt

```
deep dish pizza file1 line1
deep tandoori chicken pizza file3 line1
deep tandoori chicken pizza file3 line2
deep tandoori chicken pizza file3 line3
deep tandoori chicken pizza file3 line4
deep tandoori chicken pizza file3 line5
deep tandoori chicken pizza file3 line6
deep tandoori chicken pizza file3 line7
```

Listing 5.41 displays the content of single-line1.sh that shows you how to print a single line from a text file.

LISTING 5.41: single-line1.sh

```
echo "Print a single line from ONE file:"
awk 'FNR == 2 {print}' file1.txt file2.txt
```

Listing 5.41 contains an `echo` command that prints a message, followed by an `awk` command that prints only the second line in the second input file (which happens to be `file2.txt`). Launch the code in Listing 5.41, and you will see the following output:

```
Print a single line from ONE file:
deep dish potato garlic pizza file1 line2
```

Listing 5.42 displays the content of `single-line2.sh` that shows you how to print a single line from multiple text files.

LISTING 5.42: single-line2.sh

```
echo "Print one line from MULTIPLE files:"
awk 'FNR == 2 {print}' 'ls file*txt'
```

Listing 5.42 contains almost the same code as Listing 5.41: the only difference is that the `awk` command process the files that are in the output of `'ls file*txt'` instead of simply specifying `file1.txt` and `file2.txt`. Launch the code in Listing 5.42, and you will see the following output:

```
Print one line from MULTIPLE files:
deep dish potato garlic pizza file1 line2
deep pepperoni pizza file2 line2
deep tandoori chicken pizza file3 line2
```

Listing 5.43 displays the content of `single-line3.sh` that shows you how to print a single line from multiple text files, as well as the file name that contains each output line.

LISTING 5.43: single-line3.sh

```
echo "Print one line from MULTIPLE files:"
awk 'FNR == 2 {print}' ls file*txt
```

Listing 5.43 contains almost the same code as Listing 5.42: the only difference is that the `awk` command processes the files in the output of `ls file*txt` instead of `'ls file*txt'`. Launch the code in Listing 5.43, and you will see the following output:

```
Print one line from MULTIPLE files:
file1.txt: deep dish potato garlic pizza file1 line2
file2.txt: deep pepperoni pizza file2 line2
file3.txt: deep tandoori chicken pizza file3 line2
Listing 5.44 displays the content of count-tokens.sh that
shows you how to count the number of times that a token
appears in the second field in multiple text files.
```

LISTING 5.44: count-tokens.sh

```
echo "Count the same token in MULTIPLE files:"
```

```
awk '
BEGIN { count = 0; token = "chicken" }
{
   if($3 ~ token) {
     count += 1
   }
}
END { print "Token:",token,"token count:",count }
' file*txt
```

Listing 5.44 contains an `echo` command that displays as a message, followed by an `awk` command that contains a `BEGIN` block that initializes the variables `count` and `token` with the values `0` and `chicken`, respectively. The main execution block contains conditional logic that checks if the value of $3 matches the value of `token`, in which case the value of `count` is incremented.

The last portion of code in Listing 5.44 is an `END` block that prints the values of the string `token` and the variable `count`. Launch the code in Listing 5.44, and you will see the following output:

```
Count the same token in MULTIPLE files:
Token: chicken token count: 7
```

Listing 5.45 displays the content of `count-tokens2.sh` that shows you how to count the number of times that a token appears in the second field in multiple text files and also count the number of processed lines.

LISTING 5.45: count-tokens2.sh

```
echo "Count the same token in MULTIPLE files:"
awk '
BEGIN { count = 0; token = "chicken" }
{
   if($3 ~ token) {
     count += 1
   }
}
END { print "Token:",token,"token count:",count
      print "Number of processed lines: ",NR
}
' file*txt
```

Listing 5.45 is almost the same as Listing 5.44: the only difference is the code snippet in the `END` block that displays the number of lines `NR` that have been processed. Launch the code in Listing 5.45, and you will see the following output:

```
Count the same token in MULTIPLE files:
Token: chicken token count: 7
Number of processed lines:  15
```

Inner Join of Two Files in awk

The code sample in this section performs an action that is called an "inner join" in RDBMS parlance. Listing 5.46 displays the contents of the CSV file `customers.csv`, and Listing 5.47 displays the contents of the CSV file `purchase_orders.csv`.

LISTING 5.46: customers.csv

```
1000,Jane Jones, 1234 Appian Way
2000,John Smith, 5678 Main Street
3000,Dave Stone, 3333 Birch Avenue
```

LISTING 5.47: purchase_orders.csv

```
1000,11100,2023/02/05,$125.00
1000,11200,2023/02/13,$480.00
2000,12100,2023/03/09,$312.00
2000,12200,2023/03/25,$567.00
```

Listing 5.48 displays the content of `join2.sh` that shows you how to join the contents of `customers.csv` and `purchase_orders.csv` via the Unix `join` command.

LISTING 5.48: join2.sh

```
# https://shapeshed.com/unix-join/
file1="customers.csv"
file2="purchase_orders.csv"

echo "Joining $file1 and $file2:"
join -1 1 -2 1 -t"," $file1 $file2
echo ""

# Use "-o" to specify the order of the output fields:
echo "A different ordering of the output fields:"
join -1 1 -2 1 -t"," -o 1.1,1.2,1.3,2.2,2.1 $file1 $file2
```

Listing 5.48 starts by initializing the variables `file1` and `file2` to reference the CSV files `customers.csv` and `purchase_orders.csv`, respectively. The next section of code invokes the `join` command that performs a join on the files `file1` and `file2`, based on the contents of the first field of both of these files.

The final portion of Listing 5.48 contains another code snippet that also invokes the `join` command for the same pair of CSV files, and also specifies the columns from `file1` and `file2` to display as output. Launch the code in Listing 5.48, and you will see the following output:

```
Joining customers.csv and purchase_orders.csv:
1000,Jane Jones, 1234 Appian Way,11100,2023/02/05,$125.00
```

```
1000,Jane Jones, 1234 Appian Way,11200,2023/02/13,$480.00
2000,John Smith, 5678 Main Street,12100,2023/03/09,$312.00
2000,John Smith, 5678 Main Street,12200,2023/03/25,$567.00

A different ordering of the output fields:
1000,Jane Jones, 1234 Appian Way,11100,1000
1000,Jane Jones, 1234 Appian Way,11200,1000
2000,John Smith, 5678 Main Street,12100,2000
2000,John Smith, 5678 Main Street,12200,2000
```

Listing 5.49 displays the content of `duplicate-fields.sh` that shows you how to print the rows in which the second and third fields are the same.

LISTING 5.49: duplicate-fields.sh

```
awk -F ',' '
{
   if($2 == $3) {
      print "Duplicate fields in row",NR,":",$1,$2,$3
   }
}' datapoints.txt
```

Listing 5.49 contains an `awk` command that prints the lines in which the values of $2 and $3 are the same in the text file `datapoints.txt`. Launch the code in Listing 5.49, and you will see the following output:

```
Duplicate fields in row 2 : item2 5 5
Duplicate fields in row 5 : item5 8 8
```

However, before we look at the `awk` script, let's look at the Unix command that performs the same task on two files, `customers.txt` and `purchase_orders.txt`.

Logical Operators in awk

The `awk` command provides the logical operators, OR, AND, and NOT, which are expressed with ||, &&, and !, respectively. In addition, you can combine these logical operators to define complex Boolean expressions. The following example uses the logical AND operator:

```
awk '$3 > 10 && $4 < 20 {print $1, $2}' datapoint.txt
The following example uses the logical OR operator:
awk '$3 > 10 || $4 < 20 {print $1, $2}' datapoint.txt
```

Listing 5.50 displays the content of the text file `datapoints2.txt`.

LISTING 5.50: datapoints2.txt

```
item1,4,6,1000
item2,5,5,8000
item3,4,6,4000
```

```
item4,7,9,7000
item5,8,8,9000
```

Listing 5.51 displays the content of `duplicate-fields2.sh` that shows you how to print the rows in which the second and third fields are the same *and* the first field equals a given token.

LISTING 5.51: duplicate-fields2.sh

```
awk -F ',' '
{
    if(($2 == $3) && ($4 == 9000)) {
        print "Duplicate fields in row matching", $4":",$0
    }
}' datapoints2.txt
```

Listing 5.51 is almost the same as Listing 5.49: the difference is that the conditional block contains compound logic that displays input lines in which $2 and $3 are equal *and* the value of $4 is 9000. Launch the code in Listing 5.51, and you will see the following output:

```
Duplicate fields in row matching 9000: item5,8,8,9000
```

A Simple Use Case

The code sample in this section shows you how to use the `awk` command to split the comma-separated fields in the rows of a dataset, where fields can contain nested quotes of arbitrary depth.

Listing 5.52 displays the content of the file `quotes3.csv` that contains a "," delimiter and multiple quoted fields.

LISTING 5.52: quotes3.csv

```
field5,field4,field3,"field2,foo,bar",field1,field6,field7,
    "fieldZ"
fname1,"fname2,other,stuff",fname3,"fname4,foo,bar",fname5
"lname1,a,b","lname2,c,d","lname3,e,f","lname4,foo,bar",
    lname5
```

Listing 5.53 displays the content of the file `delim1.sh` that illustrates how to replace the delimiters in `quotes3.csv` with a "," character.

LISTING 5.53: delim1.sh

```
#inputfile="quotes1.csv"
#inputfile="quotes2.csv"
inputfile="quotes3.csv"

grep -v "^$" $inputfile |  awk '
{
    print "LINE #" NR ": " $0
    printf ("--------------------\n")
```

```
   for (i = 0; ++i <= NF;)
     printf "field #%d : %s\n", i, $i
   printf ("\n")
}' FPAT='([^,]+)|("[^"]+")' < $inputfile
```

The output from launching the shell script in Listing 5.53 is here:

```
LINE #1: field5,field4,field3,"field2,foo,bar",field1,
    field6,field7,"fieldZ"
------------------------
field #1 : field5
field #2 : field4
field #3 : field3
field #4 : "field2,foo,bar"
field #5 : field1
field #6 : field6
field #7 : field7
field #8 : "fieldZ"

LINE #2: fname1,"fname2,other,stuff",fname3,"fname4,foo,
    bar",fname5
------------------------
field #1 : fname1
field #2 : "fname2,other,stuff"
field #3 : fname3
field #4 : "fname4,foo,bar"
field #5 : fname5

LINE #3: "lname1,a,b","lname2,c,d","lname3,e,f","lname4,
    foo,bar",lname5
------------------------
field #1 : "lname1,a,b"
field #2 : "lname2,c,d"
field #3 : "lname3,e,f"
field #4 : "lname4,foo,bar"
field #5 : lname5

LINE #4: "Outer1 "Inner "Inner "Inner C" B" A" Outer1",
    "XYZ1,c,d","XYZ2lname3,e,f"
------------------------
field #1 : "Outer1 "Inner "Inner "Inner C" B" A" Outer1"
field #2 : "XYZ1,c,d"
field #3 : "XYZ2lname3,e,f"

LINE #5:
------------------------
```

As you can see, the task in this section is very easily solved via the awk command.

Another Use Case

The code sample in this section shows you how to use the awk command to reformat the date field in a dataset and change the order of the fields in the new dataset. For example, consider the following input line in the original dataset:

```
Jane,Smith,20140805234658
```

The reformatted line in the output dataset has this format:

```
2014-08-05 23:46:58,Jane,Smith
```

Listing 5.54 displays the content of the file `dates2.csv` that contains a "," delimiter and three fields.

LISTING 5.54: dates2.csv

```
Jane,Smith,20140805234658
Jack,Jones,20170805234652
Dave,Stone,20160805234655
John,Smith,20130805234646
Jean,Davis,20140805234649
Thad,Smith,20150805234637
Jack,Pruit,20160805234638
```

Listing 5.55 displays the content of `string2date2.sh` that converts the date field to a new format and shifts the new date to the first field.

LISTING 5.55: string2date2.sh

```
inputfile="dates2.csv"
outputfile="formatteddates2.csv"

rm -f $outputfile; touch $outputfile

for line in `cat $inputfile`
do
   fname=`echo $line |cut -d"," -f1`
   lname=`echo $line |cut -d"," -f2`
   date1=`echo $line |cut -d"," -f3`

   # convert to new date format
   newdate=`echo $date1 | awk `{ print substr($0,1,4)
   "- "substr($0,5,2)"- "substr($0,7,2)" "substr($0,9,2)":"
   substr($0,11,2)":"substr($0,13,2)}'`

   # append newly formatted row to output file
   echo "${newdate},${fname},${lname}" >> $outputfile
done
```

Listing 5.55 initializes the `inputfile` and `outputfile` variables with the names of the two CSV files. The next code snippet removes those files, thereby ensuring that they are empty. The next portion of Listing 5.55 contains a loop that iterates through the rows in the input file, and initializes the variables `fname`, `lname`, and `date1` with the contents of the first, second, and third fields, respectively, of each input line.

The next code block constructs the variable `newdate` via an `awk` statement that extracts the appropriate contents of each input row using the `substr()` function. The final portion of Listing 5.55 appends a new string to the `outputfile` that consists of the comma-separated values of `newdate`, `fname`, and `lname`. Launch Listing 5.55, and you will see the following output:

```
2014-08-05 23:46:58,Jane,Smith
2017-08-05 23:46:52,Jack,Jones
2016-08-05 23:46:55,Dave,Stone
2013-08-05 23:46:46,John,Smith
2014-08-05 23:46:49,Jean,Davis
2015-08-05 23:46:37,Thad,Smith
2016-08-05 23:46:38,Jack,Pruit
```

Date Conversion

Listing 5.56 displays the contents of `mixed_currency.csv`, and Listing 5.57 displays the content of `convert_currency3.sh` that illustrates how to replace a "," with a "." and vice versa when it is necessary so that strings have a valid USD currency format. Keep in mind that the code does not check strings for invalid date formats.

LISTING 5.56: mixed_currency.csv

```
product1|1129.95
product2|2110,99
product3|2.110,99
product4|2.110.678,99
product5|1,130.95
```

LISTING 5.57: convert_currency3.sh

```
filename="mixed_currency.csv"

echo "=> INITIAL CONTENTS OF CSV FILE:"
cat $filename
echo

echo "=> UPDATED CONTENTS OF CSV FILE:"
awk -F"|" '
BEGIN { modified=0 }
{
   comma  = index($2,",")
   period = index($2,".")
   OLD2=$2

   if(comma > 0 && period == 0) {
     gsub(/,/,".",$2)
     modified += 1
     #print "comma(s) but no period:", $2
   }
```

```
    else if( comma > period ) {
      # replace right-most "," with "Z"
      gsub(/,/,"Z",$2)
      # replace "." with ","
      gsub(/\./,",",$2)
      # replace "Z" with "."
      gsub(/Z/,".",$2)
      modified += 1
      #print "comma(s) before period:", $2
    }
    NEW2=$2

    printf("OLD: %18s NEW: %15s\n",OLD2, NEW2)
}
END { print "=> Modified lines:",modified }
' < mixed_currency.csv
```

Listing 5.57 starts by initializing the variable `filename` as `mixed_currency.csv` and then displays its contents. The next portion of Listing 5.57 is an `awk` script that initializes the variables `comma` and `period` with the index of a comma (",") and period (".") for every input line from the file `mixed_currency.csv`. Unlike other programming languages, there is no explicit loop keyword in the code: instead, it is an implicit aspect of the `awk` programming language (which might take some time to become accustomed to this style).

The next block of conditional code checks for the presence of a comma and the absence of a period: if so, then the `gsub()` function replaces the comma (",") with a period (".") in the second field, which is the numeric portion of each line in Listing 5.57, and the variable modified is incremented. For example, the input line `product3|2110,99` is processed by the conditional block and replaces the contents of $2 (which is the second field) with the value `2110.99`.

The next portion of code checks for the presence of a comma and a period where the location of the comma is on the *right side* of the period: if so, then three substitutions are performed. First, the right-most comma is replaced with the letter `z`, after which the period is replaced with a comma, and then the `z` is replaced with a period. Launch the code in Listing 5.57 with the following code snippet:

```
$ ./convert-currency3.sh
```

You will see the following output:

```
=> INITIAL CONTENTS OF CSV FILE:
product1|1129.95
product2|2110,99
product3|2.110,99
product4|2.110.678,99
product5|1,130.95
```

```
=> UPDATED CONTENTS OF CSV FILE:
OLD:            1129.95 NEW:            1129.95
OLD:            2110,99 NEW:            2110.99
OLD:            2.110,99 NEW:          2,110.99
OLD:         2.110.678,99 NEW:      2,110,678.99
OLD:          1,130.95 NEW:          1,130.95
=> Modified lines: 3
```

A Dataset with 1,000,000 Rows

The code samples in this section show you how to use `awk` to perform various comparisons on a dataset that contains 1,000,000 rows.

Numeric Comparisons

The code snippet in this section illustrates how to check for a specific number (e.g., 58) and the occurrence of one, two, or three adjacent digits in the first field of each row.

Listing 5.58 displays the content `numeric_comparisons.sh` that shows you how to work with a dataset that contains 1,000,000 rows.

LISTING 5.58: numeric_comparisons.sh

```
filename="1000000_HRA_Records.csv"

echo "first:"
awk -F"," '{ if($1 > 50) { print $1 } }' < $filename | wc
echo

echo "second:"
awk -F"," '{ if($1 > 50 && $5 > 70) { print $4 } }'
    < $filename | wc
```

Listing 5.58 initializes the variable `filename` with a CSV filename, followed by an `awk` command that counts the number of rows in which the first field is greater than 50.

The second and final `awk` statement counts the number of rows whose first field is greater than 50 and whose fifth field is greater than 70. Launch the code in Listing 5.58, and you will see the following output:

```
first:
  232161   232161   696484

second:
  232161   232161   696484

third:
  232161   232161  1011843
```

Counting Adjacent Digits

The code sample in this section illustrates how to check for a specific number (e.g., 58) and the occurrence of one, two, or three adjacent digits in the first field of each row.

LISTING 5.59: adjacent_digits.sh

```
filename="1000000_HRA_Records.csv"

echo "first:"
awk -F"," '{ if($1 ~ /58/) { print $1} }'   < $filename  |wc
echo

echo "second:"
awk -F"," '{ if($1 ~ /[0-9]/) { print $1} }' <$filename   |wc
echo

echo "third:"
awk -F"," '{ if($1 ~ /[0-9][0-9]/) { print $1} }'
    < $filename |wc
echo

echo "fourth:"
awk -F"," '{ if($1 ~ /[0-9][0-9][0-9]/) { print $1} }'
    < $filename |wc
```

Listing 5.59 initializes the variable `filename` with a CSV filename, followed by three `awk` commands. The first `awk` command counts the number of rows whose first field contains the string 58. The second `awk` command counts the number of rows whose first field contains a digit, and the third `awk` command counts the number of rows whose first field contains three consecutive digits. Launch the code in Listing 5.59, and you will see the following output:

```
first:
   23199   23199   69597

second:
 1000000 1000000 3000000

third:
 1000000 1000000 3000000

fourth:
       0       0       0
```

Average Support Rate

The code sample in this section illustrates how to check for a specific number (e.g., 58) and the occurrence of one, two, or three adjacent digits in the first field of each row.

LISTING 5.60: average_rate.sh

```
filename="1000000_HRA_Records.csv"

awk -F"," '
BEGIN { total = 0; num_records = 0 }
{
   if($1 > 40 && $5 == "Support") {
     total += $4
     num_records += 1
   }
}
END {
   avg_rate = total/num_records
   print "Number of Records:   ",num_records
   print "Average Support Rate:",avg_rate
}
' < $filename
```

Listing 5.60 initializes the variable `filename` with a CSV filename, followed by an `awk` statement that calculates the total value in the fourth field of the rows whose first field is greater than 40 and whose fifth field equals the string `Support`.

The final portion of Listing 5.60 calculates the `avg_rate`, which is the total value divided by the number of matching rows. Next, the `avg_rate` and `num_records` are displayed. Launch the code in Listing 5.60, and you will see the following output:

```
Number of Records:    77482
Minimum Rate:         100
Maximum Rate:         1500
Average Support Rate: 798.935
```

What is Recursion?

Recursion-based algorithms can provide elegant solutions to tasks that would be difficult to implement via iterative algorithms. For some tasks, such as calculating factorial values, the recursive solution and the iterative solution have comparable code complexity.

As a simple example, suppose that we want to add the integers from 1 to n (inclusive), and let n = 10 so that we have a concrete example. If we denote s as the partial sum of successively adding consecutive integers, then we have the following:

```
S = 1
S = S + 2
S = S + 3
. . .
S = S + 10
```

If we denote `s(n)` as the sum of the first n positive integers, then we have the following relationship:

```
S(1) = 1
S(n) = S(n-1) + n for n > 1
```

The next section contains code samples for calculating the sum of the first n positive integers using an iterative approach and then with recursion.

Arithmetic Series

This section shows you how to calculate the sum of a set of positive integers, such as the numbers from 1 to n, inclusive. The first algorithm uses an iterative approach and the second algorithm uses recursion.

Before delving into the code samples, there is a simple way to calculate the closed form sum of the integers from 1 to n, inclusive, which we will denote as s. Then there are two ways to calculate S, as shown here:

```
S = 1 + 2    + 3    + . . . + (n-1) + n
S = n + (n-1) + (n-2) + . . . + 2      + 1
```

There are n columns on the right side of the preceding pair of equations, and each column has the sum equal to `(n+1)`. Therefore, the sum of the right side of the equals sign is `n*(n+1)`. Since the left side of the equals sign has the sum `2*s`, we have the following result:

```
2*S = n*(n+1)
```

Now divide both sides by 2, and we get the well-known formula for the arithmetic sum of the first n positive integers:

```
S = n*(n+1)/2
```

Incidentally, the preceding formula was derived by a young student who was bored with performing the calculation manually: that student was Karl F. Gauss (in third grade).

Calculating Arithmetic Series (Iterative)

Listing 5.61 displays the content of the `arith_sum.sh` that illustrates how to calculate the sum of the numbers from 1 to n, inclusive, using an iterative approach.

LISTING 5.61: arith_sum.sh

```
echo "" |awk '
function arith_sum(num)
{
    sum = 0
    for(i=1; i<=num; i++) {
```

```
        sum += i
    }
    return sum
}
BEGIN {
    max = 20

    for(j=1; j<=max; j++) {
        sum = arith_sum(j)
        print "Sum from 1 to",j," = ",sum
    }
}
'
```

Listing 5.61 starts with the function `arith_sum()` that contains a loop that iteratively adds the numbers from 1 to n. The next portion of Listing 5.61 also contains a loop that iterates through the numbers from 2 to 20, inclusive, and then invokes `arith_sum()` with each value of the loop variable to calculate the sum of the integers from 1 to that value. Launch the code in Listing 5.61, and you will see the following output:

```
sum from 1 to 2 = 3
sum from 1 to 3 = 6
sum from 1 to 4 = 10
sum from 1 to 5 = 15
sum from 1 to 6 = 21
sum from 1 to 7 = 28
sum from 1 to 8 = 36
sum from 1 to 9 = 45
sum from 1 to 10 = 55
sum from 1 to 11 = 66
sum from 1 to 12 = 78
sum from 1 to 13 = 91
sum from 1 to 14 = 105
sum from 1 to 15 = 120
sum from 1 to 16 = 136
sum from 1 to 17 = 153
sum from 1 to 18 = 171
sum from 1 to 19 = 190
sum from 1 to 20 = 210
```

Modify the code in Listing 5.62 to calculate the sum of the squares, cubes, and fourth powers of the numbers from 1 to n, along with your own variations of the code.

Calculating Arithmetic Series (Recursive)

Listing 5.63 displays the content of the `arith_sum_recursive.sh` that illustrates how to calculate the sum of the numbers from 1 to n, inclusive, using a recursion.

LISTING 5.63: *arith_sum_recursive.sh*

```
echo "" |awk '
```

```
function arith_sum(num)
{
    if(num == 0) return num
    else {
        return num + arith_sum(num-1)
    }
    for(i=1; i<=num; i++) {
        sum += i
    }
}
BEGIN {
    max = 20

    for(j=1; j<=max; j++) {
        sum = arith_sum(j)
        print "Sum from 1 to",j," = ",sum
    }
}
'
```

Listing 5.63 starts with the recursive function `arith_sum()`, which uses conditional logic to return n if n equals the value 0 (which is the terminating case); otherwise, the code returns the value of n *plus* the value of `arith_sum(n-1)`. Launch the code in Listing 5.63, and you will see the same output as shown in the previous section.

Calculating Partial Arithmetic Series

Listing 5.64 displays the content of `arith_partial_sum.sh` that illustrates how to calculate the sum of the numbers from m to n, inclusive, where m and n are two positive integers such that m <= n, using an iterative approach.

LISTING 5.64: *arith_partial_sum.sh*

```
echo "" |awk '
function arith_sum(m,n)
{
    if(m > n) return 0
    else {
        return n*(n+1)/2 - m*(m+1)/2
    }
}
BEGIN {
    max = 10

    for(i=1; i<max; i++) {
        for(j=i+1; j<=max; j++) {
            sum = arith_sum(i,j)
            print "Arithmetic sum from",i,"to",j," = ",sum
        }
    }
}
```

Listing 5.64 is straightforward: the function `arith_partial_sum()` returns the sum of squares from 1 to n *minus* the sum of the squares from 1 to m. This function is invoked in a loop in the second part of Listing 5.64, which calculates the difference of the sum of squares from 2 to 20. Launch the code in Listing 5.64, and you will see the following output:

```
arithmetic sum from 2 to 2 = 2

Arithmetic sum from 1 to 2   =   2
Arithmetic sum from 1 to 3   =   5
Arithmetic sum from 1 to 4   =   9
Arithmetic sum from 1 to 5   =   14
Arithmetic sum from 1 to 6   =   20
// details omitted for brevity
Arithmetic sum from 7 to 9   =   17
Arithmetic sum from 7 to 10  =   27
Arithmetic sum from 8 to 9   =   9
Arithmetic sum from 8 to 10  =   19
Arithmetic sum from 9 to 10  =   10
```

Now that you have seen some examples involving arithmetic expressions, let's turn to geometric series, which is the topic of the next section.

Geometric Series

This section shows you how to calculate the geometric series of a set of positive integers, such as the numbers from 1 to n, inclusive. The first algorithm uses an iterative approach and the second algorithm uses recursion.

Before delving into the code samples, there is a simple way to calculate the closed form sum of the geometric series of integers from 1 to n, inclusive, where r is the ratio of consecutive terms in the geometric series. Let s denote the sum, which we can express as follows:

```
S   = 1+ r + r^2 + r^3 + . . . + r^(n-1) + r^n
r*S =     r + r^2 + r^3 + . . . + r^(n-1) + r^n + r^(n+1)
```

Now subtract each term in the second row from the corresponding term in the first row, and we have the following result:

```
S - r*S = 1 - r^(n+1)
```

Factor s from both terms on the left side of the preceding equation, and we obtain the following result:

```
S*(1 - r) = 1 - r^(n+1)
```

Divide both sides of the preceding equation by the term `(1-r)` to get the formula for the sum of the geometric series of the first `n` positive integers:

```
S = [1 - r^(n+1)]/(1-r)
```

If `r = 1`, then the preceding equation returns an infinite value, which makes sense because `s` is the sum of an infinite number of occurrences of the number 1.

Calculating a Geometric Series (Iterative)

Listing 5.65 displays the content of the `geom_sum.sh` that illustrates how to calculate the sum of the numbers from 1 to n, inclusive, using an iterative approach.

LISTING 5.65: geom_sum.sh

```
echo "" |awk '
function geom_sum(num, ratio)
{
    partial = 0
    power   = 1

    for(i=1; i<=num; i++) {
        partial += power
        power *= ratio
    }
    return partial
}
BEGIN {
    max = 10
    ratio = 2

    for(j=2; j<=max; j++) {
        prod = geom_sum(j, ratio)
        print "Geometric sum for ratio",ratio,"from 1 to",j,
            " = ",prod
    }
}
'
```

Listing 5.65 starts with the function `geom_sum()` that contains a loop that calculates the sum of the powers of the numbers from 1 to n, where the power is the value of the variable `ratio`. The second part of Listing 5.65 contains a loop that invokes the function `geom_sum()` with the values 2, 3, . . ., n and a fixed value of 2 for the variable ratio. Launch the code in Listing 5.65, and you will see the following output:

```
geometric sum for ratio= 2 from 1 to 2 = 3
geometric sum for ratio= 2 from 1 to 3 = 7
geometric sum for ratio= 2 from 1 to 4 = 15
geometric sum for ratio= 2 from 1 to 5 = 31
```

```
geometric sum for ratio= 2 from 1 to 6 = 63
geometric sum for ratio= 2 from 1 to 7 = 127
geometric sum for ratio= 2 from 1 to 8 = 255
geometric sum for ratio= 2 from 1 to 9 = 511
geometric sum for ratio= 2 from 1 to 10 = 1023
```

Calculating Arithmetic Series (Recursive)

Listing 5.66 displays the content of geom_sum_recursive.sh that illustrates how to calculate the sum of the geometric series of the numbers from 1 to n, inclusive, using recursion. Note that the following code sample uses "tail recursion."

LISTING 5.66: geom_sum_recursive.sh

```
echo "" |awk '
function geom_sum(num, ratio, term, sum)
{
   if(num == 1) {
     return sum
   } else {
     term *= ratio
     sum += term
     return geom_sum(num-1,ratio,term,sum)
   }
}
BEGIN {
   max = 10
   ratio = 2
   sum = 1
   term = 1

   for(j=2; j<=max; j++) {
      prod = geom_sum(j, ratio, term, sum)
      print "Geometric sum for ratio",ratio,"from 1 to",j,
         " = ",prod
   }
}
'
```

Listing 5.66 contains the function geom_sum() that takes four parameters: n (the current value of the upper range), ratio (which is the exponent 2 in this code sample), term (which is the current intermediate term of the sum), and sum (the target sum).

As you can see, the code returns the value 1 when n equals 1; otherwise, the values of term and sum are updated, and the function geom_sum() is invoked whose *only* difference is to decrement n by 1.

This code sample illustrates tail recursion, which is more efficient than regular recursion, and perhaps a little more intuitive as well. The second part of Listing 5.66 contains a loop that invokes the function geom_sum() as the loop iterates from 2 to max, inclusive. Launch the code in Listing 5.66, and you will see the same output as shown in the previous section.

Factorial Values

Listing 5.67 displays the content of `factorial.sh` that calculates a set of factorial values.

LISTING 5.67: factorial.sh

```
awk '
function factorial(n) {
    return (n > 1 ? n * factorial(n-1) : n)
}
BEGIN {
    for(x=2; x<15; x++) {
        result = factorial(x);
        print "factorial",x," =",result
    }
}
'
```

Listing 5.67 starts with an `awk` command defining the recursive function `factorial()` that calculates the factorial value of its integer-valued input parameter. The next portion of Listing 5.67 is a BEGIN block containing a `for` loop that iterates through the values 2 and 14, inclusive. During each iteration, the `factorial` function is invoked with the loop parameter and the result is displayed. Launch the code in Listing 5.67, and you will see the following output:

```
factorial 2  = 2
factorial 3  = 6
factorial 4  = 24
factorial 5  = 120
factorial 6  = 720
factorial 7  = 5040
factorial 8  = 40320
factorial 9  = 362880
factorial 10  = 3628800
factorial 11  = 39916800
factorial 12  = 479001600
factorial 13  = 6227020800
factorial 14  = 87178291200
```

Fibonacci Numbers

Listing 5.68 displays the content of `fibonacci.sh` that calculates a set of Fibonacci numbers.

LISTING 5.68: fibonacci.sh

```
awk '
function fibonacci(n) {
    return (n > 1 ? fibonacci(n-1) + fibonacci(n-2) : n)
}
BEGIN {
    for(x=2; x<15; x++) {
        result = fibonacci(x);
        print "Fibonacci",x,"=",result
    }
}
'
```

Listing 5.68 starts with an awk command defining the recursive function fibonacci() that calculates the Fibonacci number of its integer-valued input parameter. The next portion of Listing 5.68 is a BEGIN block the contains a loop that iterates through the values 2 and 14, inclusive. During each iteration, the fibonacci function is invoked with the loop parameter and the result is displayed. Launch the code in Listing 5.68, and you will see the following output:

```
Fibonacci 2 = 2
Fibonacci 3 = 3
Fibonacci 4 = 5
Fibonacci 5 = 8
Fibonacci 6 = 13
Fibonacci 7 = 21
Fibonacci 8 = 34
Fibonacci 9 = 55
Fibonacci 10 = 89
Fibonacci 11 = 144
Fibonacci 12 = 233
Fibonacci 13 = 377
Fibonacci 14 = 610
```

Euclid's Algorithm (GCD)

Euclid's algorithm enables you to find the greatest common divisor (GCD) of two positive integers. Listing 5.69 displays the content of gcd1.sh that calculates the GCD of two positive integers.

LISTING 5.69: gcd1.sh

```
echo "" | awk '
function gcd(num1, num2) {
    if(num1 % num2 == 0) {
      return num2
    } else if (num1 < num2) {
      #print "Switching",num1,"and",num2
      return gcd(num2, num1)
    } else {
      #print "Reducing",num1,"and",num2
```

```
        return gcd(num1-num2, num2)
    }
}
BEGIN {
   arr1[0] = 24; arr1[1] = 36; arr1[2] = 50; arr1[3] = 100;
   arr2[0] = 10; arr2[1] = 18; arr2[2] = 11; arr2[3] = 64;
}
{
   for(i=0; i<length(arr1); i++) {
      num1 = arr1[i]
      num2 = arr2[i]
      result = gcd(num1,num2)
      print "The GCD of",num1,"and",num2,"=",result
   }
}
'
```

Listing 5.69 starts with an awk command defining the function gcd() that calculates the GCD of its two integer-valued input parameters. This function implements the Euclidean algorithm whereby the order of the parameters is switched to ensure that the first parameter is greater than or equal to the second parameter. When the second parameter equals 0, the first parameter is the GCD, and its value is returned. The next block of code in Listing 5.69 is a BEGIN block that initializes the arrays arr1 and arr2 with a set of integer values (both arrays have the same length).

The next portion of Listing 5.69 is main execution block that contains a loop that iterates through the elements of the array arr1. During each iteration, the current value of arr1 and the corresponding value in arr2 are used to initialize the values of the variables num1 and num2, respectively. The next code snippet initializes the variable result with the value that is returned from invoking the function gcd() with the arguments num1 and num2. Launch the code in Listing 5.69, and you will see the following output:

```
The GCD of 24 and 10 = 2
The GCD of 36 and 18 = 18
The GCD of 50 and 11 = 1
The GCD of 100 and 64 = 4
```

Lowest Common Multiple of Two Positive Integers

Listing 5.70 displays the content of lcm1.sh that determines the lowest common multiple of a pair of positive integers.

LISTING 5.70: lcm1.sh

```
echo "" | awk '
function gcd(num1, num2) {
   if(num1 % num2 == 0) {
   return num2
```

```
      } else if (num1 < num2) {
        #print "Switching",num1,"and",num2
        return gcd(num2, num1)
      } else {
        #print "Reducing",num1,"and",num2
        return gcd(num1-num2, num2)
      }
}
BEGIN {
  arr1[0] = 24; arr1[1] = 36; arr1= 50; arr1[3] = 100;
  arr2[0] = 10; arr2[1] = 18; arr2= 11; arr2[3] = 64;
}
{
    for(i=0; i<length(arr1); i++) {
      num1 = arr1[i]
      num2 = arr2[i]
      result = gcd(num1,num2)
      lcm = num1*num2/result
      print "The LCM of",num1,"and",num2,"=",lcm
    }
}
'
```

Listing 5.70 starts with the definition of the function gcd() that you saw in Listing 5.69, followed by the same BEGIN block that is shown in Listing 5.69.

The next portion of Listing 5.70 is the main execution block that contains a loop that iterates through the elements of the array arr1. During each iteration, the current value of arr1 and the corresponding value in arr2 are used to initialize the values of the variables num1 and num2, respectively. The next code snippet initializes the variable result with the value that is returned from invoking the function gcd() with the arguments num1 and num2.

The final code snippet initializes the value of lcm, which equals the lowest common multiple of num1 and num2. Launch the code in Listing 5.70, and you will see the following output:

```
The LCM of 24 and 10 = 120
The LCM of 36 and 18 = 36
The LCM of 50 and 11 = 550
The LCM of 100 and 64 = 1600
```

Composite versus Prime Numbers

Listing 5.71 displays the content of prime1.sh that determines whether a positive integer is composite or prime.

LISTING 5.71: prime1.sh

```
echo "" | awk '
function divisors(num) {
```

```
    for(i=2; i<=num/2; i++ ) {
       if(num % i == 0) {
           #print "divisor:",i
           return 1
       }
    }
    return 0;
}
BEGIN { max = 20; }
{
    for(x=3; x<max; x++) {
        result = divisors(x);
        if(result == 0) {
            print x,"is prime"
        } else {
            print x,"is not prime"
        }
    }
}
'
```

Listing 5.71 defines the function divisors() that contains a loop that iterates from 2 to the input parameter num divided by 2. During each iteration, a conditional statement checks whether num is divisible by the loop variable x: if so, then num is composite and the value 1 is returned. If the loop completes without returning a value, then num is a prime number, and the value 0 is returned.

The next portion of Listing 5.71 contains a BEGIN block that initializes the variable max to 20, followed by the main execution block that contains a loop that iterates through the values 3 through max-1, inclusive. During each iteration, the function divisors() is invoked with the value of the loop variable x. The final portion of code contains a conditional code block that prints a message based on whether the variable x is a prime number. Launch the code in Listing 5.71, and you will see the following output:

```
3 is prime
4 is not prime
5 is prime
6 is not prime
7 is prime
8 is not prime
9 is not prime
10 is not prime
11 is prime
12 is not prime
13 is prime
14 is not prime
15 is not prime
16 is not prime
17 is prime
```

```
18 is not prime
19 is prime
```

Factors of Positive Integers

Listing 5.72 displays the content of prime_factors1.sh that determines the prime factors of a positive integer.

LISTING 5.72: prime_factors1.sh

```
echo "" | awk '
function divisors(num) {
   factors = ""; div = 2
   while(num > 1) {
      if(num % div == 0) {
         factors = factors " " div
         num /= div
      } else {
         div += 1
      }
   }
   return factors;
}
BEGIN { arr[0] = 24; arr[1] = 7; arr[2] = 96 }
{
   for(i=0; i<length(arr); i++) {
      num = arr[i]
      result = divisors(num)
      print "Factors of",num,":",result
   }
}
'
```

Listing 5.72 starts with the function prime_factors() that initializes the variables factors and div with the values "" and 2, respectively. The next portion of this function contains a while() loop that executes as long as its input parameter num is greater than 1. During each iteration, a conditional code block checks if num divided by div equals 0: if true, then the variable factors is updated by appending the value of div to factors, after which num is divided by the value of div. However, if num is not divisible by div, then the value of div is incremented by 1. The preceding logic enables us to find multiple prime divisors that are equal. For example, the number 12 has prime factors 2, 2, and 3.

The next portion of Listing 5.72 is a BEGIN block that initializes the array arr with three positive integers. The next portion of Listing 5.72 is the main execution block that contains a loop that iterates through the elements of the array arr. During each iteration, the divisors() function is invoked with the current element of arr, whose return value is used to initialize the variable result. The final code snippet of this code block displays the current value of x and its prime divisors. Launch the code in Listing 5.68, and you will see the following output:

```
Factors of 24 :   2 2 2 3
Factors of 7 :    7
Factors of 96 :   2 2 2 2 2 3
```

Goldbach's Conjecture

Goldbach's conjecture states that every even number greater than 2 can be expressed as the sum of two odd prime numbers.

LISTING 5.73: goldbach_conjecture.sh

```
echo "" | awk '
function prime(num) {
  div = 2

  while(div < num) {
    if( num % div != 0) {
      div += 1
    } else {
      return COMPOSITE
    }
  }
  return PRIME
}

function find_prime_factors(even_num) {
  for(num=3; num<int(even_num/2); num++) {
    if(prime(num) == 1) {
      if(prime(even_num-num) == 1) {
        print even_num , " = " , num , "+" , (even_num-num)
      }
    }
  }
}
BEGIN { PRIME = 1; COMPOSITE = 0; upper_bound = 30; }
{
  for(idx=4; idx<upper_bound; idx++ ) {
    find_prime_factors(idx)
  }
}
'
```

Listing 5.73 starts with the function prime() that determines whether the parameter num is a prime number. Next, the function find_prime_factors() contains a loop whose loop variable num iterates from 3 to half the value of the parameter even_num. If num is a prime number, then the conditional logic in Listing 5.73 invokes prime() with the number even_num-num.

If both `num` and `even_num` are prime, then they are a solution to Goldbach's conjecture because the sum of these two numbers equals the parameter `even_num`. Launch the code in Listing 5.73, and you will see the following output:

```
8  =  3 + 5
10 =  3 + 7
12 =  5 + 7
14 =  3 + 11
16 =  3 + 13
16 =  5 + 11
18 =  5 + 13
18 =  7 + 11
20 =  3 + 17
20 =  7 + 13
22 =  3 + 19
22 =  5 + 17
24 =  5 + 19
24 =  7 + 17
24 =  11 + 13
26 =  3 + 23
26 =  7 + 19
28 =  5 + 23
28 =  11 + 17
```

Environment Variables in awk

All versions of `awk` support the built-in variables FS, NFS, RS, NR, FILENAME, OFS, and ORS. Moreover, the environment variables ARGC and ARGV enable you to pass parameters from the command line to the given `awk` script. Keep in mind the following regarding ARGC and ARGV:

- ARGC is the number ("count") of arguments.

- ARGV is an array of the arguments passed to the `awk` script.

- The index for ARGV is from 0 through ARGC.

- ARGV[0] is the `awk` utility.

LISTING 5.74 displays the content of `command_line.sh` *that shows you how to pass parameters to an* `awk` *script.*

```
awk '
   BEGIN {
    print "ARGC = ",ARGC

    for (i = 0; i < ARGC; i++)
      print "ARGV[",i,"]: ",ARGV[i]
   }
{
}
' 1 2 3
```

Listing 5.74 contains an `awk` command starting with a BEGIN block that prints the number of arguments ARGC, followed by a loop that iterates from 1 to ARGC-1, inclusive. During each iteration, the value of the current input argument is printed. Note that the list of input arguments is 1, 2, and 3, which is shown in the final portion of Listing 5.74. Launch the code in Listing 5.70, and you will see the following output:

```
awk -f command_line.sh 1 2 3
ARGC =   4
ARGV[ 0 ]:   awk
ARGV[ 1 ]:   1
ARGV[ 2 ]:   2
ARGV[ 3 ]:   3
```

Summary

This chapter started with bit operations in `awk`, such as calculating the AND, OR, and XOR of a pair of positive integers. Then you learned how to perform various string-related tasks, such as reversing a string, checking for balanced parentheses, and column alignment.

In addition, you learned how to delete rows with missing values, how to process multiple files, and perform date conversions. Next, you learned how to work with a data set that contains one million records, and how to count adjacent digits in such a dataset.

You also learned about recursion, along with code samples for calculating values of arithmetic series, geometric series, factorial values, and Fibonacci numbers. Moreover, you learned how to use Euclid's algorithm to find the GCD of two positive integers, which also enabled you to find the least common multiple of two positive integers. Finally, you learned how to display the values of command line parameters using ARGC and ARGV in an `awk` command.

## CHAPTER 6

REGULAR EXPRESSIONS

This chapter explores regular expressions, a very powerful language feature in many programming languages (such as JavaScript and Java). Consequently, the knowledge that you gain from the material in this chapter will be useful to you outside of awk. Although you have seen examples of regular expressions in previous chapters, this chapter consolidates those code samples and provides a more extensive discussion of the variety of regular expressions that you can define in an awk command. As a result, this chapter contains a mixture of code blocks and complete code samples, with varying degrees of complexity, that are suitable for beginners as well as people who have had some exposure to regular expressions.

There is also a good chance that you have used regular expressions in commands that you have launched from the command line on a laptop, whether it be Windows, Unix, or Linux-based systems. Examples of such comments involve the DIR command on Windows for listing files with a given suffix, and the ls command for performing the same action on a Linux machine or MacBook. In this chapter, you will learn how to define and use more complex regular expressions than the regular expressions that you have used from the command line.

The first part of this chapter discusses metacharacters and character classes, followed by code samples that define regular expressions with digits and letters (uppercase as well as lowercase), and how to use character classes in regular expressions.

The second portion contains code samples with regular expressions involving metacharacters, such as ".," "^," "$," and "|." In addition, you will also learn how to match subsets of strings via regular expressions.

The third portion of this chapter shows you how to use the built-in `sub()` and `gsub()` functions in `awk` to remove digits, characters, and consecutive characters via `awk` commands.

The fourth portion of this chapter shows you how to split strings with regular expressions, how to define dynamic regular expressions, and how to count comments in text fields. Then you will learn how to combine the `grep` and `sed` commands, which you learned in Chapter 1 and Chapter 2, with the `awk` command. Finally, you will see how to use the `gsub()` command with captured groups.

One additional point about this chapter: you will encounter many concepts and facets of regular expressions that might make you feel overwhelmed with the density of the material if you are a novice. However, practice and repetition will help you become comfortable with regular expressions.

What are Regular Expressions?

Regular expressions are referred to as REs, regexes, or regex patterns, and they enable you to specify expressions that can match specific "parts" of a string. For instance, you can define a regular expression to match a single character or digit, a telephone number, a zip code, or an email address. You can use metacharacters and character classes (defined in the next section) as part of regular expressions to search text documents for specific patterns. As you learn how to use REs, you will find other ways to use them, as well.

Metacharacters

The `awk` command supports a set of metacharacters, most of which are the same as the metacharacters in other scripting languages such as Perl, as well as programming languages such as JavaScript and Java. The complete list of metacharacters in Python is here:

`.  ^  $  *  +  ?  {  }  [  ]  \  |  (  )`

The meaning of the preceding metacharacters is here:

? (matches 0 or 1): the expression `a?` matches the string `a` (but not `ab`)

* (matches 0 or more): the expression `a*` matches the string `aaa` (but not `baa`)

+ (matches 1 or more): the expression a+ matches aaa (but not baa)

^ (beginning of line): the expression `^[a]` matches the string `abc` (but not `bc`)

$ (end of line): [c]$ matches the string abc (but not cab)
. (a single dot): matches any character (except newline)

Sometimes you need to match the metacharacters themselves rather than their representation, which can be done in two ways. The first way involves by "escaping" their symbolic meaning with the backslash ("\") character. Thus, the sequences \?, *, \+, \^, \$, and \. represent the literal characters instead of their symbolic meaning. You can also "escape" the backslash character with the sequence "\\." If you have two consecutive backslash characters, you need an additional backslash for each of them, which means that "\\\\" is the "escaped" sequence for "\\."

The second way is to list the metacharacters inside a pair of square brackets. For example, [+?] treats the two characters "+" and "?" as literal characters instead of metacharacters. The second approach is obviously more compact and less prone to error (it is easy to forget a backslash in a long sequence of metacharacters). As you might surmise, the methods in the re module support metacharacters.

NOTE *The "^" character that is to the left (and outside) of a sequence in square brackets (such as ^[A-Z]) "anchors" the regular expression to the beginning of a line, whereas the "^" character that is the first character inside a pair of square brackets negates the regular expression (such as [^A-Z]) inside the square brackets.*

The interpretation of the "^" character in a regular expression depends on its location in a regular expression, as shown here:

"^[a-z]" means any string that starts with any lowercase letter
"[^a-z]" means any string that does *not* contain any lowercase letters
"^[^a-z]" means any string that starts with anything *except* a lowercase letter
"^[a-z]$" means a single lowercase letter
"^[^a-z]$" means a single character (including digits) that is *not* a lowercase letter

Character Sets

A single digit in base 10 is a number between 0 and 9 inclusive, which is represented by the sequence [0-9]. Similarly, a lowercase letter can be any letter between a and z, which is represented by the sequence [a-z]. An uppercase letter can be any letter between A and Z, which is represented by the sequence [A-Z].

The following code snippets illustrate how to specify sequences of digits and sequences of character strings using a short-hand notation that is much simpler than specifying every matching digit:

[0-9] matches a single digit
[0-9][0-9] matches 2 consecutive digits
[0-9]{3} matches 3 consecutive digits
[0-9]{2,4} matches 2, 3, or 4 consecutive digits
[0-9]{5,} matches 5 or more consecutive digits
^[0-9]+$ matches a string consisting solely of digits

You can define similar patterns using uppercase or lowercase letters in a way that is much simpler than explicitly specifying every lowercase letter or every uppercase letter:

[a-z][A-Z] matches a single lowercase letter that is followed by 1 uppercase letter
[a-zA-Z] matches any upper or lowercase letter

Working with "^" and "\"

The purpose of the "^" character depends on its context in a regular expression. For example, the following expression matches a text string that starts with a digit:

^[0-9].

However, the following expression matches a text string that does *not* start with a digit because of the "^" metacharacter that is at the beginning of an expression in square brackets as well as the "^" metacharacter that is to the left (and outside) the expression in square brackets (which you learned in a previous note):

^[^0-9]

Thus, the "^" character inside a pair of matching square brackets ("[]") negates the expression immediately to its right that is also located inside the square brackets.

The backslash ("\") allows you to "escape" the meaning of a metacharacter. Consequently, a dot "." matches a single character (except for whitespace characters), whereas the sequence "\." matches the dot "." character.

Other examples involving the backslash metacharacter are here:

\.H.* matches the string .Hello
H.* matches the string Hello
H.*\. matches the string Hello.
.ell. matches the string Hello

.* matches the string `Hello`

\..* matches the string `.Hello`

Character Classes

Character classes are convenient expressions that are shorter and simpler than their "bare" counterparts that you saw in the previous section. There are character classes that are supported in programming languages such as Perl, Python, and JavaScript (discussed in the first subsection) and there are character classes that are supported in `awk`.

For example, the character class \d represents a single (base 10) digit, which is supported in the first group of programming languages. However, `[[:digit:]]` matches a single (base 10) digit in `awk`. Similar comments apply to character classes such as \D, \w, and \W.

POSIX Character Classes

`POSIX` classes differ from regular expression character classes that we have discussed in the previous chapters in this book. `POSIX` classes use a string to define a class, which is probably more intuitive than the backslash style that you will see in regular expressions in other languages such as JavaScript and Java. For example, `POSIX` uses `[[:digit:]]` to specify a digit instead of `[0-9]` or \d to represent a digit in regular expressions. In addition, the `POSIX` standard defines 12 character classes, some of which are listed here:

- `[:alpha:]` Alphabetic characters
- `[:alnum:]` Alphabetic characters and digits
- `[:digit:]` Digits
- `[:xdigit:]` Hexadecimal digits
- `[:blank:]` Space and Tab
- `[:cntrl:]` Control characters

For example, the following `awk` commands work with IPV4 addresses with a regular expression that use `POSIX` character classes:

```
$ echo "192.168.10.13" |awk -F"." '/^[[:digit:]]+/ { print $1 }'
#192

$ echo "ABC.168.10.13" |awk -F"." '/^[[:alnum:]]+/ { print $1 }'
#ABC
```

You can use a combination of the `printf` command and `POSIX` to correctly split the string in the following `awk` command:

```
$ printf "a\n1\nb\n2\nc\n" | awk '/[[:digit:]]/'
1
2
```

However, replacing the `printf` command with the `echo` command in the preceding `awk` command does not work:

```
$ echo "a\n1\nb\n2\nc\n" | awk '/[[:digit:]]/'
a\n1\nb\n2\nc\n
```

More information regarding POSIX character classes is accessible online:

https://riptutorial.com/regex/example/17891/posix-character-classes
https://www.regular-expressions.info/posixbrackets.html

The next section contains the corresponding `awk` commands that do not use POSIX character classes.

Generic Character Classes

This section contains character classes that you will encounter in other programming languages, such as Python and JavaScript. Some convenient character sequences that express patterns of digits and letters:

\d matches a single digit
\w matches a single character (digit or letter)
\s matches a single whitespace (space, newline, return, or tab)
\b matches a boundary between a word and a non-word
\n, \r, \t represent a newline, a return, and a tab, respectively
\ "escapes" any character

Based on the preceding definitions, \d+ matches one or more digits and \w+ matches one or more characters, both of which are more compact expressions than using character sets. In addition, we can reformulate the expressions in the previous section:

\d is the same as [0-9] and \D is the same as [^0-9]
\s is the same as [\t\n\r\f\v] and it matches any non-whitespace character, whereas \S is the opposite (it matches [^ \t\n\r\f\v])
\w is the same as [a-zA-Z0-9_] and it matches any alphanumeric character, whereas \W is the opposite (it matches [^a-zA-Z0-9_])

Another useful feature is the ability to specify the minimum, maximum, or range of occurrences of a character, as shown in the following examples:

- \d{2}   is the same as [0-9][0-9]

- \d{3}   is the same as [0-9]{3}

- \d{2,4} is the same as [0-9]{2,4}

- \d{5,} is the same as [0-9]{5,}

- ^\d+$ is the same as ^[0-9]+$ </UL>

The curly braces ("{}") are called quantifiers, and they specify the number (or range) of characters in the expressions that precede them. The following set of awk commands contains examples of various matching patterns, with the result of each awk command displayed as a commented line:

```
echo "a.b.c 192.168.10.13"    |awk '/^[a-zA-Z0-9.-]+/
    { print $2 }'
#192.168.10.13

echo "aa.bb.cc 192.168.10.13" |awk '/^[a-zA-Z0-9.-]+ /
    { print $2 }'
#192.168.10.13

echo "aa.bb.cc 192.168.10.13" |awk '/^[a-zA-Z0-9.-]+ .*/
    { print $2 }'
#192.168.10.13

echo "aa.bb.cc 192.168.10.13" |awk -F"." '/^[a-zA-Z0-9.-]+
    /   { print $2 }'
#bb

echo "aa.bb.cc 192.168.10.13" |awk -F"." '/^[a-zA-Z0-9.-]+
    .*/ { print $2 }'
#bb
```

Regular Expressions in awk

Regular expressions are very powerful in terms of the tasks that you can solve in awk. This section contains subsections that show you show simple example of working with regular expressions, and later in this book, you will see more complex examples of regular expressions in awk.

Matching Strings with the Dot "." Metacharacter

The following awk command uses the "." character to match a single character:

```
$ echo -e "pet\npat\nbat\npit\npot\nput" | awk '/p.t/'
pet
pat
pit
pot
put
```

Notice the multiple occurrences of "\n" in the preceding awk command: they serve as a linefeed, which means that the preceding string is treated as 6 lines, each of which contains a single string. However, only 5 of the strings match the pattern `p.t`: the exception is the string `bat`, and therefore that string is omitted from the output.

Listing 6.1 displays the content of `remove_dots.sh` that removes all occurrences of the "." character from an input string.

LISTING 6.1: remove_dots.sh

```
echo "aaa. bbb. ccc. a.b.c." | awk '
{
  for(i=1;i<=NF;i++) {
    if($i ~ /\./) gsub(/\./, "", $i);
  }
  print $0
}
'
```

Launch the code in Listing 6.1, and you will see the following output:

```
aaa bbb ccc abc
```

A simpler solution does not require a loop. First, note that the following `awk` command uses the `sub()` function to remove the first occurrence of a period ("."):

```
$ echo "aaa. bbb. ccc. a.b.c." | awk '{sub(/\./, "");
    print $0}'
aaa bbb. ccc. a.b.c.
```

However, the following `awk` command uses the `gsub()` function to remove all occurrences of a period ("."):

```
$ echo "aaa. bbb. ccc. a.b.c." | awk '{gsub(/\./, "", $0);
    print $0}'
aaa bbb ccc abc
```

Matching Strings with the "^" Metacharacter

The following `awk` command uses the "^" character to match the beginning of a line:

```
$ echo -e "pet\npat\nbat\npit\npot\nput" | awk '/^p.t/'
pet
pat
pit
pot
put
```

Once again, notice the multiple occurrences of "\n" in the preceding `awk` command: they serve as a linefeed, which means that the preceding string is treated as 6 lines, each of which contains a single string. However, only 5 of the strings match the pattern `^p.t`: the exception is the string `bat`, and therefore, that string is omitted from the output.

As another example, the long listing of a directory starts with a "-" for ordinary files and a "d" for subdirectories. Listing 6.2 displays the content of `file_sizes.sh` that counts the number of bytes occupied by the files in the current directory and also counts the number of subdirectories.

LISTING 6.2: file_sizes.sh

```
ls -l |awk '
BEGIN {
    total_bytes = 0;
    file_count  = 0;
    directories = 0;
}
{
    if( $1 ~/^-/ ) {
        total_bytes += $5
        file_count  += 1
    } else if( $1 ~/^d/ ) {
        directories += 1
    }
}
END {
    print "Directories:",directories
    print "File count: ",file_count
    print "Total size: ",total_bytes
}
'
Launch the code in Listing 6.2, and you will see the
following output:
Directories: 2
File count:  11
Total size:  881299
```

Matching Strings with the "$" Metacharacter

The following `awk` command uses the "^" character to match the beginning of a line:

```
$ echo -e "pet\npat\nbat\npit\npot\nput" | awk '/p.t$/'
pet
pat
pit
pot
put
```

Once again, notice the multiple occurrences of "\n" in the preceding `awk` command.

Matching Strings with the "|" Metacharacter

The following `awk` command uses the "|" character to match two possible patterns:

```
$ echo -e "pet\npat\nbat\npit\npot\nput" | awk '/[p.t]|[b.t]/'
pet
```

```
pat
bat
pit
pot
put
```

The preceding `awk` command matches the string `bat` because the regular expression `[p.t]|[b.t]` represents two regular expressions `p.t` and `b.t`, which means that the string `bat` appears in the output, as shown in bold above.

Matching with ?, +, or * Metacharacters

The metacharacter "?" matches 0 or 1 occurrences, whereas the metacharacter "+" matches 1 or more occurrences, and finally, the metacharacter "*" matches 0 or more occurrences.

You might think that the metacharacter "?" has limited value, but it is actually useful in some situations. For example, you can use the metacharacter "?" to match 0 or 1 occurrences of a letter in a word, which is useful for words that have slightly different spellings, such as "color" and "colour," "favor" and "favour," "traveled" and "travelled," depending on whether you are using the US (for the former spelling) or the UK (for the latter spelling) form of the word.

As another example, you can use a metacharacter to match US postal codes, which have two potential patterns: either `(\d){5}`, which matches five adjacent digits, or `(\d){5}-(\d){4}`. If you want one regular expression to handle both patterns, you can use either of the following regular expressions:

```
(\d){5}|(\d){5}-(\d){4}
(\d){5}|(-(\d){4})?
```

The first regular expression uses the "|" metacharacter to specify both postal code patterns, and the second regular expression uses the "?" metacharacter, which makes the second sub expression optional, in which the regular expression "reduces" to `(\d){5}`.

The following `awk` command uses the "?" metacharacter to match multiple strings:

The following example matches **Colour** as well as **Color**. We have made **u** as an optional character by using **?**.

```
$ echo -e "Colour\nColor" | awk '/Colou?r/'
```

On executing this code, you get the following result:

```
Colour
Color
```

The following `awk` script uses the "+" metacharacter to match multiple strings:

```
$ echo -e "111\n22\n123\n234\n456\n222"  | awk '/2+/'
```

On executing the above code, you get the following result:

```
22
123
234
222
```

The following `awk` script uses the "*" metacharacter to match multiple strings:

The following example matches `ca`, `cat`, `catt`, and so on.

```
$ echo -e "ca\ncat\ncatt" | awk '/cat*/'
On executing this code, you get the following result -
ca
cat
catt
```

Matching Subgroups with ?, +, or * Metacharacters

You can match a subgroup within a regular expression, which is useful when you need to match a two-word sequence, where the first word is the same in all cases. Examples of such are "red sunset" and "red planet," "eat well" and "eat slow." Here is an `awk` command that contains grouping in a regular expression:

```
$ echo -e "Apple Juice\nApple Pie\nApple Tart\nApple Cake"
| awk
    '/Apple (Juice|Cake)/'
Apple Juice
Apple Cake
```

Matching with Character Classes

If we can match a simple pattern, you probably expect that you can also match a regular expression, just as we did in `grep` and `sed`. Listing 6.3 displays the content of `Patterns1.sh` that uses metacharacters to match the beginning and the end of a line of text in the file `columns2.txt`.

LISTING 6.3: Patterns1.sh

```
awk '
   /^f/     { print $1 }
   /two $/ { print $1 }
' columns2.txt
```

The output from launching Listing 6.3 is here:

```
one
five
```

```
four
```

Listing 6.4 displays the content of RemoveColumns.txt with lines that contain a different number of columns.

LISTING 6.4: columns3.txt

```
123 one two
456 three four
one two three four
five 123 six
one two three
four five
```

Listing 6.5 displays the content of MatchAlpha1.sh that matches text lines that start with alphabetic characters as well as lines that contain numeric strings in the second column.

LISTING 6.5: MatchAlpha1.sh

```
awk '
{
   if( $0 ~ /^[0-9]/) { print $0 }
   if( $0 ~ /^[a-z]+ [0-9]/) { print $0 }
}
' columns3.txt
```

The output from Listing 6.5 is here:

```
123 one two
456 three four
five 123 six
```

Listing 6.6 displays the contents of strings.txt, and Listing 6.7 displays the content of regexs1.sh that matches text lines that start with alphabetic characters as well as lines that contain numeric strings in the second column.

LISTING 6.6: strings.txt

```
a
abg
f
A
Z
Abg
Zafzcxv
ATqwer
A3432asdfwer
ATWRF
AFEG
Zafzcxv
```

```
aTqwer
a3432asdfwer
```

LISTING 6.7: regexs1.sh

```
awk '{if($1 ~ /^[a-z]/)      {print "Match ^[A-Z]:",$0}}'
    strings.txt
echo ""
awk '{if($1 ~ /^[A-Z]/)      {print "Match ^[A-Z]:",$0}}'
    strings.txt
echo ""
awk '{if($1 ~ /^[A-Z]+/)     {print "Match ^[A-Z]+:",$0}}'
    strings.txt
echo ""
awk '{if($1 ~ /^[A-Z]+$/)    {print "Match ^[A-Z]+$:",$0}}'
    strings.txt
echo ""
awk '{if($1 ~ /^[^A-Z]+$/)   {print "Match ^[^A-Z]+$:",$0}}'
    strings.txt
echo ""
awk '{if($1 ~ /^[^A-Z]/)     {print "Match ^[^A-Z]:",$0}}'
    strings.txt
echo ""
awk '{if($1 ~ /^[^A-Z]+/)    {print "Match ^[^A-Z]+:",$0}} '
    strings.txt
```

Listing 6.7 contains 7 awk commands that match various regular expressions against the rows in the text file strings.txt, which contains 6 text lines. Hence, the output consists of 7 blocks of text, each of which contains the lines in strings.txt that match the associated regular expression. Launch the code in Listing 6.7, and you will see the following output:

```
Match ^[a-z]: a
Match ^[a-z]: abg
Match ^[a-z]: f
Match ^[a-z]: aTqwer
Match ^[a-z]: a3432asdfwer

Match ^[A-Z]: A
Match ^[A-Z]: Z
Match ^[A-Z]: Abg
Match ^[A-Z]: Zafzcxv
Match ^[A-Z]: ATqwer
Match ^[A-Z]: A3432asdfwer
Match ^[A-Z]: ATWRF
Match ^[A-Z]: AFEG
Match ^[A-Z]: Zafzcxv

Match ^[A-Z]+: A
Match ^[A-Z]+: Z
Match ^[A-Z]+: Abg
Match ^[A-Z]+: Zafzcxv
Match ^[A-Z]+: ATqwer
Match ^[A-Z]+: A3432asdfwer
```

```
Match ^[A-Z]+: ATWRF
Match ^[A-Z]+: AFEG
Match ^[A-Z]+: Zafzcxv

Match ^[A-Z]+$: A
Match ^[A-Z]+$: Z
Match ^[A-Z]+$: ATWRF
Match ^[A-Z]+$: AFEG

Match ^[^A-Z]+$: a
Match ^[^A-Z]+$: abg
Match ^[^A-Z]+$: f
Match ^[^A-Z]+$: a3432asdfwer

Match ^[^A-Z]: a
Match ^[^A-Z]: abg
Match ^[^A-Z]: f
Match ^[^A-Z]: aTqwer
Match ^[^A-Z]: a3432asdfwer

Match ^[^A-Z]+: a
Match ^[^A-Z]+: abg
Match ^[^A-Z]+: f
Match ^[^A-Z]+: aTqwer
Match ^[^A-Z]+: a3432asdfwer
```

Working with Postfix Arithmetic Operators

Listing 6.8 displays the content of `mixednumbers.txt` that contains postfix operators, which means numbers where the negative (and/or positive) sign appears at the end of a column value instead of the beginning of the number.

LISTING 6.8: mixednumbers.txt

```
324.000-|10|983.000-
453.000-|30|298.000-
783.000-|20|347.000-
```

Listing 6.9 displays the content of `AddSubtract1.sh` that illustrates how to add the rows of numbers in Listing 6.8.

LISTING 6.9: AddSubtract1.sh

```
myFile="mixednumbers.txt"

awk -F"|" '
BEGIN { line = 0; total = 0 }
{
   split($1, arr, "-")
   f1 = arr[1]
   if($1 ~ /-/) { f1 = -f1 }
   line += f1
```

```
    split($2, arr, "-")
    f2 = arr[1]
    if($2 ~ /-/) { f2 = -f2 }
    line += f2

    split($3, arr, "-")
    f3 = arr[1]
    if($3 ~ /-/) { f3 = -f3 }
    line += f3

    printf("f1: %d f2: %d f3: %d line: %d\n",f1,f2,f3, line)
    total += line
    line = 0
}
END { print "Total: ",total }
' $myfile
```

The output from Listing 6.9 is here. See if you can work out what the code is doing before reading the explanation that follows:

```
f1: -324 f2: 10 f3: -983 line: -1297
f1: -453 f2: 30 f3: -298 line: -721
f1: -783 f2: 20 f3: -347 line: -1110
Total:  -3128
```

The code assumes we know the format of the file. The `split()` function turns each field record into a length 2 vector, the first position equals a number, second position is either an empty value or a dash, and then it captures the first position number into a variable. The `if` statement just sees if the original field has a dash in it. If the field has a dash, then the numeric variable is made negative, otherwise it is left alone. Then it adds the line up.

Working with the sub() Function in **awk**

The `sub()` and `gsub()` functions enable you to perform search-and-replace on strings, which is discussed later in the subsequent sections.

Examples Using the sub() Function

The following `awk` command uses the `sub()` function to replace the first occurrences of the letter "a" with ABC:

```
echo aaaabcd | awk '{ sub(/a/, "ABC"); print }'
ABCaaabcd
```

The following `awk` command uses the `sub()` function to replace multiple occurrences of the letter "a" with ABC:

```
$ echo aaaabcd | awk '{ sub(/a+/, "ABC"); print }'
ABCbcd
```

The following `awk` command uses the `sub()` function to replace multiple occurrences of the letter "a" with ABC:

```
$ echo aaaabcd | awk '{ sub(/[a]+/, "ABC"); print }'
ABCbcd
```

Working with the gsub() Function

The `gsub()` function enables you to perform search-and-replace functionality, just like the `sed` command line utility that you studied in Chapter 2. The following `awk` command uses the `gsub()` function to replace spaces in an input string with a hyphen:

```
$ echo "a bc" s awk '{ gsub(/ /, "-", $0); print }'
a-bc
$ echo "a bc " | awk '{ gsub(/ /, "-", $0); print }'
a-bc-
```

The following `awk` command inserts a hyphen between every pair of characters:

```
$ echo "abc" | awk '{ gsub(//, "-", $0); print }'
-a-b-c-
```

Removing Digits with the gsub() Function

The following `awk` command removes the digits in an input string:

```
$ echo "a1b2c3" | awk '{ gsub(/[0-9]/, "", $0); print }'
Abc
```

The following `awk` command removes the digits 3 through 5 in an input string:

```
$ echo "a1b2c3" | awk '{ gsub(/[3-5]/, "", $0); print }'
a1b2c
```

The following `awk` command removes the first initial digit in an input string:

```
$ echo "123a4b5c678" | awk '{ gsub(/^[0-9]/, "", $0); print }'
23a4b5c678
```

The following `awk` command removes all the initial digits in an input string:

```
$ echo "123a4b5c678" | awk '{ gsub(/^[0-9]+/, "", $0); print }'
a4b5c678
```

The following `awk` command removes the final digit in an input string:

```
$ echo "123a4b5c678" | awk '{ gsub(/[0-9]$/, "", $0); print }'
123a4b5c67
```

The following `awk` command removes all the trailing digits in an input string:

```
$ echo "123a4b5c678" | awk '{ gsub(/[0-9]+/, "", $0); print }'
123a4b5c
```

The following `awk` command removes all the digits in an input string:

```
$ echo "123a4b5c678" | awk '{ gsub(/[0-9]+/, "", $0); print }'
Abc
```

Removing Characters with the gsub() Function

The following `awk` command removes any of the letters t, h, or e that appear as the first character of an input string:

```
$ echo "there" | awk '{ gsub(/^[the]/, "", $0); print }'
here
```

The following `awk` command removes either of the letters t or T that appear as the first character of an input string:

```
$ echo "there" | awk '{ gsub(/^[tT]/, "", $0); print }'
here
```

The following `awk` command removes either of the letters t or T that appear as the first character, followed by the sequence "he," of an input string:

```
$ echo "there" | awk '{ gsub(/^[tT]he/, "", $0); print }'
re
```

The following `awk` command removes the lowercase letters in an input string:

```
echo "ABCa1b2c3XYZ" | awk '{ gsub(/[a-z]/, "", $0); print }'
ABC123XYZ
```

The following `awk` command removes the uppercase letters in an input string:

```
$ echo "ABCa1b2c3XYZ" | awk '{ gsub(/[A-Z]/, "", $0); print }'
a1b2c3
```

The following `awk` command removes the uppercase letters X through Z in an input string:

```
$ echo "ABCa1b2c3XYZ" | awk '{ gsub(/[X-Z]/, "", $0); print }'
ABCa1b2c3
```

The following `awk` command removes the uppercase letters A, X, Y, and Z in an input string:

```
$ echo "ABCa1b2c3XYZ" | awk '{ gsub(/[AX-Z]/, "", $0); print }'
BCa1b2c3
```

The following `awk` command removes the lowercase letters a and b as well as the uppercase letters A, X, Y, and Z in an input string:

```
$ echo "ABCa1b2c3XYZ" | awk '{ gsub(/[abAX-Z]/, "", $0); print }'
BC12c3
```

The following `awk` command removes the lowercase letters and the uppercase letters in an input string:

```
$ echo "ABCa1b2c3XYZ" | awk '{ gsub(/[a-zA-Z]/, "", $0); print }'
123
```

Removing Consecutive Characters with the gsub() Function

The examples in an earlier section showed you how to remove a single uppercase or lowercase letter, as well as all uppercase or lowercase letters. However, you might need to remove only consecutive uppercase (or lowercase characters) instead of all occurrences of such characters. For example, the following `awk` command removes two consecutive uppercase letters in an input string:

```
$ echo "ABCa1b2c3XYZ" | awk '{ gsub(/[A-Z]{2}/, "", $0); print }'
Ca1b2c3Z
```

The following `awk` command removes the initial occurrence of three consecutive digits (1, 2, and 3) that are followed by one or more lowercase letters in an input string:

```
$ echo "123a4b5c678" | awk '{ gsub(/^123[a-z]+/, "", $0); print }'
4b5c678
```

Removing Complements of Strings with the gsub() Function

The following `awk` command removes the everything except for the digits 1, 2, and 3 in an input string:

```
$ echo "123a4b5c678" | awk '{ gsub(/[^123]/, "", $0); print }'
123
```

Keep in mind that the occurrence of the "^" metacharacter inside a pair of brackets is different from the occurrence of the "^" metacharacter outside a pair of brackets. For example, the following `awk` command removes any character that does not start with any of the digits 1, 2, and 3 in an input string:

```
$ echo "123a4b5c678" | awk '{ gsub(/^[^123]/, "", $0); print }'
123a4b5c678
```

The following `awk` command removes the trailing character that matches any of the digits 6, 7, and 8 in an input string:

```
$ echo "123a4b5c678" | awk '{ gsub(/[678]$/, "", $0); print }'
123a4b5c67
```

Removing Metacharacters with the gsub() Function

The following `awk` command removes the $ metacharacter in an input string:

```
$ echo "a?b?c?" | awk '{ gsub(/?/, "", $0); print }'
abc
```

The following `awk` command removes multiple metacharacters in an input string:

```
$ echo "a@b#?c$d^" | awk '{ gsub(/[@#?$^]/, "", $0); print }'
abc
```

Now compare the result of the following `awk` command that omits the square brackets with the preceding `awk` command that includes the square brackets:

```
echo "a@b#?c$d^" | awk '{ gsub(/@#?$^/, "", $0); print }'
a@b#?c^
```

Removing Spaces in Text Fields

The following `awk` command uses the `gsub()` function to replace the space between first names and last names with a hyphen:

```
$ awk -F"," '$1 { gsub(/ /, "-", $2); print }' employees.csv
empid,full_name,start_date,expenses
1000 Jane-Jones 12/05/2021 93.55
2000 John-Smith 03/08/2020 87.23
3000 Dave-Stone 07/15/2022 84.16
```

If there are multiple white spaces between first names and last names, use the following modification of the preceding `awk` command:

```
$ awk -F"," '$1 { gsub(/ +/, "-", $2); print }' employees.
csv
```

Splitting Strings with Regular Expressions

The following `awk` command splits an input string by specifying the letter "a" as the delimiter:

```
$ echo "abcdef" |awk -F'a' '{print $1, "x", $2}'
 x bcdef
```

The following `awk` command splits an input string by specifying the letter "a" as the delimiter for a string that contains multiple consecutive occurrences of the letter "a:"

```
$ echo "aaabcdef" |awk -F'a' '{print $1, "x", $2}'
 x
```

The following `awk` command splits an input string by specifying the regular expression "a*" as the delimiter:

```
$ echo "abcdef" |awk -F'a*' '{print $1, "x", $2}'
 x bcdef
```

The following `awk` command splits an input string by specifying the letters "bc" as the delimiter:

```
$ echo "abcdef" |awk -F'cd' '{print $1, "x", $2}'
ab x ef
```

The following `awk` command splits an input string by specifying the letters "ae" as the delimiter:

```
$ echo "abcdef" |awk -F'[ae]' '{print $1, "x", $2}'
x bcd
```

The following `awk` command splits an input string by specifying the letters "ae" as the delimiter:

```
$ echo "aaabcdef" |awk -F'[ae]' '{print $1, "x", $2}'
x
```

The following `awk` command splits an input string by specifying the range of characters `[a-c]` as the delimiter:

```
echo "abcdef" |awk -F'[a-b]' '{print $1, "x", $2}'
x
```

Dynamic Regular Expressions

Dynamic regular expressions are expressions such as `[[:digit:]]` that are evaluated and if need be, converted to a string. Some dynamic regular expressions are listed here:

▪ `[[:digit:]]` matches a digit

▪ `[[:alpha:]]` matches an uppercase or lowercase letter

▪ `[[:alpha:]]` matches an alphanumeric character

▪ `[[:punct:]]` matches a punctuation mark

You can find additional information online: *https://support.google.com/a/answer/1371415?hl=en*.

Listing 6.10 displays the content of `dynamic_regex1.sh` that checks for the occurrence of digits in an input string.

LISTING 6.10: dynamic_regex1.sh

```
echo "abc 123" | awk '
BEGIN {
  digits_regexp = "[[:digit:]]+"
}
  $0 ~ digits_regexp    { print }
'
```

Listing 6.10 contains an `awk` command with a `BEGIN` block that initializes the variable `digits_regexp` as the pattern of one or more digits. The next code snippet checks whether $0 matches the pattern defined in `digits_regexp`, and if so, the contents of $0 are printed. Launch the code in Listing 6.10, and you will see the following output:

```
abc 123
```

Listing 6.11 displays the content of `dynamic_regex2.sh` that checks for the occurrence of alphabetic characters in an input string.

LISTING 6.11: dynamic_regex2.sh

```
echo "abc 123" | awk '
BEGIN {
  alpha_regexp = "[[:alpha:]]+"
}
  $0 ~ alpha_regexp    { print }
'
```

Listing 6.11 contains an `awk` command with a `BEGIN` block that initializes the variable `alpha_regexp` as the pattern of one or more alphanumeric characters. The next code snippet checks whether $0 matches the pattern defined in `alpha_regexp`, and if so, the contents of $0 are printed. Launch the code in Listing 6.11, and you will see the following output:

```
abc 123
```

Listing 6.12 displays the content of `dynamic_regex3.sh` that checks for the occurrence of punctuation in an input string.

LISTING 6.12: dynamic_regex3.sh

```
echo "abc !@#" | awk '
BEGIN {
  punct_regexp = "[[:punct:]]+"
}
  $0 ~ punct_regexp    { print }
'
```

Listing 6.12 contains an `awk` command with a `BEGIN` block that initializes the variable `punct_regexp` as the pattern of one or more punctuation characters. The next code snippet checks whether $0 matches the pattern defined in `punct_regexp`, and if so, the contents of $0 are printed. Launch the code in Listing 6.12, and you will see the following output:

```
abc !@#
```

Regular Expressions Involving Text Files

The preceding (rather long) section showed you how to perform a multitude of simple tasks involving text files. This section contains subsections with `awk` commands that display rows that match a character, rows that match multiple characters, and so forth. The code samples rely on basic metacharacters, such as "^" that functions as "starts with," along with a regular expression, and "|" that functions as an OR operator, as well as "!" that functions as a NOT operator.

Counting Comments with Regular Expressions

Listing 6.13 displays the content of comments.txt with various comment style for awk, C, and Python. Listing 6.14 displays the content of comments.sh that counts the number of comments using different styles.

LISTING 6.13: comments.txt

```
# this is an awk and Python style comment
// this is a C-style comment
x = 1
y = 3
   # pound-style comment number two
   // another C-style comment
   # pound-style comment number three
   // a third C-style comment
""" python style comment """
```

LISTING 6.14: comments.sh

```
awk '
BEGIN {
  c_count   = 0; awk_count = 0;
  c_count2 = 0; awk_count2 = 0
  py_count = 0;
}
{
   if($0 ~ /^#/) { awk_count++ }
   else if ($0 ~ /^\/\//)    { c_count++ }
   else if ($0 ~ /^"""/)     { py_count++ }
   else if ($0 ~ /^[ ].*#/) { awk_count2++ }
   else if ($0 ~ /^[ ].*\/\//) { c_count2++ }
}
END {
   print "C-style comments:   ",c_count
   print "awk-style comments:",awk_count
   print "C-style comments:   ",c_count2
   print "awk-style comments:",awk_count2
   print "python-style comments:",py_count
  }
' comments.txt
```

Listing 6.14 contains an awk command that starts with a BEGIN block that initializes several scalar variables that are used to count the number of occurrences of different types of command statements.

The next portion of Listing 6.14 contains the main execution block that contains conditional code snippets that compare the first character in $0 with the characters //, """, #, and //, which are comment statements for C, Python, awk, and C again, respectively. Each time one of the conditional code snippets matches such strings, the corresponding scalar variable is incremented.

The final portion of Listing 6.14 contains an END block that prints the values of the various scalar variables. Launch the code in Listing 6.14, and you will see the following output:

```
C-style comments:    1
awk-style comments: 1
C-style comments:    2
awk-style comments: 2
python-style comments: 1
```

Combining grep with awk

Listing 6.15 displays the contents of employees.csv, and Listing 6.16 displays the content of grep_awk.sh that calculates the expenses for the employees in employees.csv.

LISTING 6.15: employees.csv

```
# remove header line and blank lines with 'sed':
empid,full_name,start_date,expenses
1000,Jane Jones,12/05/2021,93.55

2000,John Smith,03/08/2020,87.23

3000,Dave Stone,07/15/2022,84.16
```

LISTING 6.16: grep_awk.sh

```
grep ",J" employees.csv | awk -F"," '
{
    expenses += $4
}
END { print "Expenses for",NR,"employees:",expenses }
'
```

Listing 6.16 starts with a grep command that matches the lines in the CSV file employees.csv that contain the pattern ,J, and the matching lines are redirected to an awk command that increments the scalar variable expenses with the contents of $4.

The final portion of Listing 6.16 is an END block that prints the number of matching rows as well as the value of the variable expenses. Launch the code in Listing 6.16, and you will see the following output:

```
Expenses for 3 employees: 264.94
```

Combining sed with awk

Listing 6.17 displays the content of sed_awk.sh that calculates the expenses for the employees in employees.csv.

LISTING 6.17: sed_awk.sh

```
# remove header line and blank lines with "sed":
cat employees.csv | sed -e '1d' -e '/^$/d' | awk -F"," '
{
    expenses += $4
}
END { print "Expenses for",NR,"employees:",expenses }
'
```

Listing 6.17 starts with the cat command that redirects the contents of the CSV file employees.csv to a sed command the removes the first line, and then redirects the remaining lines to an awk command, which simply increments the scalar variable expenses with the contents of $4.

The final portion of Listing 6.17 is an END block that prints the number of matching rows as well as the value of the variable expenses. Launch the code in Listing 6.17, and you will see the following output:

```
Expenses for 3 employees: 264.94
```

Removing HTML Tags

Listing 6.18 displays the content of abc.html whose HTML tags are removed by an awk command.

LISTING 6.18: abc.html

```
<html>
<body>
 <p>paragraph one</p>
 <p>paragraph two</p>
 <div>first div element</div>
 <div>second div element</div>
</body>
</html>
```

The following awk command displays a message each time that an HTML tag is encountered in the input to the awk command:

```
$ cat abc.html | awk '{ if ($0 ~ /<.*>/) { print "found a tag" } }'
found a tag
found a tag
found a tag
found a tag
found a tag
found a tag
found a tag
found a tag
```

The following awk command removes all HTML tags as well as all the text:

```
$ cat abc.html | awk '{ gsub(/<.*>/, "", $0); print }'
```

The reason is simple: the * meta character performs a greedy match, which means that it will continue to match beyond the first occurrence of a ">" character. See the following site for more information:

https://stackoverflow.com/questions/68511098/awk-multiline-non-greedy-matching-workaround

Listing 6.19 displays the content of remove_tags.sh that shows you how to disable greedy matching to remove the HTML tags and retain the text.

LISTING 6.19: remove_tags.sh

```
awk '
{
   #disable greedy match for "*":
   gsub(/<[^>]*>/, "", $0); print
}
' abc.html
```

Listing 6.19 contains an awk command that invokes the gsub() built-in function to remove any text that matches the pattern <[^>]*>. This pattern will match text that consists of the following parts:

1. the character "<"

2. followed by any character *except* the ">" character

3. followed by zero or more occurrences of anything other than ">"

4. followed by a ">" character

For example, the HTML tags <HTML>, <BODY>, <html>, <body>, and <p> match the regular expression <[^>]*>. Launch the code, and you will see the following output:

```
paragraph one
paragraph two
first div element
second div element
```

However, the removal of the four <html> and <body> HTML tags results in blank lines, which we can remove as follows:

```
./remove_tags.sh | sed '/^$/d'
```

The preceding command generates the following output:

```
paragraph one
paragraph two
first div element
second div element
```

We can also remove the initial white space from the preceding command by invoking the following command:

```
$ ./remove_tags.sh | sed -e '/^$/d' -e 's/^ //'
paragraph one
paragraph two
first div element
second div element
```

The gensub() Function and Captured Groups

The `gensub()` function extends the `gsub()` with the ability to specify regular expressions that "capture" portions of a string by means of parentheses, and then refer to the captured substring by specifying \N, where N can be between 1 and 9 inclusive.

Listing 6.20 displays the content of `gensub1.sh` that shows you how to capture and print one or more captured groups via an `awk` command.

LISTING 6.20: gensub1.sh

```
echo aabbbccc | awk '{ print gensub(/(a*)(b*)(c*)/, "\\3 \\2
    \\1", "g", $1); }'
#result: ccc bbb aa

echo aabbbccc | awk '{ print gensub(/(a*)(b*)(c*)/,
    "\\3Z\\2Y\\1X", "g", $1); }'
#result: cccZbbbYaaX

echo "aa bbb ccc" | awk '{ print gensub(/(a*) (b*) (c*)/,
    "\\3 \\2 \\1", "g", $0); }'
#result: ccc bbb aa

echo "aa bbb ccc" | awk '{ print gensub(/(a*) (b*) (c*)/,
    "\\3 \\2 \\1", "g", $1); }'
#result: aa
```

Listing 6.20 contains four `awk` commands, each of which has a string as its input. The four `awk` commands match strings that contain the following regular expressions:

- `(a*)(b*)(c*)`

- `(a*)(b*)(c*)`

- `(a*) (b*) (c*)`

- `(a*) (b*) (c*)`

In addition, each `awk` command displays one of the following output strings when there is a matching input string:

```
\\3 \\2 \\1
```

```
\\3Z\\2Y\\1X
\\3 \\2 \\1
\\3 \\2 \\1
```

Launch the code, and you will see the output that is displayed (as a comment) under each `awk` command in Listing 6.20.

Summary

This chapter started with an explanation of metacharacters and character classes, followed by code samples that define regular expressions with digits and letters (uppercase as well as lowercase), and also how to use character classes in regular expressions. Next, you saw code samples with regular expressions involving metacharacters, such as ".," "^," "$," and "|." In addition, you learned how to match subsets of strings via regular expressions.

In addition, you saw examples of the built-in `sub()` and `gsub()` functions in `awk` to remove digits, characters, and consecutive characters via `awk` commands. Then you learned how to split strings with regular expressions, how to define dynamic regular expressions, and how to count comments in text fields.

Furthermore, you saw examples of combining the `grep` and `sed` commands, which you learned in Chapter 1 and Chapter 2, with the `awk` command. Finally, you learned how to use the `gsub()` command with captured groups.

INDEX